Lessons on Praise from Critter County T.M.

Helping Children Praise God

by Paula J. Bussard
and
Patti Jefferson

illustrated by Diane Johnson and Lawrence Goodridge

Critter County on Radio by Shawna Heisler

Memory Verse Songs by Christine Wyrtzen

Order a copy of *Activities on Praise From Critter County* for each child:

Ages 5-8	(3338)
Ages 8-10	(3339)
Order a Sydney puppet	(3685)

STANDARD PUBLISHING
Cincinnati, Ohio 3337

Library of Congress Card No. 86-63191
ISBN 0-87403-217-2

Published by The STANDARD PUBLISHING Company, Cincinnati, Ohio
A division of STANDEX INTERNATIONAL Corporation
Printed in U.S.A.

Contents

Introduction

The philosophy of Critter County is certainly not unique. The concept grew out of the desire of one mother to make Scripture memory fun and easy for her two young children. The use of the alphabet and animal kingdom provided the tools needed to make memorizing easier. Putting catchy musical melodies to the verses provided the fun!

So a record album which teaches twenty-six verses and Scriptural concepts to children of all ages was born. Performed by the talented Christine Wyrtzen and her close friend, Sydney the squirrel, the album lays the foundation for an ever-expanding series of products developed to teach Scripture to children. Twelve books with cassettes staring all the animal friends, games and puzzles provide hours of learning experiences as children play alone or with friends. This new curriculum, sequel to the first curriculum, **Lessons on Love From Critter County,** invites children to learn Bible lessons and memorize Scripture while participating in thirteen lessons with group interaction.

Lessons on Praise From Critter County is designed to provide a variety of experiences for each child, making the class setting more enjoyable, and enhancing the quality of his spiritual education. This curriculum is to be used in addition to your Sunday School curriculum and second hour program. The many activities and stories provide a great opportunity to teach the Scriptures during a special summer activities program or an after-school program. The thirteen lessons provide material for one quarter of Sunday night classes. This curriculum can be presented in varied ways. The children become intrigued by Sydney and the critters and are encouraged to learn God's Word and apply its truths to their lives.

To help the children visualize the various locations in Critter County, the following suggestions are offered. With some poster board, markers, and *your* creative imagination, Critter County can indeed come *alive* for you and the children.

Sydney's Car, the Shuttlebug: Sydney has his own car—a royal blue "bug" with a white convertible top. Use the pattern on page 99 to make a large outline model of Sydney's Shuttlebug from posterboard or a large cardboard box. At the beginning of each session, have the children sit in chairs holding the shuttlebug model and take an imaginary ride to Critter County.

Make the ride exciting and fun for the children as you bounce up and down over imaginary hills, lean to the left or right around curves, and stop for imaginary lights, railroad signs or animals crossing the road. The more fun you have as you imagine, the more response you will see from the children.

During the ride, give the children an overview of the places they will visit as well as the lessons and activities they will do that day. At the close of the lesson time, have the children climb back into the Shuttlebug for the trip home. Use this time to make concluding remarks about today's lesson.

Light Post on Memory Lane: Thirteen memory verses are suggested in this curriculum. It is important that the children know that Scripture memorization is given a special place in each lesson. So the Light Post on Memory Lane is a very important place in Critter County. From the light post hangs a sign that reads, "Thy word is a lamp unto my feet, and a light unto my path: Psalm 119:105 (KJV).

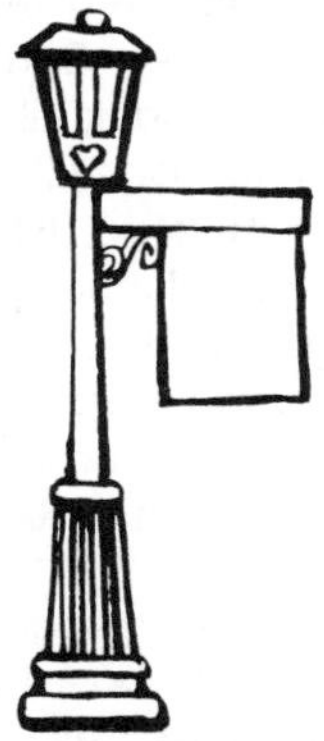

Make a large light post to place in your room. *(See the pattern on page 98.)* It can be drawn on a chalkboard, a window shade, or poster board and attached to a wall. Or it can be free standing by adding a brace to the back. It will mark the place for the children to go to study, recite, and color an item of praise on their Memory Verse Chart found on page 17 of the *Activities on Praise From Critter County* books, and receive a new memory verse. Have an assistant assigned to the Light Post on Memory Lane who will be responsible for providing a variety of teaching aids such as jigsaw puzzles, word cards, string-a-verse, word puzzles, fill-in-the-blanks, picture cards, etc. to help the children learn the verse.

When the children gather at the Light post on Memory Lane, the assistant is to introduce the new verse, discuss the meaning of any difficult words, and show where the verse is found in the Bible *(Old or New Testament, letters, gospels, poetry).* Say the verse together. Then use the teaching aids to reinforce the learning of the verse. Keep these aids at the Light Post so the children may work with them any time they finish their classwork, or arrive early.

Memory Verses

1. The heavens declare the glory of God; the skies proclaim the work of his hands.—Psalm 19:1 (NIV)
2. Great is our Lord and mighty in power; his understanding has no limit.—Psalm 147:5 (NIV)
3. The Lord is not slow in keeping his promise, as some understand slowness. He is patient with you, not wanting anyone to perish, but everyone to come to repentance.—2 Peter 3:9 (NIV)
4. My purpose is . . . that they may know the mystery of God, namely, Christ, in whom are hidden all the treasures of wisdom and knowledge.—Colossians 2:2, 3 (NIV)
5. He is your praise; he is your God, who performed for you those great and awesome wonders you saw with your own eyes.—Deuteronomy 10:21 (NIV)

6. Clap your hands, all you nations; shout to God with cries of joy.—Psalm 47:1 (NIV)
7. Unless the Lord builds the house, its builders labor in vain.—Psalm 127:1 (NIV)
8. Praise the Lord. How good it is to sing praises to our God, how pleasant and fitting to praise him!—Psalm 147:1 (NIV)
9. To our God and Father be glory for ever and ever. Amen.—Philippians 4:20 (NIV)
10. But thanks be to God! He gives us the victory through our Lord Jesus Christ.—1 Corinthians 15:57 (NIV)
11. Praise the Lord, O my soul; all my inmost being, praise his holy name. He forgives all my sins and heals all my diseases.—Psalm 103:1, 3 (NIV)
12. Serve the Lord with gladness; come before him with joyful songs.—Psalm 100:2 (NIV)
13. We give thanks to you, Lord God Almighty, who is and who was, because you have taken your great power and have begun to reign.—Revelation 11:17 (NIV)

The Activi-Tree: Draw a large tree from Critter County on butcher paper or poster board and place on a bulletin board or wall near the story area. Be sure to write specific duties, activities, and special assignments or projects on pieces of paper *(simple squares or shapes of leaves, nuts, or fruit)* for each lesson. Place the papers on the tree with Plasti-Tak so the activities are hidden. (Pattern is on page 97.)

As the children arrive, let them pick a paper from the tree understanding that the assignment on the paper is the job they well do. Some suggested activities:

Helping Activities:
- Hand out napkins at snack time.
- Be the leader today
- Hold the model of the Shuttlebug/or be the driver.
- Clean tables after snacks and /or crafts.
- Have the prayer for refreshments.

Learning Activities:
- Look up a Scripture, and be ready to read it when called upon later in class.
- Look up two important facts about the Sea of Galilee, and share with the class later.

Some activities can be used for each lesson; others will need to be changed according to the needs of the individual lesson. Be sure to adapt the activities to the age level of your pupils. The numbers in ( ) following the assignments indicate the number of children needed for this activity.

Another use of the Activi-Tree is to divide the class into groups. Use pictures of nuts, numbers, or colors for the number of groups desired.

Pause to Praise: This activity has been added to enhance the theme and emphasis of "Praise". During each class session, the children will be encouraged to study a portion of Psalm 150. The Psalm has been divided into 13 segments and a continuing scrapbook is to be made during the Pre-session Activities.

Instructions are given for the development of the actual **Pause to Praise** segment. The children will share that day's portion of the Scripture, the information gained during Pre-session, various instruments of praise, an actual praise exercise, and the scrapbook.

This activity is very flexible and is to be worked into the schedule where it best suits the teacher's lesson plan. One day you might include the **Pause to Praise** at the end of a particularly moving Bible lesson. Or, you may choose to wait until snack time or the final activity of the class period. Be sure to encourage the students to develop this segment. The degree of their understanding of personal praise may very well be determined by the level of their involvement in the actual activity.

Wonders-of-God's-World Box: You will find suggestions for the use of the **Wonders-of-God's-World Box** throughout the curriculum. It is most often used during the Bible Story time as a teaching aid. This box will hold items the teacher may refer to during the lesson. For example, in Lesson Five, the teacher is to place in the box a piece of wood, some puffed wheat cereal, an artificial bird, and pictures of the Israelites gathering manna. During the lesson she will give emphasis to the lesson by removing the objects at appropriate times.

The design and "character" of the box has been left to the teacher's desires. The box can be a shoebox decorated with something as simple as foil or it can be a more elaborate box with pictures of creation or used Bible lesson materials. The special touch you give will help the children recognize and look forward to the Wonders-of-God's-World-Box and its use during the class period.

Story Time: Two stories are presented in each lesson. One is a make-believe adventure in Critter County, and one is a true lesson from the Bible. It is important that you help the children to distinguish the difference between the make-believe and the true stories.

The stories of Critter County take place in different locations: Lester's Workshop or playground. Simple props may be used to help set the mood for a particular story.

The Bible stories have been selected to help the children understand that it is important to praise God. Teaching pictures from your picture file, or from the book, *The World Into Which Jesus Came (#4951),* will help the children understand some of the Bible stories. Be sure to check the supplemental list of teaching aids found on page 8.

Activity Books: Two activity books are available with this curriculum:

Activities on Praise From Critter County—Ages 5-8
(Look for Sydney on the cover.)

Activities on Praise From Critter County—Ages 8-10
(Look for Lester on the cover.)

These books provide a variety of activities for each lesson. Be sure to purchase an activity book for each child and teacher in your class.

These activities are to be used with both Critter County and the Bible stories, and may be used during the Presession Time or following each story. The ability level will be indicated by Ages **5-8** or **8-10.**

Be sure to emphasize *Sydney's Note of Praise.* This is Sydney's way of restating in simple words the aim of the lesson.

Critter County Radio Station: During each lesson, the children will visit the Critter County Radio Station, **WWCC** *(Wonderful World of Critter County).* Here the children will meet the puppet reporter, Sydney. *(Use the puppet of Sydney, 3685.)*

A puppet stage may be as simple as a large, collapsible cardboard partition *(such as a cutting board or a refrigerator box),* a folded table turned on its side, or a tension rod extended across a doorway with a small curtain hanging from the rod. The most popular puppet stage is the three-sided screen that folds out to form a booth with the stage opening cut in the front like a window. Use whatever you have available. Make the stage look like a radio station. Place the letters **WWCC** on a sign board (See page 98.) Be sure the puppeteer keeps out of sight and only the puppets are seen.

Assign one teacher-helper to be responsible for the Radio Station and to work with each child who helps with the radio program. For older children, prepare an assignment to attach to the Activi-Tree for each part needed. *(Example: Be Rascal Raccoon in today's WWCC radio program. See the teacher in charge to get the script and read over your part.)*

Stuffed animals can be used for the extra critters. You will need Grandmother Mouse, Lester Lion, Liona Lou, Rascal Raccoon, and others.

Crafts: Two crafts are suggested with each lesson. Use the one suggested for the age group of your students. Patterns needed for the crafts are located on pages. A list of all materials needed for each craft is provided at the beginning of each lesson.

It is most helpful for the teacher to make a sample of each craft so she can show it to the children and be aware of the degree of difficulty in making it. She will then be better prepared to help the children when they encounter problems.

Songs: Christine Wyrtzen has written eighteen Scripture songs, one for each lesson's memory verse and six Critter County storybooks. All the songs suggested in each lesson are included in this book.

Be sure to teach the songs early so the children will have adequate time to learn the words and music before presenting the closing program on page 93.

Extra Activities: Each lesson has suggestions for additional activities which are correlated to the lesson's aims. They are especially helpful when the class time has to be lengthened due to the adult services running overtime.

Schedules: A good schedule is flexible. Two schedules are suggested so that you can select the one that fits your time frame. Adjust it as you wish to fit your class. Post your schedule so all workers can see it.

Suggested Schedules (2½ hours)

Morning Before	**Activity**	**Evening** Before
9:00-9:20	Welcome—Pre-Session	6:30-6:50
9:20-9:30	Together Time	6:50-7:00
9:30-9:35	Opening-Shuttlebug ride	7:00-7:05
9:35-9:55	Critter County Story/Activity Book	7:05-7:25
9:55-10:05	Critter County Radio Station	7:25-7:35
10:05-10:15	Snack—Break	7:35-7:45
10:15-10:25	Song Time	7:45-7:55
10:25-10:45	Bible Story Time/Activity Book	7:55-8:15
10:45-10:50	Story Applications	8:15-8:20
10:50-11:00	Light Post on Memory Lane	8:20-8:30
11:00-11:25	Craft Time	8:30-8:55
11:25-11:30	Closing Activity/Closing Prayer	8:55-9:00

Alternate Schedule (1½ hours)

Before	Before	
9:30-9:45	Pre-session Activities—Together Time	7:00-7:15
9:45-9:50	Opening—Shuttlebug Ride	7:15-7:20
9:50-10:00	Critter County Story/Activity Book	7:20-7:30
10:00-10:05	Critter County Radio Station	7:30-7:35
10:05-10:10	Song Time	7:35-7:40
10:10-10:20	Bible Story Time/Activity Book/Light Post on Memory Lane	7:40-8:00
10:20-10:45	Craft Time	8:00-8:25
10:45-10:50	Closing Activity/Prayer	8:25-8:30

Extended Time Suggestions: Extra Activities
Games

Supplemental Teaching Aids:

Twelve Critter County Storytime Sets. These books can provide excellent free-time activities for the students. Each one features a different story and teaches a verse of Scripture set to music. Stickers are included. (3391, 3392, 3393, 3394, 3395, 3396, 3441, 3342, 3443, 3444, 3445, 3446)

Two Critter County Puzzles. These are designed for ages 5-8 and will provide fun during pre-and post-session times. (2290, 2291)

Critter County Card Game. Emphasizes Scripture memorization. (2486)

Critter County Album (3390), Cassette (3389) and Demo Tape (3387). Includes songs that teach a Bible verse for each letter of the alphabet, sung by Christine Wyrtzen and friends.

Basic Bible Dictionary—for children 8-11. A good dictionary for use when doing Activi-Tree activities. (2770)

The World Into Which Jesus Came, by Sylvia Root Tester. A good resource book for older children, and a good picture book for the New Testament Bible lessons. (4951)

These items may be purchased from your local Christian bookstore or Standard Publishing.

Suggested Room Arrangement

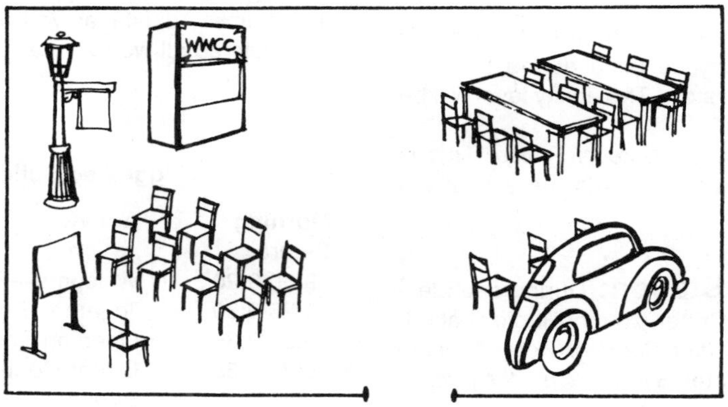

Lesson 1

Praise God for His Power

Scripture: Genesis 1:1-25

Psalm References: Psalm 19:1, 2; Psalm 148:1-13; Psalm 150:1 (Pause-to-Praise verse)

Memory Verse: The heavens declare the glory of God; the skies proclaim the work of his hands.—Psalm 19:1 (NIV)

Lesson Aim: As a result of studying this lesson and completing the designed activities referring to God's power, the children should

1) Know that God wants us to praise Him.
2) Know that God used His power to create all things.
3) Feel the need to praise God for all He has done and all He has given.
4) Praise God specifically for something He has made.
5) Sing or say the memory verse Psalm 19:1.

Materials Needed:
Pre-Session. *Name Tags:* Cut 2″ x 3″ rectangles from light blue construction paper. Use crayon or markers to draw a rainbow across the center of the tag. The words "Praise God" should be written across the rainbow and a line drawn under the rainbow for the child's name. (See illustration included under *Welcome the Children.*) Use the tags for the first three lessons or until the children know everyone in the class. (Note: The tags should be attached with a rolled piece of masking tape applied to the back instead of a straight pin.)

Activi-Tree: Write specific duties on slips of paper and fasten to the Activi-Tree. (Directions for the tree are given on page 6.) Each day allow the children to choose a slip of paper from the tree and encourage them to follow the instructions chosen. (Younger children may need you to assist them as they read.) Suggestions for today's Activi-Tree slips:

- Look up the word *creation* in the dictionary and remember its meaning.
- Pass out the napkins and cups for snack time. (2)
- Choose a friend and go outside to find nature items to place in the *Wonders-of-God's-World* box. (2)
- Find the "Shuttlebug" when the teacher tells you it is time to look for Sydney's car. (2)
- Be leader of the line.
- Pray for food.
- Look up the word *sanctuary* in the dictionary and be ready to tell its meaning to the class.

Select only the assignments you know your children can do. You may think of others to add.

Torn-paper pictures: Blue construction paper, box of multi-colored-paper scraps (varied textures suggested), and glue.

Pause to Praise: Dictionary; Bible; modeling clay; three pictures: the tabernacle, the temple, and a church building; construction paper; markers; glitter; tissue paper scraps; and glue.

Together Time. Torn-paper pictures made during Pre-session.

Memory Verse. Chairs for number of children in your class; 2 signs reading "Memory Verse Chair"; record player and record (if available); and a chalkboard or poster board with memory verse written on it.

Critter County Radio Station. Prepare a place for the puppet stage (See page 7.); Sydney puppet.

Snack Time. Fresh fruit and fruit juice.

Bible Story Time. Bible, Wonders-of-God's-World box (See directions page 6.), and pictures of creation (suggestions given under Bible Story).

Crafts.
5-8. *Critter Caps:* Pattern from page 100, crayons or markers, strong tape or staples, and elastic string.

8-10. *Night-Scene Picture:* Prepared poster board (See directions under Crafts) yellow and orange crayons, kitchen cleanser, india ink (**Be sure to allow one day before class to prepare the board.**), yarn and a No. 6 nail for each child.

Welcome the Children

Greet each child by name. Tell the child we are going to be praising God as we share each time we have class. Tell each child to be thinking of one thing they would like to praise God for as you give each child the rainbow-name tag (prepared before class). Older children might enjoy writing their own name on the tag. Guide each child to one of the pre-session activities as you tell them what *you* have personally chosen to praise God for today.

Pre-session Activities

Activi-Tree. Encourage each child to choose a slip of paper from the tree and follow the directions chosen. Remember to help non-readers to discover what special instructions they are to follow from their paper.

Torn-paper Pictures. Give each child a sheet of blue-construction paper. Have a box of scrap paper. (Many colors and varied textures are suggested for best results.) Encourage the child to tear the scrap papers and glue the pieces to the construction paper as they design God's world in picture form. Talk with the children about praising God for each of the items they make in their picture. (These pictures will be shared during Together Time and then arranged attractively on the wall or bulletin board.)

Preparation of Pause to Praise. Open your Bible to Psalm 150:1. (Older children will read the verse. Younger children will listen as you read.) Let the child who looked up the word *sanctuary* in the dictionary tell its meaning to the group. (A sanctuary is a special place where God can be worshiped and praised.) Show the children a picture of the tabernacle, the temple, and a church building. Ask if they can remember a lesson from the Bible when each place was used to worship God. Suggest that the tabernacle was used by the Israelites as a place of worship while they were crossing the desert to the land God had promised. Explain that the temple was the beautiful building used for worship and praise, and the Bible tells us Jesus went to the temple to worship. Let the children tell you about the picture of the church building.

Explain to all of the children that you will be compiling a scrap book as you study these lessons on praise. Two children will need to design a "Praise God" front cover for the scrap book and add the first page that will read, "Praise God in His Sanctuary." Allow the children to be creative. The "Praise God" cover could be decorated with glitter or tissue-paper scraps or crayons. The first page should include a picture that depicts a sanctuary. (Use a photo of your building's auditorium or worship center.) The first page should bear the words "Praise God in His Sanctuary". As two children work on the scrapbook pages, the others will participate in a modeling-clay activity.

Divide the children into three groups. Give each group a piece of the clay. Assign one picture to each group. Encourage the children to make one of the places of worship. Be sure to involve yourself in their conversations as they work. Tell the children to remember what they have learned about "sanctuaries" so they will be able to share during **Pause to Praise.**

During Pause to Praise: Have one child read all of Psalm 150. Have one child explain that our verse from Psalm 150 today is the first verse, and read this verse once again. Allow the children to discuss all they have learned regarding the sanctuary. Have one child from each modeling-clay group tell about his group's structure. Allow the students who made the scrapbook cover and page one explain their activity to the group. Be sure the class understands that we will be adding to the scrapbook with each session. Close this session by singing, "He Is the King" page 141.

Note: You might want to take your class to the church's auditorium for this time of praise. This will reinforce the idea of the sanctuary.

Together Time: Have the children who worked on the pictures and who found objects for the *Wonders-of-God's-World* box share their projects with the entire class. End this session by encouraging the children to think of the one thing for which they wish to praise God. At the count of three, everyone will clap (with the words) as they say together, "We praise you, God, for (child names item)." You may need to go through these steps several times before the children catch on, but it will be fun to praise God together for individual favorite things.

Boys and girls, I can hardly wait for you to see what is going to happen during the rest of our class time. Come meet Sydney (show Sydney puppet). Each time we meet together we will take an imaginary trip to a very special, pretend place called Critter County. During our trip we will look in on Sydney and his friends and see what is happening in the lives of all the little critters. Now, how are we going to get to this pretend place? Well, would you believe Sydney has his very own blue and white convertible car? He sure does! Let's see if it is parked outside. (Have the two children who chose this responsibility from the Activi-Tree look outside the door to find the Shuttlebug.)

As the children bring the Shuttlebug inside, continue to explain about the trip to Critter County.

The Shuttlebug will take us to pretend places where learning is so much fun! Every time we go to Critter County, we will listen to a story involving our favorite critters. We'll laugh at them when they get into funny situations and have to find their way out. And we'll learn with them as they help us to understand how to apply the lessons of God's Word to everyday life. The pretend Critter-County stories are a special treat.

And, we will hear a *real* Bible story too. Our Bible story is about our God whom we praise without pretending because we know He is real. We'll make a stop at Memory Lane where we will praise God by learning new verses from His word. Let's all get in and buckle up! There is so much to do! I'll just have to tell you as the class continues. Right now, let's get ready to pretend. Our first stop is the story area.

At the end of your pretend ride in the Shuttlebug, become excited to see Lester's house. Say, "Look, there is Lester's house! He is one of my favorite critters. Lester is a lion who always has a special message to share. This is where we stop. Everyone out of the Shuttlebug for our Critter County Story!"

We have a beautiful world! We look around us and have to wonder how God could make it so special. Lester and Lunchbox are going to help us understand about our world and how God made it so perfect. Let's peek inside Lester's workshop. I think I hear him hollering. I wonder what has happened . . .

Out of Nothing

"YOWWW!! Oh man, I do think I have killed my thumb with this hammer!" yelled Lester, the grand lion of Critter County. Little Lunchbox ran to the workshop to see how badly he was hurt and what he could do to help. He found Lester in a lot of pain.

"Oh, oh, oh me, oh my!" whimpered Lester. "You'd better start planning my funeral 'cause I've really done it this time. Yes sir, it's just a matter of time . . . my life is starting to pass before me."

"Boy, Dad, you really smashed it good, " said Lunchbox. "It looks really bad."

"Yes, son, your father is in agony. I am most miserable. I mean, oh, this hurts! But I need to teach you to be brave, son, so I'm going to keep a stiff upper lip."

"If you're going to keep a stiff upper lip Dad, why are you crying?" asked Lunchbox.

"Well, Lunchbox, I told you what I was going to do with my lip. You'll notice I did not mention what I was going to do with my eyes! Now, tell me about school today so I can spend my last few minutes on earth spending time with my son."

"Oh, it was OK, I guess. But I didn't do very well on my Bible test. Mrs. Pigeon made us write all about what it must've been like when God created the earth. I guess I blew it," answered the little lion cub.

"Well, this is just great. I'm here on my death bed having just fatally injured my thumb, and my boy breaks the news to me that he doesn't understand creation. Well, before I take my last breath, let me try and explain this.

"Now, son, I want you to look at these scraps of wood, paper, and string," said Lester.

"Yes, Dad, it looks to me like it's junk for the garbage can," said Lunchbox.

"Not so, my boy, not so at all. Now watch carefully."

And with that, Lester picked up a large piece of wood and began to saw it. Back and forth, back and forth until it was just the right size and shape. Then he took more wood and sawed until he had quite a stack of lumber.

Lunchbox asked, "What are you building, Dad?"

"I'm not just building, son. Why, I'm creating!"

And Lester worked on and on, hammering and sawing, pounding, and then painting. Finally, he said, "Well, son, what do you think?"

"It's a great looking doghouse, Daddy. But who are we going to give it to?"

"Well, I thought that little puppy you run around with at school might like it. What is his name?"

"Oh, you mean, Tide. My friend's names is Tide," Lunchbox answered.

Lester pounded and painted a little bit more and then began to make a sign for the front door of the little house. As he was painting the sign, he said to Lunchbox, "You see, son, when God created the world, He spoke it into being. He said, 'Let there be light,' and there was light! Everything God created was good. Remember before I started building the house, you thought these materials were ready for the garbage?" Lunchbox nodded. "Well, now I've created something of value. I can build a house for you little friend, but only God could make the tree that gave us this wood. And only God could make your friend, and your parents, and you." Lester continued.

Lunchbox perked up and said, "Oh, I get it. God took nothing and made something out of it. Yeah, I can see that only God could do that. Hey, Dad, what does the sign say for the front of the house?"

"Well, son, I know that particular family lives down by the beach, so I figure that's where they'll put this house. The sign will let folks know whether or not your friend is home. He can turn this side up when he's home. It reads, "Tide's In" and when he leaves, he can switch it so this side shows. It says, "Tide's Out."

Lunchbox smiled and said, "Dad, this is really neat. Tide will just love it and I love you for making it for him. Oops, creating it for him."

"You're very welcome, son. Of course, this is the last thing I'll ever do because my thumb is killing me. I think it's just a matter of a few more minutes now . . . oh my thumb . . . oh, my aching thumb. Goodbye, my boy."

Lunchbox left the workshop and went into the kitchen to taste the lion chow. Liona Lou said, "How's your Daddy feeling?"

"Oh, he's fine," said Lunchbox.

Have the children go to the tables and give each child page 3 of the activity book.

5-8. *Create Your Own Picture:* Cut out the pictures found at the bottom of this page and create Lester's workshop. Use crayons to add anything else you want in your picture. Now color your picture.

8-10. *Lester and His Creation:* Follow each step and draw a picture of Lester and the special creation he made for the puppy, Tide. Draw your pictures in the boxes.

When all have finished, have the children go to the Critter County Radio Station and sit on the floor in front of it. Let's all listen to the Critter County news.

Sydney: (Solemn.) Hello, **WWCC** listeners. We received word a short while ago that Lester, the lion, has been seriously injured. We were unable to locate him at the Critter County Hospital, and fear that we may be too late. We are rushing to the side of Liona Lou at this very moment. Liona Lou, hello.

Liona: Why, hello, Sydney, what a pleasant surprise!

Sydney: Liona, I hope that you don't mind if the **WWCC** listeners join you at this time.

Liona: Why, not at all. It is about dinner time, but that's OK. The lion chow is already done.

Sydney: Tell us . . . how did it happen?

Liona: How did what happen, Sydney?

Sydney: Lester's tragedy, Liona.

Liona: Oh, you mean his thumb! Well, he was building this little house for Tide, Lunchbox's new friend, and pow! He hit his thumb with his hammer!

Sydney: It must have been just horrible! We received a call at the station.

Liona: Someone called **WWCC** about Lester's thumb! Who?

Sydney: Why, I don't know. We just rushed right over.

Liona: Sydney, **WWCC,** have you ever heard of a dog whose bark is bigger than it's bite? Well, when Lester roars, he roars loudly! Sydney, Lester is just fine! I'm sure he called **WWCC** himself!

Sydney: Good 'ole Lester. Well, listeners, it looks like things are quite normal now here in Critter County. So, back to the program!

We are suggesting different kinds of fruit slices and juice for today's snack. Talk about how God made so many different kinds of fruit for us to enjoy. He made grapes to grow one way and apples to grow another. He even put a cover on bananas to keep the soft fruit inside from getting bruised as it grew! (Let the children who chose responsibilities from the Activi-Tree help with the snacks.) After clean up, have the children return to the story area.

Play the song "Sing Praise to Him" on page 140 as the children assemble in the story area. When all have gathered, sing the song together.

Sing familiar songs as well as new ones. "O Give Thanks," page 128; "He Is the King," page 141; "Sing and Shout It," page 136; and "The Heavens Are Telling," page 114.

Prayer Song: "Hear Us as We Pray," page 143.

Prayer: Ask God to help the children listen as we learn about the power and love He showed as He created all things.

Before the Bible story begins, place several pictures in the *Wonders-of-God's-World* box used earlier in the lesson. (Picture suggestions: Sun, moon, stars, various animals, fish and birds, night-time scene, day-time scene, trees, shrubs, and flowers) Be sure there are enough pictures for everyone in the class to have one.

Have the children sit down in a circle. Tell them we will be thinking about the very first lesson written in the Bible. See if anyone would like to guess what the Bible story is about. Tell the children that today you are going to tell the Bible story a special way. Tell them you want them to be ready to do whatever you say. Remember this story is real. We are not pretending anymore.

Open your Bible and tell the Bible Story.

In the Beginning God . . .
Genesis 1:1-25

Boys and girls, I want you to close your eyes. Be sure they are really closed so that you can't see me or anything in the room. Are they completely closed? Tell me what you see. (Give the children a moment to answer . . . some may open their eyes now because they think you are teasing.) Did you think that was a silly question? Just do it one more time for me. Close your eyes and look hard. Do you see anything at all . . . one tiny little anything? No, you don't see anything do you? Keep your eyes closed. Don't open them again until I tell you.

The Bible tells us that is how it was before God made the world. There was nothing here. Not one thing. Just black nothing. And then . . . God did something wonderful! The Bible says He spoke some words and pushed away the nothing. He said, "Let there be light"! (Now, open your eyes). And, just like that . . . the nothing was gone and light came.

The Bible says every time God wanted something to begin He said for it to come, and it appeared. Can you believe it? It's true! God said what He wanted, and it came.

Now, can you imagine what it would be like to *think* what you want, then *say* for it to come, and all of a sudden, it appears? That is what God did! What a powerful, powerful God we worship. We should praise Him for being so powerful.

God was more than just powerful. Our God was wise enough to know exactly what this world would need. He knew plants would have to grow so we would have food. He knew water would keep us from being thirsty. He knew some parts of His world would be very hot and some would be cold. He knew a soft playful puppy would make us giggle and feel happy inside. He knew everything! So, He spoke for each of the things He knew we would need, and it appeared.

The Bible says it took six whole days for God to make everything in His world. On the seventh day, he rested from all of the work.

We have a wonderful, powerful God. Let's all praise God for the world He has made. Sing or clap your hands as you say, "We praise You, God, for our beautiful world. We praise Your holy name."

Now, I want you to have some special fun with me. I have this box marked *Wonders of God's World.* You saw it earlier as we saw things from nature that were placed inside. Now the box has something different in it. It has pictures of the things God thought to put in His world. We will pass the box around our circle. I want you to think of one of the things God made and say it out loud. (Demonstrate what you want them to do.) "Let there be ________ ." Then, you can look inside the box to see if the item you asked for is there. If it is, take out that picture and place it in front of you. You will know a little bit about how it would be to speak and see what you asked for to appear. If the item you thought of is not in the box, replace the lid and pass the box to the next class member. Each time one of you asks for the item you are thinking of, we will clap our hands and praise God for making it. (Proceed around the class as long as interest holds.) Each time an item is mentioned, clap your hands and say, "We praise you, God, for making *(child's request)*".

Close the Bible story time by reading Psalm 148:1-13. You may choose to let one of the older children read the verses and each time an item is mentioned that a child has chosen from the box, the child can hold up the picture in his possession.

Have the children go to the tables and complete the activity paper found on page 4 of their activity book.

5-8. *Creation Match:* Instruct the children to draw a line from the picture of the things God created to their matching shadows.

8-10. *God's Creation:* Help the children find the things in the picture that do not belong. Place an X on those things (paint brush, ball, golf flag, ladder, arrow, violin).

Light Post on Memory Lane

Have the children gather at the light post as the song, "Memory Lane," page 130, is played. Tell them this is where they will come each day to learn a new memory verse.

Today we are going to play a memory verse game.

Using the same number of chairs as you have students, place the chairs in two straight lines back to back. Have one chair in each line marked "Memory-Verse Chair". The children will walk around the chairs as music plays. When the music stops, the children will sit in the chairs. Each child in the Memory-Verse Chair will be asked to say the verse. (The first few times, let them read the verse from the board.) After you play several times, begin erasing one word at a time. Try to allow each child the opportunity to say the verse.

Note: For younger children, the teacher might say the memory verse, and let each child in the marked chairs repeat it. Then, after playing several times, the teacher can say the verse leaving out words to be filled in by the students in the special chairs.

Close by singing "The Heavens Are Telling" on page 114.

Craft Time

5-8. Critter Caps: Following the pattern on page 100, provide each child with a critter-cap outline drawn on poster board. Let the children color the details of their cap with markers or crayons. Cut around the outline of the two cap pieces. Place the top part of the critter over the bottom pattern piece so that the bottom piece forms the "bill" of the cap. Fasten together with strong tape on the back side of the cap so the tape will not show. Measure a piece of elastic string to fit around the head of each child. Fasten the string to the cap and allow the child to wear the cap during the remainder of the class period.

8-10. God's Wonderful World Picture: Before class, prepare enough poster board so that each child will have his own 8″ X 10″ finished picture. (Prepare the entire board and cut into 8″ X 10″ pieces after it dries) Cover the entire board with yellow or orange crayon. Be sure the area is thoroughly colored. Sprinkle kitchen cleanser over the crayon and shake off any excess. Coat the prepared board with india ink and let dry completely.

Give each child his piece of poster board and one No. 6 nail. Have a completed picture on hand as a sample. Explain to the children that they will be able to "create" their picture by scratching through the black "nothing" and making their picture appear. Help them to understand that each mark they make with the nail cannot be erased. It is important for them to decide what objects they want in their picture before they begin to draw. A night scene works best, but allow them to be creative. They will enjoy working through the "black" and watching their world appear.

Finish the picture by punching two holes four inches apart at the top of the picture and attaching an 8″ piece of yarn (orange or yellow depending on the crayon color beneath the ink). Remember to keep the conversation directed toward praising God for His creation and praising Him for making us so that we could enjoy this time together.

Shuttlebug Ride Home

It's time for us to gather at the Shuttlebug for our journey home. Would you like to return to Critter County? (Allow time for them to answer.) This pretend ride home is exciting! (Lean to the right and left or bounce up and down over bumpy roads.) Tell me what you have learned today. (Allow several children to share what they learned.) What will you praise God for now that class is over? (Let children express their praise.) Let's say the memory verse one more time before getting out of the Shuttlebug. (Say and then sing today's memory verse.)

Closing Prayer

Dear God, we praise You for being so powerful. You spoke the words and our whole world came into being. You made all that we see, and we praise You for continually giving us all that we need. God, we want to praise You by taking care of the world we live in and by always remembering that You chose to make it for us. We love You, and we praise You. In Jesus' name, amen.

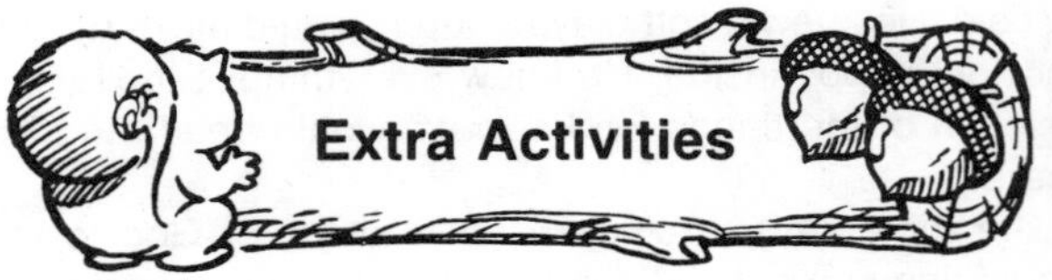

Extra Activities

Animal Chain: Ten or more children will make this game most exciting. Have the children form a straight line with each member of the line (except the leader) holding on to the waist of the member in front of him or her. One "extra" class member, who will try to attach himself or herself to the end of the chain, waits at the head and to the left of the chain until the chain begins to move. The leader at the head of the chain tries to move the animals in a direction away from the animal who will begin chasing the tail of the chain. When the chaser catches the tail, the head becomes the chaser allowing a new class member to lead as the game continues. The game is played until every class member has been the leader and the chaser.

One to Another: Seat the class in a circle for this "thinking" game. Explain to the children that they will have to work hard to remember what their friends have spoken so they must watch and listen carefully. The first player begins the game by saying, "God said, 'Let there be *(item of creation)*'." The second player must say the item mentioned and add a new item of his or her choice. The third player continues with "God said, 'Let there be *(1st player choice)* and *(2nd player choice)* with each child remembering what those before him have mentioned. When a player fails to remember, he or she must scoot out of the circle and watch as the game continues. When three players in a row fail to remember, the last player to correctly remember all the items mentioned is declared the winner.

The game begins again with one of the children who has been sitting out the longest, thinking of the first item.

Lesson 2

Praise God for His Knowledge

Scripture: Genesis 1:26-31

Psalm References: Psalm 139:1-3, 14; Psalm 119:73; Psalm 150:1b (Pause-to-Praise verse)

Memory Verse: Great is our Lord and mighty in power; his understanding has no limit.—Psalm 147:5 (NIV)

Lesson Aim: As a result of studying this lesson, the children should

1) Know that God created them, and He is with them everyday.
2) Feel assured that God cares for them and wants what is best for them.
3) Praise God for creating them.
4) Tell how God made Adam and Eve.
5) Sing and say the memory verse, Psalm 147:5.

Materials Needed:
Pre-session. *Activi-Tree:* Write the following assignments on slips of paper and attach them to the Activi-tree before the children arrive.

- Look up Psalm 150:1, and read it to friends in Pause to Praise activity center.
- Name as many friends as you can in the class and learn the names of any visitors. Be ready to introduce these friends during Together Time.
- Hold Sydney's Shuttlebug. (2)
- Be the Critter County Radio announcer.
- Look up the word *image* in the dictionary.
- Hold the mirror during Bible Story time.

A Man From Clay: Salt, flour, water, vegetable oil, cream of tartar, Styrofoam meat tray, food coloring, toothpicks.

Pause to Praise: Fingerpaint, paper, towel, water.

Together Time. Wonders-of-God's-World box containing pictures of children from foreign lands.

Snack Time. Happy-face cookies and fruit punch.

Bible Story Time. Stamp pad, butcher paper, water, towel, cake pan filled with sand covering clay man or figurine, hand mirror.

Light Post on Memory Lane. Two identical poster boards with fill-in-the-blank verses, two pencils. See page 19.

Crafts.
5-8. *Praise God Bookmark:* Corner of letter-size envelope, markers scissors.

8-10. *The Making of a Man Game:* One Styrofoam egg carton per student, felt squares (red, blue, neutral, green, and black), construction paper, glue, scissors, pattern pieces from page. 101

Welcome the Children
Be in the classroom before the children arrive. Greet each child by name and direct each toward an activity center. Today we're going to be praising God for being such a wise creator. He made each of us very different, yet the Bible says He made us to be like Him. Let's see what we can learn in our activity centers today.

Pre-Session Activities
Activi-Tree. Instruct the children to pick an assignment from the tree and make preparations for doing that assignment. Be sure to use only the activities that are suitable to the age and abilities of your students.

A Man from Clay. Allow the children to help you mix 3 cups of flour, 1½ cups table salt, 2 tablespoons cream of tartar, and 3 cups of water plus 2 tablespoons vegetable oil. Once you have thoroughly mixed these ingredients, give a small portion of the dough, a meat tray, and toothpick to each child. Encourage the children to use the clay to make a figure of themselves or one of their friends. Shape the clay on the meat tray. Use the toothpick to dab different colors of food coloring to small pieces of the clay used for clothing or accessories, such as a green ball cap or blue jeans. Save the clay models to share during **Together Time.**

Preparations for Pause to Praise: Have the child who chose the slip from the Activi-Tree read Psalm 150:1. Review with the children to see if they remember any information about the word "sanctuary" from our last class session. The portion of the verse we read today says we are to also praise God . . . where? Allow time for the children to answer. *(In His mighty heavens.)*

Today, lets think about praising God as we work with finger paint to paint a picture of the heavens we read about.

Use blue finger paint made by pouring two tablespoons of liquid starch on butcher or shelf paper and adding tempera paint (powdered or undiluted liquid) to desirable consistency. (Inexpensive fingerpaint can also be purchased at your local discount store)

Make the picture with your hands as you continue the conversation of praise with the children. Encourage them to understand that each time they look at the sky, they can praise God for what they see. Be sure to write, "Praise Him in His Mighty Heavens," somewhere on the picture. This is the second page of the scrapbook the class began yesterday and this page should follow yesterday's picture which read "Praise God in His Sanctuary".

During the **Pause to Praise,** take the children outside and look up to the heavens. Have one child read the verse again to the class. Let the children who worked with the fingerpaint share their pictures and explain about the conversations which took place during pre-session. Close this session by turning the pages of the scrapbook to read the entire verse of Psalm 150:1.

Together Time: Have the *Wonders-of-God's-World* box ready with pictures of children from foreign lands. Have the children come together to discuss what activity they were involved in during Pre-session. Let the children choose a picture from the box. Encourage them to notice how different the children in their picture look from boys and girls in America. Talk about how God was so wise to make us all different. The eskimo has thick, dark skin that helps protect him from the bitter cold. The native African has very dark skin to keep the sun from burning him. Chinese people have eyes that look different. Korean people have tiny feet and always have very black hair. We cannot explain why people are different in so many ways, but we can know that God was wise enough to make each of us to look exactly as He wanted us to look.

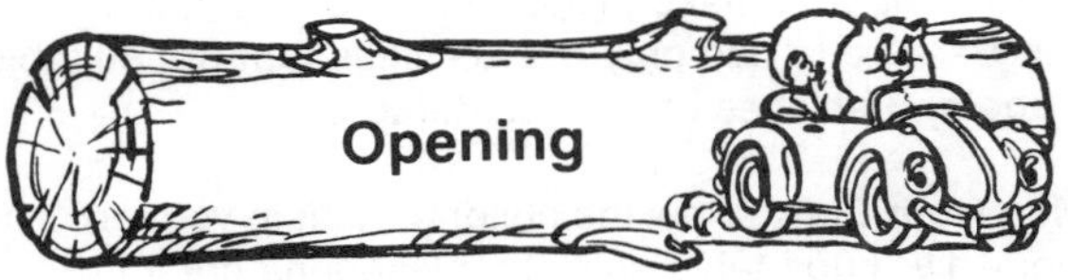

Look around the class. Do you see how we all look different? God gave <u>(child's name)</u> blonde hair, and He gave <u>(child's name)</u> brown hair. There is something He made about all of us that is alike, though. He created us so we could have fun. Let's have some fun right now as we hop in the Shuttlebug and head for a visit to our pretend story land we call Critter County. I wonder what Sydney and Rascal are up to today. Here we Go! Everybody buckle up and sit still. We'll be there in no time at all.

Sometimes it is hard for us to understand how God can see everything and know everything that is happening to everyone in the whole world. Rascal the raccoon has the same problem until Sydney takes him for a special ride.

Rascal's New View of Life

Sydney was in his workshop putting the finishing touches on the model airplane that he was building. Suddenly the door flew open and in walked Rascal the raccoon.

"Hey, buddy, did you forget to knock?" asked the little squirrel with the big brown eyes.

"Yes, I did; I'm sorry, Sydney. I'll remember next time. What are you working on now?" asked Rascal.

"Oh this is a plane I've been making for my nephew, Sugums," Sydney answered. "What color do you think I should paint it?"

"How about sky blue. Seems like that's the color to paint an airplane." suggested Rascal.

"Sounds like a great idea to me!" Sydney agreed. "How was school today?"

"Oh, it was OK, I guess. I got a "C" on my math test. But I'm happy it wasn't any worse than that. Mother and Dad are going to make me give up my paper route if my grades don't improve. Man, if they do that, it will be no more honey-milk shakes for me!" moaned Rascal.

Sydney did not feel the least bit sorry for Rascal. "Sounds to me like I know a young man who really needs to hit the books. You know, the grades that you get aren't as important as whether or not you've tried your hardest. Some children work very, very hard and get "C's." For them, that is excellent. Other kids goof off and get "B's," and they should be ashamed because they didn't give it their best effort. I hope that you can keep that paper route. I want you to give your school work your very best."

"I know I need to buckle down. I'll do an extra math page tonight, and that will show Mrs. Pigeon that I want to improve my grades," said Rascal. "You know, Sydney, I can kind of understand math, but you know what I just cannot figure out?"

"What's that, my friend," replied Sydney. "Tell me what has you puzzled. If I can't help you, I promise I'll help you find someone who can."

Little Rascal slumped into the chair closest to Sydney's work bench. He put his paws inside his sweatshirt. "Well, it's something Pastor Penguin said at church last Sunday. Remember in his message when he was talking about the fact that God can see everyone at the same time, and He can see the whole world all at once?"

"Yes, I remember when he mentioned that. And I can understand why you would be puzzled," said an understanding Sydney.

Rascal sat right up in the chair. "Yeah, it really does have me stumped. I've been thinking about it all week. I mean, like right now for instance. I'm here with you, and I know my mom is probably at home starting to fix dinner, and dad is at the barber shop. But I can't even imagine what anyone else is doing. Oh, wait a minute; I bet Lester is taking his afternoon nap."

Both Sydney and Rascal chuckled as they thought of Lester all stretched out on the recliner in his den. "Get your things together," Sydney said to Rascal. "We're going for a little ride."

Rascal was all excited because *everyone* in Critter County *loves* to ride in Sydney's shuttlebug. And sure enough, that's what Rascal got to do. Sydney couldn't tell him where they were going, but when Sydney turned left at the Post Office, Rascal correctly guessed that they were headed toward the airport.

Sydney pulled the shuttlebug right up to hangar number three, the blue one with the brown acorn on the door. Rascal was so excited, he could hardly sit still.

"Am I going to get to see your plane, Sydney?"

Sydney smiled and answered real big, "Oh, you're going

to do more than just see it! You're going to ride in it."

Rascal could hardly believe his eyes and ears when Sydney told him to open the door of the airplane and get it.

Then the little squirrel instructed, "Now, fasten that seat belt real snug around you." Soon the propellers were whirling so fast that they looked like they were going backwards. The plane taxied to the end of the runway. Putt, putt, putt, the little aircraft bumped down the runway until the air under the wings began to lift it above the trees.

"Wheee, I can't believe it. I'm, really flying . . . a raccoon with wings," Rascal laughed. "Oh man, this is great!"

"Are you ready to look down, yet?" asked Sydney.

"Sure, I can handle it," answered Rascal.

So the little fellow looked out of his window at everything down below. "Hey, Sydney, what's that building over there?"

"That, my friend, is the Critter County Care Club. As I recall, you spent some time there once when your feelings were hurt."

"Yes, you're right. But the Love Birds helped me. What's that over there?" asked Rascal.

Sydney smiled and said, "Let me point things out to you. See that flat building with the blue roof?" Rascal nodded. "Well, that is the Post office we just passed on our way to the airport. There is the library and over there is the tree house that I call home. Speaking of homes, would you like to see yours?"

"I sure would," said a very excited raccoon. So Sydney banked the plane to the left, dipped the wing and pointed to Rascal's house. "There it is."

"Hey, Mother, look at me. I'm up in the sky!!"

"I don't think she can hear you. you'll have to wait till we touchdown to tell her of your little adventure. Now, I'd like to tell you something. Of course, we can't be God and can't even pretend to be like Him. But I thought if I brought you up here in my plane you could get a better feel for the way God can see more than one thing at a time. See, Rascal, there's your house . . . there's Lester's house . . . there's the park and your school and over there is . . . the hospital."

"Boy, I never could've believed I'd ever see all those places at once," said Rascal.

"Well, like I said, we can't be like God, but because He is God, He can see all of Critter County, the rest of the world, and each person on earth . . . all at the same time."

"Wow! God is watching me all the time," exclaimed Rascal.

"Can you now see why it is always important to do our very best?" asked Sydney.

The subject changed between the two friends to ideas about who would win the soccer game on Saturday afternoon. Soon it was time to leave the puffy white clouds and the feeling of flying like a bird. Rascal grew quiet as the little plane landed and drove back to the hangar. As he was removing his seat belt, Rascal said to Sydney, "Thanks for letting me go up for just a few minutes and see my world all at once. I'm glad we've got God, cause I don't think I could take care of everything the way He does . . . I have enough trouble with my room!!" Sydney and Rascal giggled and turned off the plane's engine.

Have the children go to the tables and give them page 5 of Critter County Activities.

5-8. *Critter County Friends:* Here are three of your favorite animal friends from Critter County. Each animal has some lines missing. You may connect the lines and finish the drawing of each critter and then color the picture.

8-10. *Match the Pictures:* As you look at the pictures on the top of the page, notice some are exactly like the pictures found in the dotted squares below. Cut out the picture squares and paste them beside the correct match. Be careful. Some may look alike at first, but if you look closer, you'll see the difference.

When all have finished with the activity sheets have the children go to the Critter County radio Station and sit on the floor in front of it. Be sure that the child who is today's announcer is prepared.

Sydney: Boys and girls, **WWCC** is coming to you live from the Critter County Fairgrounds. There is so much going on! Poncho the Pig is in the mud-sloppin' contest; Rascal is throwing a bean bag. And, why, Grandmother Mouse, hello. That's a beautiful blue ribbon that you're wearing.

Grandmother Mouse: Thank you, Sydney. A doll that I made won 1st place in the Arts and Crafts Show.

Sydney: Congratulations! I imagine you're quite proud.

Grandmother Mouse: It's always nice to know you've done a good job. The doll means a lot to me because I made it with my own hands.

Sydney: You know, Grandmother, that reminds me of Genesis in the Bible. It says that after God created man, He said, "It is good." We mean very much to Him. God made us with His own hands.

Grandmother Mouse: You are so right, Sydney. I could only give my doll a pretty face, or a nice dress. God gave us life!

Sydney: You heard it here, boys and girls. This is Sydney for **WWCC**—the Wonderful World of Critter County. Thanks for joining us.

Happy-face cookies and fruit juice are suggested for today's snack. Be sure to allow the children who chose appropriate duties from the Activi-Tree to help during snack time. Talk about the faces on the cookies. Notice how all have eyes and a mouth . . . but every cookie is different. After clean up have the children return to the story area.

Play the song "Sing Praise to Him," page 140, as the children assemble in the story area. When all have gathered, sing the song together.

Sing familiar songs as well as new ones. "The Heavens Are Telling," page 114;"Exceeding Great," page 129; "Forever Will I Praise Your Name," page 138;"He Is the King," page 141; and "Great Is Our Lord," page 115.

Prayer Song: "Hear Us as We Pray," page 143.

Prayer: Ask God to help the children listen as we talk about the time when man was created.

Have a small pan filled with enough sand or dirt to cover a clay figure hidden in the sand. The clay figure will represent Adam. Remember to give the child the mirror needed to complete his or her assignment from the Activi-Tree. Encourage the children to watch and listen carefully to today's lesson. Ask them to recall the Bible lesson from your first class time together. Give them plenty of time to answer and to share what they have thought about since that lesson.

It must have been something to look at the sky and trees, and the hills and lakes, and the cattle and birds, and all that God had prepared for man. But, did you notice we left out one very important part of God's creation when we studied our first lesson? We didn't talk about what happened when God created man. Ask, "Who has the mirror?" and "Who looked up the word *image* in the dictionary?" (Allow both children to identify themselves.) Ask the child who looked up the word to share the definition. (Image means "exact likeness.")

The Bible tells us God made man in His own image. (Ask the child with the mirror to walk around the room and let his or her classmates look at their image as you talk.)

As you look at the mirror, you don't really see you. You see just a reflection of your real self. Maybe this will help you understand that God did not make us exactly like Him. He made us to be an image of Himself.

We don't know if God has arms and legs and eyes and ears just like we have . . . because the Bible tells us God is a spirit. But we know we can believe we are something like God because He chose to make us in His image. Read (or allow an older child to read) Genesis 1:26. (You may want to retrieve the mirror now so there are no distractions during the lesson).

God Made Adam and Eve

Genesis 1:26-31; 2:7, 18-23

The Bible tells us that after God created the earth and everything in it, He looked around at everything He had made. He saw the mountains and the seashore. He heard the birds sing and he saw the creatures of the ocean. He looked all around and said His creation was "very good".

(Move Your hand about in the sand as you talk being careful not to uncover the clay figure until the right moment.) Then God had a wonderful thought. He said, "Let us make man in our own image." The Bible says God formed man of the dust of the ground. (Begin to work with both of your hands to uncover the clay figure.)

Now, isn't that something to think about? Everything else God made He spoke into existence. He asked for what He wanted. He spoke for it to come, and it appeared. But man was different. The Bible says God formed man out of the dust. God took time to make the first man, and his name was Adam. (Pick up the clay figure from the sand.)

Boys and girls, I want you to look very carefully at this man because the next thing God did is *so* important. I want you to understand how special God's knowledge is. You see, I made this man. He doesn't look like the kind of man God made because I made him out of clay. I am not able to do what God can do. No matter what I do to this man, he will not walk or talk or sit up or open his eyes. Nothing I can do will make this man come alive.

Adam was like this man until God gave Adam life. Does anyone know how Adam began to live? (Allow time for any child who knows to answer.)

The Bible says God *breathed* into Adam's nose, and Adam began to live. Isn't that something to know. Wouldn't you like to have been there to see God give Adam life? We should praise God for breathing life into the man He made. (Clap Your hands together as you repeat, "We praise you, God, for giving life. We praise Your holy name".)

God was so wise to know what to do to make Adam live. God was very wise about something else, too. He saw that all the birds had other birds and could make families to keep them company. He saw that all the animals could have families . . . but He saw that Adam was alone.

Our God, because He is so wise, knew it would not be good for Adam to be alone. He knew Adam would need someone. And so, The Bible tells us God did another special thing. He made Adam fall asleep. When Adam was in a very deep sleep, God took one of Adam's ribs and then closed up his side. God used the rib to make a special helper for Adam to love. God brought Adam's special helper to him when he woke up, and the Bible says Adam called her "woman" because she had been taken out of man.

Do you see how very special God is? He knew how to make man. He knew Adam could not be alone, and He knew exactly what to do to make the perfect helper for him. Let's praise God for His knowledge. (Clap Your hands together as you repeat, "We praise you God for being so wise, we praise Your holy name.)

Application: Now we have seen that we should praise God for His power in making our world, and we should praise Him for the special knowledge He had when he made man and woman. I have one more thought I want to share with you. Read (or have an older child read Psalm 139:1-3 and 14.) This last verse says, "I will praise you for I am fearfully and wonderfully made."

Lay a large sheet of butcher paper on the floor. Explain to

the children that God is so wise, He can make every person who has ever lived and no two people would be exactly the same. Illustrate this with the stamp pad. Encourage the children to take turns putting their hands on the pad and then making the copy of their handprint on the paper. Look carefully at the prints and see that each is different.

End this session by repeating, "I will praise you because I am fearfully and wonderfully made." Let's all bow our heads and praise God as we thank Him for making us.

Have the children go to the tables and give them page 6 from the Critter County activity book.

5-8. *Help Eve Find the Way!* Help Eve find her way to Adam. Draw a line from Eve as you find the correct way to Adam. Be careful to choose the right way so you will not be stopped by the river.

8-10. *Where Are the Animals?* Find the eight animals hiding in Adam's world. Circle the animals and then color the picture. The animals are pig, horse, bird, cat, monkey, elephant, sheep, lion.

When the children have finished the activity sheets, have them go to the Light Post on Memory Lane.

Light Post on Memory Lane

Begin today's visit by singing "Memory Lane," on page 130.

Divide the class into two groups and explain that we will complete an activity called "Make the Man". Give each group one of the two prepared posterboards. Encourage them to work as a team to fill in the blanks after looking up the Scripture reference. The team members must try to memorize each word as it is completed. The team whose members can recite the entire verse and show the completed man first is the winning team.

Close this session by singing "Great Is Our Lord," on page 115.

Craft Time

5-8. Praise God Bookmark: Use the materials mentioned at the beginning of the lesson. Cut the corner from a letter-size envelope. Allow the children to decorate the bookmark using the markers and/or stickers. Be sure to write the words, I will praise You because I am fearfully and wonderfully made," from Psalm 139:14 on the bookmark. (Or use the memory verse text.) Encourage the children to keep the bookmark for personal use or make several extra and mail bookmarks to children on a foreign mission field. See someone from your mission committee for names and addresses. This will give the children the opportunity to touch the lives of God's people in other lands.

8-10. The Making-of-a-Man Game: Each student will need one Styrofoam egg carton (undivided lid works best); felt pieces with patterns drawn from page 101: head and two hands-neutral color, Shirt-red, pants-blue, two feet-black, lid liner-green; seven bottle caps; construction paper; glue; and scissors.

Cut a piece of green felt into a 10″ X 13″ rectangle. This will be glued to the inside of the egg carton lid. (Cartons vary in size, so be sure the green liner is large enough to cover each lid.) Allow the students to draw around the bottom of the egg holders to make twelve circles that will be labeled and glued to the inside of each holder. These circles should be labeled: head, shirt, pants, right hand, left hand, right shoe, left shoe and the five remaining circles should each read, "lose turn."

Older students should be able to cut the felt pieces themselves. Younger children may need assistance. The students may draw a face with markers on the head. Cover and decorate the outside of the carton lid with construction paper and markers. (All felt pieces and bottle caps can be stored inside the carton.)

To Play the Game Alone: Place the carton on a table or the floor and stand a few feet away. Toss each bottle cap into the carton aiming for the holes labeled with body or clothing parts. Keep track of how many caps you throw to make a complete man. Build the man on the green felt as you "win" each piece. When you hit "lose turn" you count the bottle cap, but you do not add any piece to the body.

To Play the Game With a Friend: You will need two games. Take turns throwing the caps one at a time. If you hit a hole marked, "lose a turn", your opponent gets two throws before you can throw again. The first player to complete his or her man is the winner, and the game begins again.

Shuttlebug Ride Home

Well, boys and girls, we can praise God for such a good time together in Critter County today. We certainly were busy. As we ride home, I want you to tell me which activities were your favorites. (Allow the children time to answer.) We learned so much about our Creator and the knowledge He used to make us in His image. We want to continue praising Him for giving us eyes to see and ears to hear. We should be thankful to know He has made us so we can learn about Him and know the mighty things He has done.

Let's all say the memory verse together one more time. "Great is our Lord and mighty in power; his understanding has no limit, Psalm 147:5." When you go home, tell Your mother and daddy that you praise God for making you and placing you in your own special family.

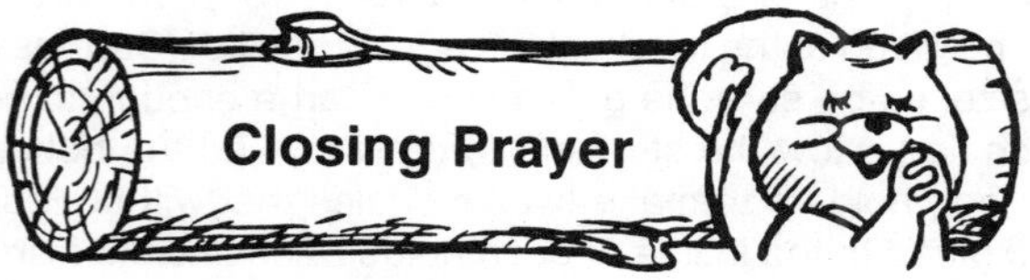

Closing Prayer

Dear Heavenly Father, You have made us, and You love us just the way we are. Thank You for choosing the color of (girl's name) hair and for giving (boy's name) legs that can run fast and play in Your world. Thank You for letting us know You as our Creator who chose to make us special. We praise You God. Your knowledge is too great for us to understand! Thank You for making us. Thank You for loving us. We praise Your name. Through Jesus, we pray, amen.

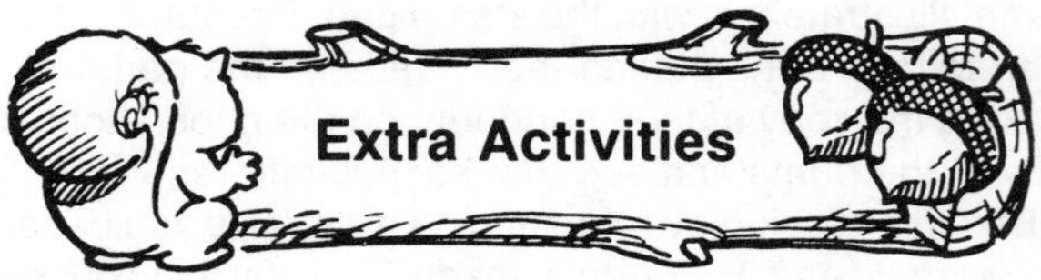

Extra Activities

The Making of a Man: Use one of the 8-10 year old games made today at craft time. Divide the class into two groups. (See directions under 8-10 crafts.) Or use two large sheets of butcher paper (one for each team). Draw the body parts life size as team members take turns throwing bottle caps into the labeled carton. The first team to complete a man is the winner.

All Around Eden: Have the class form two circles. The children stand an arm's length between each other. Appoint one child in each circle to be the "first man made". At the signal you give, this first player begins to weave in and out around the entire circle until he comes to his original starting position. When he arrives where he started, the person on his right begins to weave in and out around members in the circle. The entire process continues until each circle member has taken a turn weaving his way around the group. The first circle to have all of its members complete the weaving sits down, and is declared the winner. Mix up the circle and begin again.

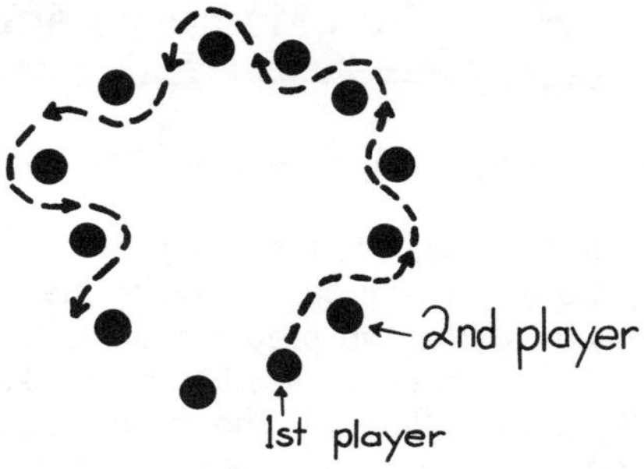

Lesson 3

Praise God for His Promises

Scripture: Genesis 8

Psalm Reference: Psalm 37:39, 40; Psalm 150:2a (Pause-to-Praise verse)

Memory Verse: The Lord is not slow in keeping his promise, as some understand slowness. He is patient with you, not wanting anyone to perish, but everyone to come to repentance.—2 Peter 3:9 (NIV)

Lesson Aim: As a result of studying this lesson, the children should be able to
1) Know that God kept His promise to Noah.
2) Feel the assurance that God will take care of them.
3) Name promises God has made and kept.
4) Praise God for keeping His promises.
5) Sing or say the memory verse, 2 Peter 3:9.

Materials Needed:
Pre-session. *Activi-Tree:* Write the following suggestions on slips of paper and attach to the tree.
- Hold the picture during Bible story time.
- Read Psalm 150:2a in the preparation for **Pause-to-Praise** center.
- Find Genesis 8:20-22 in your Bible and be ready to read it to the class later.
- Carry pitchers of water to fill tub for boats. (3)
- Pass out napkins and cups during snack time (2)
- Be the leader in line for our bathroom break.
- Hold prism (if available) during **Pause to Praise.**

Boats To Float: 1 spring clothespin for each student and glue toothpick, paper, tub of water

Preparation for Pause to Praise: Bible, construction paper, glue, various colors of yarn, scissors, cotton swabs, Wonders-of-God's-World box containing prism (if available).

Together Time. Boats from pre-session activity and tub of water.

Snack Time. Iced animal cookies and fruit punch.

Light Post on Memory Lane. Cardboard rainbow to hide in room.

Bible Story Time. Bible, picture of Noah building ark, posterboard and marker, stickers or inexpensive gifts like pencils or special buttons given as the teacher keeps her promise.

Crafts.
5-8. *Noah's Dove:* Posterboard, dove pattern from page 101, crayons or markers, two pennies per child, and tape.

8-10. *Birdfeeder:* 15″ piece of yarn for each student, cellophane tape, any cereal shaped like "o's."

Extra Activities.
Hop to the Ark: ball or balloon.
Stay Afloat: Water in bucket, jar lid or custard cup, five pennies per child.

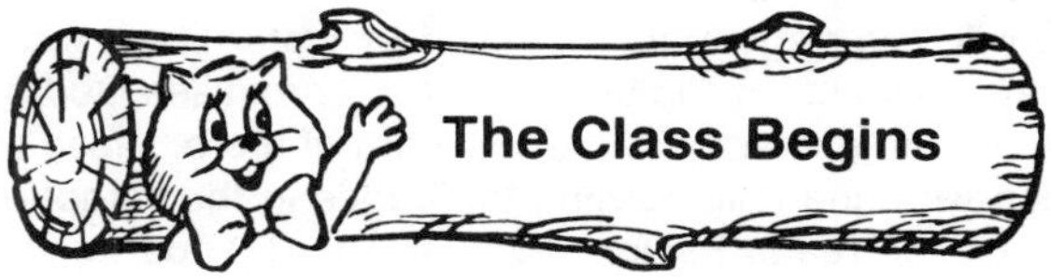

Welcome the Children
Greet each child by name. Choose one characteristic to praise God for as you welcome each one. Example: "I praise God for Your beautiful hair, Julie. It looks especially pretty today." Encourage each child toward a Pre-session activity as you tell each we have praised God for His power as He made our world. We have praised Him for His knowledge as He made all people different. Today we will be praising Him for keeping His promises.

Pre-session Activities
Activi-Tree. Remind the children to choose a paper from the Activi-Tree. Be ready to assist as the children follow the instructions on the paper they choose.
Boats to Float. Use the materials listed to make boats that will float in the tub (or large pan of water). Remove the spring from the clothespin and glue the two flat sides of the clothespin together. Cut a square from thin paper to use as a sail. Have the child decorate his or her sail with markers or crayons. Glue the toothpick inside the hole formed by the joining of the flat sides of the clothespin. Weave the sale onto the toothpick as illustrated. Save the boats to float during **Together Time.**

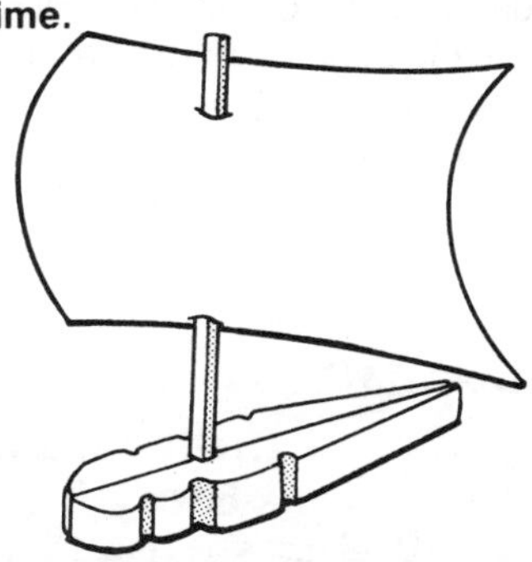

Preparation for Pause to Praise. If you have access to a prism, position it so the children can see the colors of the rainbow as they are reflected through the glass. Talk with the children about the symbol of God's promise as you watch them use strips of colored yarn to make a rainbow picture. Dip the cotton swabs in glue and make an arch across the center of a piece of construction paper. Have the children cut lengths of different colors of yarn to press into each glue arch in their rainbow. Be sure to write, "Praise Him for His Acts of Power" somewhere on the picture. Use one of the pictures or save the teacher's copy for the scrapbook. (This is the third page of the illustrated scrapbook of Psalm 150.)

Pause-to-Praise Session: Have one child read Psalm 150:2a out loud. Allow another child to hold the Wonder's-of-God's-World box containing the prism. (Or use a rainbow picture if no prism is available.) Open the box after reading the Scripture. Have one child explain how the rainbow was given by God to show He would keep His promise. Every time we see a rainbow we should remember to praise God for keeping His word, and we should remember that the world will never again be destroyed by water like it was in the day of Noah. This is just one of the promises God has made. In our lesson today we will learn of more. Close this session with one child turning the pages in the scrapbook as he or she reads Psalm 150:1-2a. Clap hands together and say, "We praise You, God, for Your acts of power. We praise Your holy name".

Together Time: Have the children bring their boats to the large group as they assemble for **Together Time.** (The tub of water should have been filled by the children who chose this responsibility from the Activi-Tree.) Talk with the children as they place their boats in the water and gently blow the sail to set the boats in motion. Tell them we will be talking about the very first boat mentioned in the Bible. Ask them to be thinking about whose boat it was and what was carried inside.

Lets put the boats away for now so we can take another trip to Critter County. It is time to get into the Shuttlebug for today's journey. Everybody buckle up! Remember it is a bumpy ride.

It is Sunday in Critter County. We will ride to the little white church above the pond where all the critters gather for worship. We'll look in on our friends and see what lessons they want us to learn today. We'll study a special Bible lesson about God's promises too!. There is the church . . . just over the next hill. Everybody put on a happy face, and we'll join the critters for worship.

All of us know what a promise is. When someone promises they will do something for us, we expect them to keep their word. God made many promises to people who lived thousands of years ago and He keeps His promises to us today. God always keeps His promises!

The critters will find a way to cheer up little Lunchbox the lion cub, as they share some promises from God. Let's listen. (Read the story.)

The Best Gift of All

One of the best things about living in Critter County is the way that everyone seems to care about everyone else. It was no different on this particular Sunday when families from all over Critter County were gathering together for the morning church service. At the time in the service where pastor Penguin usually prays, a hand was raised.

"Yes, did you want to say something, Lester?" asked Pastor Penguin.

Lester stood to his feet. "Well, yes I would" the big lion exclaimed. "You see, Liona Lou and I are kind of sad today. Now, it's not often you find me in a dreary mood, but today I am not whistling. I didn't skip through the woods on my way to church. I didn't even jump the river. I didn't care if my paws got wet. I just walked across the deep water with my head hung so-o-o-o low. In fact, my paws are still dripping."

"What is the matter, Lester? What has you so sad?" asked pastor Penguin.

"Well, you see . . . it's Lunchbox," explained Lester. "He's not been feeling well this week. He's had a pain in his tummy. Liona Lou and I didn't know what to do. He couldn't even eat his favorite lion chow. So, I finally called Dr. Duck to see what he thought we should do. Well," the big lion started to cry, "Dr. Duck told us to bring Lunchbox to the Critter County Hospital. We took him there last night. The poor little fella is so scared."

Pastor Penguin spoke more softly now.

"Does Dr. Duck know what is the matter with Lunchbox?" he asked.

"Well", said Lester, "he has to do an operation. He has to have his appendix out. Poor Lunchbox is so scared. Would you please pray for him?"

With that Lester sat down and put his big paws around Liona Lou's shoulders to comfort her.

Pastor Penguin thought for a moment. Then his face lit up. It was obvious he had thought of something wonderful.

"We can not only pray for Lunchbox. I propose we give Lunchbox a gift from all of us. You see my message this morning is on God's promises. God promises us special things to help us when we are in situations that are hard for us. It sounds like Lunchbox could use some of those right about now. Before you leave church today, I'd like all of you to think of one of God's promises and write it down on a piece of paper. I will take all the slips of paper and put them in a big box this afternoon. Then I'll take the box to the hospital tonight and give it to Lunchbox."

So that's just what everybody did. After the service was over, everyone stayed in their seats for a few extra minutes to think of a special promise they could write down for Lunchbox. When Pastor Penguin went to wrap the box full of notes that afternoon, he was surprised at how many verses the critters thought of. He was certain that these would make the little lion cub feel loved and remind him that God was his friend.

Later that evening, Pastor Penguin walked into Lunchbox's hospital room. A nurse was putting a clean nightshirt on Lunchbox. Lunchbox perked up when he saw Pastor Penguin walk in.

"Well, hello there Lunchbox," said Pastor Penguin. "It looks like everybody is taking good care of you."

Lunchbox pulled back the blankets and climbed into his clean bed.

"I'm really scared about my operation. They are going to put me to sleep. I have to let them do it, or I won't get better. Oh, I'm, so-o-o-o scared," said Lunchbox as he began to cry.

Pastor Penguin reached out to pat the little cub's head.

"Now, Lunchbox" he said, "I brought something here that should make you feel better."

With that he went back into the hall and returned carrying a big red box with a hole in the top just big enough for Lunchbox's paw.

"What is the box for?" asked Lunchbox.

"This is a present from everybody at church this morning," said Pastor Penguin. "We figured you would be feeling scared about being in the hospital all by yourself. This box is full of God's promises found in the Bible."

"Will they help me feel better?" asked Lunchbox.

"Oh, you will still have to have the operation, Lunchbox, but these will make your heart feel better," said Pastor Penguin. "I'll tell you what you should do. Every time you're feeling scared or alone, you can reach in here and take a promise. I guarantee that there are plenty here to get you through next Thursday when you'll have your big day."

Lunchbox took the box. "Do you mind if I get one now?" he asked.

"No, that's a great idea" said Pastor Penguin.

Lunchbox put his paw through the hole and fished around for just the right slip of paper. He took it out and read it aloud.

"'I will never leave thee nor forsake thee.' Wow, is this what Jesus promises me? Will He really be right here with me from now until the operation is over? Even at night time when I miss my mother and daddy?" asked Lunchbox.

"That's right" said Pastor Penguin.

"Boy, I do feel better. What a great present, Pastor Penguin," said Lunchbox as he looked around the room.

On the bottom of his bed sat a new teddy bear. On his dresser were cards that his friends had made to let him know they were thinking about him. His grandmother and grandfather had even sent him flowers they had picked in the Critter County woods. As he thought about all these gifts he turned to Pastor Penguin and said, "The cards and the teddy bear are nice presents. My friends and my mother and daddy gave them to me to let me know they love me, and they miss me. God gave me His promises, and He is able to stay here with me. That's really neat. That makes His promises . . . the best gift of all!"

Have the children go to the tables and give them page 7 from the Critter County Activity Books.

5-8. *I Promise:* Color the card and write a special promise of something you will do on the inside. Cut out and fold the card on the dotted line. Give your card to someone special. Remember to keep the promise you wrote on it.

8-10. *An Envelope of Promises:* Look up the Scriptures on the promise strips. Write the promise in your own words on the lines on the strips. Cut out the envelope on the black lines. Fold along the dotted lines and glue the sides. Place your promise strips inside. Keep the envelope of promises near your bed so you can read a different promise each day.

When the children have finished their activity papers, have them go to the Critter County Radio Station and sit in front of it. You will need someone to be Sydney and someone to read the part of Rascal for today's newscast.

Sydney: Sydney, here. You're listening to the Wonderful World of Critter County—**WWCC.** The weather today is being brought to you by Dapper Ducks, makers of raincoats, umbrellas, and galoshes. It looks like Critters may be needing their umbrellas again today. It should reach a high of 65°, with afternoon showers. And now, we take you to Rascal for the sports.

Rascal: Not much happening in sports, Sydney. I'm afraid most of the games have been canceled because of the rain.

Sydney: I see. You know, Rascal, it's been raining for several days here in Critter County.

Rascal: You know it! I'm beginning to wonder if it will ever stop!

Sydney: Radio listeners! Did you hear that? How do we know that the rain is going to stop? God promised Noah that never again would He destroy the earth with water. And God sealed His promise with a beautiful rainbow. The rain will stop!

Rascal: Forty days and forty night of rain. Can you imagine? That would be good for Dapper Ducks' business!

Sydney: Yes! Dapper Ducks—makers of raincoats, umbrellas, and galoshes. That's weather and sports for today. We now return to our regularly scheduled programming.

Animal crackers (iced variety for older classes) and fruit punch are the perfect snack for today. Talk with the children about the animals Noah took in the ark. Ask them what they think it would have been like to have been on board. What would they see and smell? What would the rain sound like? After clean up, have the children return to the story area.

Play the song, "Sing Praise to Him," page 140, as the children assemble in the story area. when all have gathered, sing the song together.

Sing: Familiar songs as well as new ones. "Forever Will I Praise Your Name," page 138, "Exceeding Great" page 129; "Promises," page 116; "Sing and Shout It," page 136; and "Great Is Our Lord," page 115.

Prayer Song: "Hear Us as We Pray," page 143.

Prayer. Ask God to help us remember He takes care of us. Ask Him to help the children be good listeners as they hear the promises God makes to Noah.

What is a promise? (Allow time for the children to answer.) A promise is a statement that one will do or stop doing some specific thing. When someone makes a promise, what do you expect him to do about that promise? (Again, wait for the children to answer.) That's right, you expect him to keep his promise—do what he says he will do. Listen carefully, I promise to give something special to every good listener in our circle when we finish this lesson.

Who has the picture of Noah? (Let the child who chose this responsibility from the Activi-Tree show the picture to the class.) I am sure you have heard the story of Noah. God told him to build a boat big enough to hold two of every kind of animal He had created.

Does anyone know how long it took Noah to build the boat? It took Noah and his sons over 100 years to build a boat that big. He followed all the directions God had given him, and when it was finished, he called all of the animals to come inside. The animals came two by two, and Noah, his family, and all the animals went inside the boat so that God could keep His promise. He promised that Noah and his family would be safe. The Bible says that God closed the door of the ark. (Open your Bible to Genesis 8.)

God Keeps His Promise
Genesis 8

The Bible says it rained and rained and rained. It rained for forty days and forty nights. Water covered the whole earth. Water covered all the mountain tops, every tree and bush . . . everything! All the creatures and people who were not in the ark, were swallowed up by the flood. There was water everywhere . . . as far as you could see. But, inside the ark, Noah, his family, and the animals were safe. Let's praise God for keeping His promise to Noah. (Encourage the children to clap their hands and repeat, "We praise you, God, for keeping Your promise. We praise Your holy name!".)

One day the rain stopped. There was no more noise of thunder, no sound of raindrops on the roof. The Bible says God sent a "wind" over the earth to make the water do down. Noah and his family floated on the water for ten months before the tops of the mountains could be seen. Finally, the day came when Noah sent a bird out of the ark. He wanted to see if the the bird could find a place to build a nest. (Optional: Use the Wonder's-of-God's-World box to show the raven, then the dove, and then the olive branch.) The first bird Noah sent from the ark was a raven. The Bible says the raven flew back to the ark because it could not find a place to rest. The next time Noah sent a bird, he chose a dove. The dove could not find a place to rest, either. So it returned to the ark. Seven days later, Noah sent the dove again. This time, Noah was happy to see the dove return with an olive branch in its beak. This sign helped Noah to know the trees were almost ready to have the birds build nests in them again. Seven days later, Noah sent the dove out again, and the bird did not return. It had found some safe, dry place to build a home.

Noah waited until God told him to come out of the ark. When that day arrived, Noah did something very special. The Bible says Noah built an altar to praise God. Noah thanked God for keeping His promise.

Application: God had promised Noah He would not allow his family to be harmed if they made the boat and took the animals inside. But that was not the only promise God made. The Bible tells us God smelled the sweet air as it came from Noah's altar, and God made more promises.

Have the child who looked up Genesis 8:20-22 read it now. (Be prepared to write on the posterboard or chalkboard.) Listen carefully to the verses one more time, and when you hear a promise God made, raise Your hand. We will list the promises on the board. (You may have to draw simple pictures for non-readers).

1. Never again curse the ground
2. Never destroy animals and living things by water
3. As long as earth lasts there will always be:
    a. Seed time and harvest (spring & fall)
    b. Cold and heat
    c. Summer and winter
    d. Day and night.

Now let's look at our list. Has God kept His promises? (Read through each item and allow the class to answer "yes.") After each promise, clap Your hands and repeat, "We praise You, God, for keeping Your promise. We praise Your holy name!"

End this session by keeping Your promise and giving a treat to each of the children in Your class. (Optional.)

Have the children go to the tables and give them page 8 of the Critter County Activity Book.

5-8. *God Keeps His Promise:* Look carefully at the pictures. They are all mixed up. Can you number the pictures to put the story in proper order? After placing the pictures in correct order, you may draw a rainbow with crayons or markers.

8-10. *Noah Word Search:* The ark has a word search puzzle on it's side. See if you can find all the words listed in the key, then color the picture.

When the children have finished their activity sheets, have them go to the Light Post on Memory Lane.

Light Post on Memory Lane

Say the memory verse several times together before playing the memory game. Before class make a cardboard rainbow 6″ wide and 3½″ to 4″ high. Write the memory verse on the back of the rainbow. Have one student hide the rainbow as the other students close their eyes. The rainbow must be placed in plain sight. The students will be given thirty seconds to find the rainbow. If they do not find it, the entire class repeats the memory verse in unison. If it is found, the student that found it may choose any classmate or teacher to recite the verse from memory. The finder gets to be the next one to hide the rainbow. No one person may be called on twice until everyone has been called on once.

Close this session by singing, "Promises," page 116.

Craft Time

5-8. Noah's Dove: Use the materials listed to make a dove that will balance on the child's finger. Use the pattern on page 101 to draw a dove on the poster board. Allow older children to cut out the dove you have drawn. Younger children may need some assistance. Encourage the children to color their dove by using the markers or crayons. Turn the dove over and tape one penny in approximately the same area of each wing. Turn the dove right-side-up again and place your index finger under the head and neck area. The pennies should allow the dove to balance as it rests on your finger. Let the children pretend they are Noah as he takes the bird back into the ark. Encourage them to say the memory verse as they walk around the room balancing Noah's Dove.

8-10. Bird Feeder: Use the materials listed to make bird feeders for each student to take home. Cut a piece of yarn 15″ in length. Tie a large knot at the bottom of the string to keep the cereal from slipping off. Wrap a piece of cellophane tape around the top part of the yarn to make a point. This acts as a "needle" and makes it easy to thread the cereal onto the yarn. The students thread the cereal one at a time leaving 4″ of the yarn vacant to make a loop that will easily slip over a tree branch or fence post. Talk about how Noah took care of the birds and animals in the ark while God was keeping them safe as He promised. Encourage the children to hang their bird feeder where they will be able to watch the birds come to eat.

Have each child help clean up the craft area and then go to the Shuttlebug for the ride home.

Shuttlebug Ride Home

Everybody into the Shuttlebug! We've had a big day at Critter County and now it is time to go home. Buckle up because the ride will be a little bumpy today. We have learned so much about our God who keeps His promises. Let's see if you remember any promises God made in our story today. (Allow time for the children to answer: will not destroy the earth by flood again; kept Noah and his family safe; there'll always be seed time and harvest, cold and heat, summer and winter, day and night.) Let's all say the memory verse before we get home.

Closing Prayer

Dear God, we thank You for showing us how to keep our promises. We praise You for taking care of Noah and the animals. We praise You for promising to never again destroy the earth by water. Help us to trust in You and not be afraid in stormy weather. Thank You, God, for taking care of us. In Jesus name, amen.

Extra Activities

Hop to the Ark: Divide the class into two teams. Play this game inside or outside. Make a line with rope or tape to mark the Ark area. Have both teams stand side by side a few feet apart and equal distance from the Ark area. Place a ball or balloon between the first players knees. He or she must waddle or hop the distance to the Ark area. After crossing over the line, the player takes the ball or balloon back to the next person in line. The first team to have all members complete the relay is the winning team.

Stay Afloat: Have the class take turns trying to drop five pennies into a jar lid floating on the surface of a bucket or tub of water. The student must aim for the lid, and all pennies must land safely without sinking the lid. If the student is successful, he keeps the pennies. If not. He gives the pennies to the next player in line.

Lesson 4

Praise God for His Wisdom

Scripture: Genesis 37:1-36; 39:1, 2:41; 40-46; 41:53-57; 42:3; and 45:1-15

Psalm References: Psalm 56:3, 4; Psalm 86:11, 12; Psalm 150:2b (Pause-to-Praise verse)

Memory Verse: My purpose is . . . that they may know the mystery of God, namely, Christ, in whom are hidden all the treasures of wisdom and knowledge.—Colossians 2:2, 3 (NIV)

Lesson Aim: As a result of studying this lesson, the children should be able to

1) Know that God knows all things, and God's wisdom will bring about what is best.
2) Feel secure in knowing God is able to help in any situation. There is security within His wisdom.
3) Name specific ways God helped Joseph.
4) Tell how Joseph's bad times worked out for the best.
5) Praise God for His wisdom.
6) Sing or say the memory verse, Colossians 2:2, 3.

Materials Needed:

Pre-session. *Activi-Tree:* Write the following directions on slips of paper and fasten to the Activi-Tree before class. Be ready to assist the younger students as they follow directions. Have reference books and Bibles on hand for the children to use.

- Look up the story of Joseph in our Bible Story Book. See if you can find two reasons Joseph's brothers were angry with him.
- Look up the word *interpret* in the dictionary and remember its meaning.
- See if you can find some of the names of Joseph's brothers and write them on the board. (Hint: Look carefully through Genesis 35:23-26.) (2)
- Be the leader in line during restroom break.
- Hand out the napkins and cups during refreshment time (2)
- Hold the Wonders-of-God's-World box during Bible story time.
- Drive the Shuttlebug when we leave for Critter County.
- Look up Psalm 56:3, 4. Be ready to read these verses during our lesson.

Mural, Mural on the Wall: White paper, crayons, tape, poster paint and brushes.

Preparation for Pause to Praise: Class scrapbook, Bible, used curriculum pictures of well-known Bible stories, paper, glue.

Critter County Radio Station. Sydney puppet; a stuffed rabbit or rabbit puppet with glasses; a small ceramic vase.

Snack Time. Squares of bread, peanut butter and jelly, plastic knives, fruit juice.

Bible Story Time. Wonders-of-God's-World box containing: sprig of wheat or a picture of wheat, multicolored (striped) material, picture of brothers, picture of camel caravan, and picture of a king.

Light Post on Memory Lane. Cake pan, sand, popsicle sticks with words from verses on slips of paper, timer or bell.

Crafts.

5-8. *God's Grain Paperweight:* Five or six different color seeds or beans, baby food jar, glue, felt, ribbon, paper cup.

8-10. *3-D Model of Joseph:* $3\frac{1}{2}$" Styrofoam cone, 1" styrofoam ball, $1\frac{1}{2}$" piece of chenille wire, black felt, flesh color felt, striped material, yarn, solid color material.

Extra Activities. Newspaper, forty 3 X 5 cards, marker.

Welcome the Children

Be in the classroom before the children arrive. Be sure to face them at eye level as you talk to them and call each student by name. Encourage the children to choose an activity from the Activi-Tree and then join one of the Pre-session activity centers. Introduce new students to assistants and leaders.

Pre-session Activities

Activi-Tree. See the list of Materials Needed at the beginning of this lesson for responsibilities to be written on the slips fastened to the tree. Be sure there is a slip for each class member and be ready to help beginning readers if they need extra assistance.

Mural, Mural on the Wall. Have eight pieces of blank white paper with one of the phrases listed below written at the bottom of each sheet. (Eight is a general number. If your class is large, you may need to add papers and phrases.) Let each child choose a paper from the titles they find interesting or shuffle the papers and lay them face down allowing the phrases to be chosen at random. Have crayons or markers, paint brushes and paint on hand. Instruct the children to draw the portion of Joseph's life indicated by the phrase on their paper. When all have completed the picture, allow the children to help as you fasten the pictures together by taping one to the other on the back of each sheet. Conceal the mural somewhere in the room until it is shared at **Together Time**

Phrases: Joseph's father choosing Joseph as his favorite.
Joseph receiving his coat of many colors.
Joseph sleeping in his tent dreaming.
Joseph's brothers throwing him into the pit.
Joseph being sold to the caravan.
Joseph's father crying because he believes his son is dead.
Joseph arriving in Egypt.
Joseph becoming a ruler with the king.

Preparation for Pause to Praise: Have one child read Psalm 150:2b. Ask the children what the phrase "surpassing greatness" means to them. (If this proves to be a hard question, guide their thinking to each word or have one of the children in the center look up the word "surpassing" in the dictionary.) Surpassing means "greatly exceeding others, to go beyond." Greatness means "huge, big, large in size." Ask the children if they can remember any Bible stories that remind them of how "great" God is. (Allow time for the children to answer.) Show the children the used curriculum pictures you have on hand. Encourage them to work as a group to make a collage that will serve as the fourth page of the scrapbook. Cut out the pictures that show God's greatness and glue them side by side, on top of and underneath one another to cover the scrapbook page entirely. Write the phrase, "Praise Him for His Surpassing Greatness" on the finished page and add it to the scrapbook. Allow the children to point to the pictures they entered and tell how the story shows God's greatness.

During Pause to Praise: Have one of the children from your activity center read the verse of Scripture from Psalm 150:2b to the group. Have one child explain the collage and than ask class members to look for stories in the collage they recognize from the Scriptures. After each story, clap your hands and repeat the phrase, "We praise You, God, and see your greatness. We praise Your holy name".

Ask one child to offer a prayer to God for all He has done. Close the session by allowing one child to read the entire scrapbook as another child turns the pages.

Together Time: Have the children bring the mural made during Pre-session to the large group. Look at the mural and discuss how Joseph had so many happy and sad experiences in his life. Allow the children to decide what pictures should have been a happy or a sad time for Joseph. Tell the children that one thing was true in every picture. God knew what was happening to Joseph, and God was going to make it all work out just right. Ask the children if they can think of any happy or sad times they remember having in their lives. Do they feel God was with them? Close the session by praising God. Clap your hands together and say, "We praise You, God, you are great and wise. We praise Your holy name".

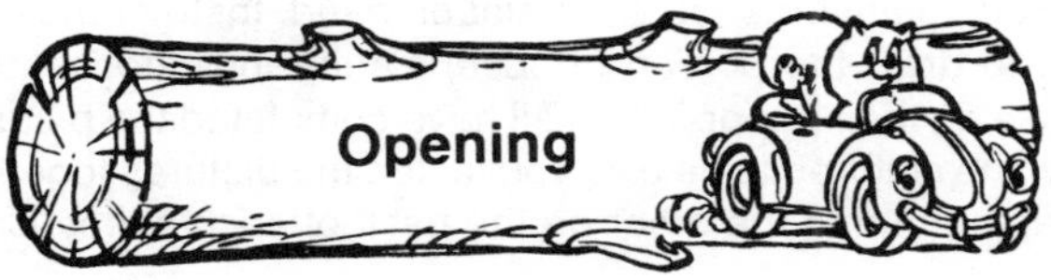

Everyone who has a brother, line up on this side of me. (Point to left side.) Everyone who has a sister, line up on this side. (Point to right.) Now, all of you who are still seated, hold up your hands and tell me what you would like to have best, a sister or a brother. (Allow the children to answer.)

Those who have no brother or sister, yet, may sit in the front of the shuttlebug for our ride to Critter County today. (Let the child who chose the slip from the Activi-Tree drive the Shuttlebug.) The rest of us will sit behind as we travel. I can't wait to see what happens to the critters in our story. After the pretend ride, say, "Here we are at the farm. Let's go see what we can learn."

As you grow, you will learn many things about God's wisdom. You'll find out why there is salt in the ocean water and why the earth is so many miles away from the sun. God used wisdom beyond our imagination when He made the earth. Harry and Rascal discover some new facts about God's wisdom when they find corn in the barn on the Critter County farm. Let's listen.

An Ear That Speaks

The hay wagons lined the dirt road. They were packed so full and the fresh straw was spilling over the sides. Big red juicy apples were bobbing their little heads in tubs of water just waiting for someone to come to their rescue. The creek running through the Critter County farm seemed to be singing as it wound its way through the rocks. Everything was ready for the picnic to begin.

Soon, the cars, bikes, and even Sydney's shuttlebug began arriving at the farm. Everyone was expecting lots of fun and laughter. Once a year in Critter County, everyone goes to the farm for a Western-style picnic. Sydney always looks so cute. He wears a big cowboy hat, plaid shirt, jeans with a western belt, and of course, cowboy boots. Sydney usually takes charge of the day and organizes the activities. Grandmother Mouse, who is the very best cook in Critter County, is put in charge of the food. She gets several of the women to help her prepare a most delicious meal. Lester takes care of the entertainment. He keeps everybody laughing with his games and fun. Even the kids, like Rascal and Lunchbox, have a part in keeping the little critters busy.

"Oh, the weather is just perfect today, and we're going to have so much fun!" said Grandmother Mouse to Muffin as she gave the little mouse a big hug.

As everyone continued arriving, the kids ran toward the field to play ball. The mothers went toward the picnic area, while the daddies looked at the barns, tools, and tractors.

"Hey, Lunchbox, let's go play on the tire swing," called Rascal. Poncho Pig and Tommy the turtle began a game of ball. The game moved rather slowly (because turtles are rather slow), and Poncho soon moved on to eating.

After the potato salad was all eaten, and the watermelon-seed-spitting contest was over, the fun games started up again. One of the "fun spots" was the big red barn. Inside the barn, there is a huge loft that can only be reached by climbing a rickety old ladder. Oh, the mice love it there. They swing from the loft, down to the floor, by holding onto ropes and squealing loudly.

Sydney was out behind the barn looking for a broom when he spotted Harry the horse and Poncho the pig heading over toward the corn barn.

Sydney thought to himself, *Guess they're going to the corn barn to get a little snack!* And he chuckled to himself as he picked up the old, wooden broom.

As Harry and Poncho walked into the barn, Rascal was just coming out. His mouth was so full of corn that he couldn't even talk, and he had lots of corn stuffed into his jeans!

"Well, son, looks like we all had the same idea. There's nothing that tastes quite like Critter County corn from this barn," said Poncho.

"Boy, you're not just kidding, Poncho. This is real good eatin'," replied the raccoon.

"Hey, Rascal, where did you get that corn?" Poncho questioned.

"From the ears over in that corner," sputtered Rascal. His mouth was almost too full to speak.

"That's what I thought. Sydney asked us not to eat from that pile; that's the seed corn," reminded Poncho.

"What in the world is 'seed corn'? Rascal asked.

"Well, my boy, I like to think of it as next year's dinner. You see, it works like this. Some of the corn grown here on the farm gets eaten."

"Yeah, that's my kind of corn!" said the little raccoon as he threw in another mouthful. "We're talking . . . *GOOD* eating!"

"Yes, that's right, but if you don't plan ahead, you'll have no corn for dinner next year," Poncho continued his explanation. "You see, what you must do is save some of the ears and let them dry out. Then you put them aside until the spring."

"Hey, wait a minute, it's going to go to waste. I'll eat it," volunteered Rascal.

"No, friend, it's not going to go to waste," continued Poncho. In fact, just the opposite is true. These few ears of corn that you see here will be planted in the spring. Each little kernel or seed will be watered and kept warm by God's rain and sunshine. It will grow to produce many ears of corn."

"Let me see if I got this," said Rascal. "You don't eat some of the ears of corn. You let them dry out and die. Then, you plant the seeds and whomp . . . more corn than you ever would have had from just the one ear."

Smiling, Poncho patted Rascal on the shoulder.

"Yes, that's the idea," said Poncho. You almost said it better than I did. Sometimes something must die to give life to something else."

"Yeah, that's the way I had it figured," said Rascal proudly.

Just then, Rascal turned, and began to walk out of the barn. As he did, the whole side of his pants split wide open, and corn went flying everywhere.

"Oops, now I've really done it. Mother's going to get me now," Rascal muttered to himself as he walked away.

Harry and Poncho stood smiling and watching the little fellow as he walked out of sight.

Have the children go to the tables and give them page 9 from the activity books.

5-8. *Down on the Farm Game:* Color the gameboard. Make the number cube which will tell you how many spaces you are to move each time. Take turns playing with a friend to help Rascal and Harry get to the barn to find corn.

8-10. *Barn Toss:* Follow the directions for making the Barn Toss game. Glue the pieces on posterboard to make them sturdy. Play the game with a friend.

When all have finished the activity sheets, have the children go to the Critter county Radio Station and sit in front of it. (Choose today's announcer if you did not include this on the Activi-Tree.) You will need someone to be Sydney and someone to be Beautiful the bunny during today's newscast.

Sydney: **WWCC** takes you today to the Critter County Art Gallery! This is Sydney, and we're with Beautiful Bunny, Critter County's prized artist. Good afternoon, Beautiful.

Beautiful: Hello, Sydney. Welcome to our Art Gallery.

Sydney: I understand, Beautiful, that you are working on a *very* special vase.

Beautiful: Why, yes, Sydney. You can see the beginnings of the vase here on the table.

Sydney: Beautiful! That's just an ugly lump of clay!

Beautiful: Yes, Sydney, that is what it looks like now, but I know what it can look like with a little work.

Sydney: That's very interesting, Beautiful. It reminds me of how God works in our lives.

Beautiful: Yes, and how He worked in the life of Joseph.

Sydney: Why, yes, Beautiful! Sometimes, it is hard for us to see how good can come out of bad. I can't believe you can make a beautiful vase out of a lump of clay!

Beautiful: I know. Sometimes, it's hard for me to see that my mother and daddy spank me because they love me. They want to bring good out of bad.

Sydney: That's another good example, Beautiful. God knows that sometimes we can look like an ugly lump of clay, but with a little bit of work . . . we can be a beautiful vase.

Beautiful: God brings good out of bad.

Sydney: Beautiful, thanks so much for joining us. This is Sydney with **WWCC,** signing off.

Today we are suggesting squares of bread and peanut butter and jelly for snacks. Cut each slice of bread into 4 pieces and allow the children to spread their own peanut butter and jelly on the squares. Talk with the children about how wheat is grown to make bread. Our Bible story will teach us about what happened to the wheat in Egypt, and what Joseph did to help.

After clean up, have the children return to the story area.

Play the song "Sing Praise to Him," page 140, as the children assemble in the story area. When all have gathered, sing the song together.

Sing familiar songs as well as new ones. "Give Glory to the Lord," page 135; "God's Wisdom," page 117; "Promises," page 116; "Never Will I Leave You," page 135; and "Forever Will I Praise Your Name," page 138:

Prayer Song: "Hear Us as We Pray," page 143.

Prayer: Ask God to help the children listen as we share the lesson about Joseph. Help them to think about their own brothers and sisters and to know that He will always work all things out for the best.

Have the Wonders-of-God's-World box ready containing the items mentioned in Materials Needed at the beginning of this lesson.

Brothers and sisters are very special! Sometimes we wonder what it would be like to be all by ourselves in the family. We wouldn't have to share a room or any of our toys or special treasures. But, did any of you ever have your brother or sister go away to visit or go to camp without you?" (Allow time for the children to answer.) That's when we realize how much we miss them.

Today our Bible lesson tells us about brothers who were all members of a large family. Eleven of these brothers belonged to Joseph. *(Child's name)* can tell us the names of some of Joseph's brothers because he or she chose this assignment from the Activi-Tree. (Allow this child time to share what he or she has learned: Reuben, Simeon, Levi, Judah, Issachar, Zebulun, Benjamin, Dan, Naphtali, Gad, and Asher.)

Now Joseph's brothers were very angry at him. If you talked to one of them, you wouldn't think they liked Joseph at all. They said very mean things about him when they talked to each other. Why were they so angry? *(Child's name)* looked up the answer to this question during Presession. What did you find out? (Allow time for this child to answer, telling the class about Joseph's coat of many colors and his ability to interpret dreams.)

Let's turn to our Bible and see how God worked in Joseph's life. God knew all the things that would happen to Joseph even before the things happened. God knew how to work everything out just right. (Have the Wonders-of-God's-World box ready with articles inside.)

God's Wisdom in Joseph's Life

Genesis 37:1-36; 39 1, 2; 41:40-46; 41:53-57; 42:3; 45:1-15

Joseph was a good boy, and his brothers knew it was no secret that their father loved Joseph more than he loved any one of them. They were jealous when their father gave Joseph a beautiful coat of many colors. (Take the multi-colored striped cloth from the box.) They wished he had never been given such a gift. And to make everything worse, they didn't like Joseph when he would tell them about his strange dreams.

Joseph had dreams that sounded like his whole family would someday bow down in front of him. Joseph was sure the dreams would come true, and so he talked about the dreams a lot. His brothers grew tired of hearing from him. They became more and more angry.

One day, Joseph's father sent him to see his brothers who had taken the flocks to eat grass in another part of the land. Joseph obeyed his father, but when his brothers saw him coming they became so angry they talked about killing him.

Joseph's brothers took his beautiful coat and threw Joseph into a deep pit. Reuben planned to come back and rescue Joseph. He wanted to take him home because he did not want his brothers to kill Joseph. But, before Reuben could rescue Joseph, the other brothers saw men traveling on a journey to Egypt. They took Joseph out of the pit and sold him to the men. Joseph was taken to Egypt to be a slave. He would become a servant of the ruler of Egypt. Joseph's father thought Joseph had died, for the brothers did not tell their father the truth.

That is a very sad part of our story ... but Someone special was with Joseph. He was there to watch over Joseph even when these bad things were happening to him. Who was with Joseph, boys and girls? (Allow the children to answer, "God".)

The Bible says, "God was with Joseph, and God helped him to succeed at everything he did."

Let's praise God for the wisdom He used when He took care of Joseph. Clap your hands together and say, "We praise You, God, for being so wise. We praise Your holy name".

One day, many years later, the ruler of Egypt had a dream. His dream was so real and seemed so strange. The ruler asked for someone to interpret it. (Ask the child who looked up the word "interpret" to share what he found.) Interpret means "to explain or to tell the meaning of something."

Joseph was brought to the ruler, and with God's help and wisdom, Joseph told him what his dream meant. Joseph told the ruler that Egypt would have seven good years when all the crops would grow and there would be much grain for flour and bread. (Take the wheat from the box.) And, then, seven very bad years of famine were coming. Remember what the word "*famine*" means? (Ask one child to explain. Be sure the class understands it would not rain for a long time and no plants would grow. Food would be very hard to find. Crush the grain in your hand as you talk about the famine.)

The king was so glad Joseph could warn him about the famine that he gave Joseph a very special job. He put Joseph in charge of building great barns and storage buildings that would hold all of the wheat during the seven good years. Then, when the famine came, Joseph would give out just enough grain to keep the people from going hungry.

Remember, boys and girls, it was God's wisdom that allowed Joseph to know what the dreams meant. It was God who knew Joseph could handle the job the ruler gave to him, and it was God who helped Joseph, even though sad things had happened to his life. (Take time to praise God for His wisdom.)

Joseph did everything he could do to please the ruler as he carried out his special job. And, just as he had told the ruler, seven very bad years followed the good years of harvest. People far away from Egypt had no food, but the people of Egypt could go to Joseph and receive grain from the storage buildings. He had listened to the wisdom of God, and the people of Egypt had plenty to eat.

Now, guess whose family became hungry because the famine had come to their land too? (Encourage the children to answer "Joseph's family.")

Joseph's brothers came. They bowed down before Joseph and asked him for grain. (If time permits, take a moment to discuss how this was just what Joseph had told his brothers would happen. His dreams did become real.)

Application: Isn't that something, boys and girls? God allowed all these things to happen to Joseph knowing how everything would work out.

God took care of Joseph all through his life. Joseph listened to God's wisdom and obeyed God's commands. Because Joseph listened to God, God was able to take the bad things that happened and make them work out for the best.

Let's look at a special Psalm that will help us remember to trust in God and his wisdom as He watches over our lives. (Ask the child who looked up Psalm 56:3, 4 to read this Scripture now.)

We need to see that God will take care of us as we grow too. Have you ever thought about what you'd like to do when you grow up? Will you be a teacher or a doctor; a mailman or a secretary? God knows *right now* what will happen to you as you grow, *and* He knows exactly what you will be doing twenty years from today! We need to praise God for His wisdom and trust Him to work everything out just right for us.

Have the children go to the tables and give them page 10 of the activity book.

5-8. *Find the Hidden Item:* Use the key to color the picture. Find the hidden item. (The hidden item is Joseph's coat.)

8-10. *I Want to Be . . .:* These children are dreaming about what they want to be when they grow up. Read the words that give the clue to their thoughts and draw the picture to show what each is thinking. The last picture is for you. Draw what you would like to be when you grow up. Then fill in the dots to see something important for you to remember. (The dots form these words: The wisdom of God.)

When all have finished with the activity papers, have them go to the Light Post on Memory Lane.

Verse in the Dessert: Before class, write each word of today's memory verse on index cards you have cut in half. These will make squares 3" x 2½". Glue or tape each word-card to a craft stick that will stand up in the sand poured at least three inches deep in the cake pan.

To begin: All the children are to read the verse in correct order. Give them a few minutes to try to memorize the verse. The first child who thinks he can say the verse volunteers. The teacher mixes up the words in the pan. Set the timer for one minute. (Note: Later you can shorten the time.) Allow sixty seconds for this student to re-arrange the words in proper order and then recite the verse. If he is correct, allow this student to choose the next classmate who would like to try. The student who just said the verse, mixes the words in the pan and sets the timer for this student.

Close by singing "God's Wisdom," on page 117.

5-9. God's-Grain Paperweight: Give each student a baby food jar, a paper cup, a felt circle cut to fit the top of the jar lid, and a 15" piece of neutral color ribbon.

Allow the children to glue the felt circle to the outside of the lid. Tell the children to be patient as you pour the first layer of beans or grain into their paper cup. Allow the children to pour the beans from the cup into the jar. They must work carefully as they add layers of grain so one layer will not mix with the other. Fill the jars full so that the lid will press the grain layers together and will not allow the grain to move as the lid is twisted into place. (You may prefer to put a thin line of glue around the inside of the lid to safeguard against spills if the lid should come off on the way home. The glue should make it secure.)

Teachers will need to assist as the lids are twisted in

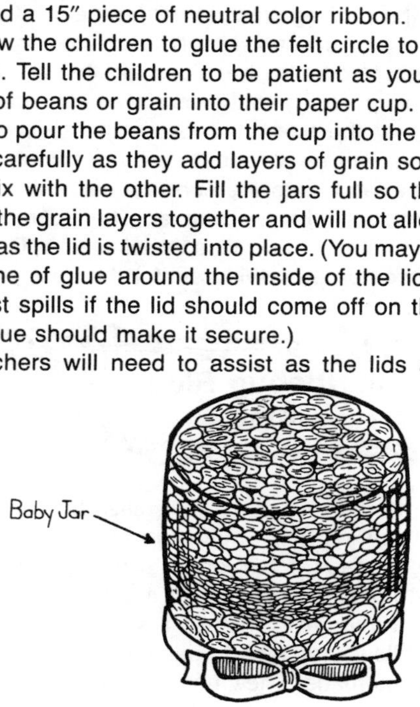

place. When the grain is secure, turn the jar upside down and tie the ribbon around the printed portion of the lid. A thin line of glue will keep the ribbon in place.

As they look at the paperweight, they should be reminded of how God's wisdom allowed everything to work out for Joseph. They should think about how God has the same wisdom to guide their lives today.

8-10. 3-D Model of Joseph: Give each child a multi-colored piece of material with the robe pattern from page 102 already drawn and ready to cut; (You may prefer to cut these pieces ahead of time and sew a running stitch across the top of the robe, leaving a long tail of thread for the students to gather as they fit the robe to the cone.) one cone and ball; one solid piece of material for the head piece; the arm pattern and a 2" piece of chenille wire, three straight pins and felt tip markers.

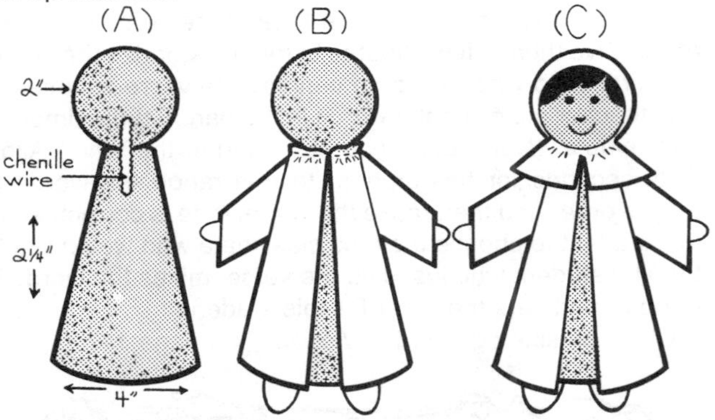

Cut the feet pattern from the black felt and glue to the bottom of the cone. Insert the chenille wire into the top of the cone leaving enough to attach the ball at the head. Cut the arm pattern from the posterboard and glue a small piece of neutral felt to the hand portion of the pattern. Glue the same multi-colored fabric as the coat to each side of the arms. Insert the arms in the position desired in each side of the cone. Pull the running stitch to gather the robe around the neck and cut a slit in each side of the coat to gently ease the arms through. Secure the two sides together at the back with a straight pin pushed into the cone. Glue fine pieces of yarn to the top of the head and fasten the solid strip of material over the hair as a headpiece by pushing straight pins through the fabric into the cone on each side of the head. Draw the face with the marker. The figure should stand alone. Remember how Joseph believed in God and God's wisdom worked everything out for the best.

We've come to the end of another class time in Critter County. Everybody into the Shuttlebug and buckle up for the ride home. Doesn't it feel good to think about going home? We can imagine how Joseph must have felt many times when he wanted to go home. It is good to know that God's wisdom allowed Joseph to see his brothers and his family again. They made a new home in Egypt.

Let's praise God one more time for His wisdom before we finish our ride. Clap your hands and say, "We praise You, God, for being so wise. We praise Your holy name". Let's try to remember that God is wise enough to take care of us and help us just like He took care of Joseph.

Here we are back home. Let me read this Psalm of Praise before we go. (Read Psalm 86:11, 12.)

We praise You, God, for knowing everything about our lives. We know You can work all things out if we trust in You and keep Your commandments. We thank You for taking care of Joseph, and we ask You to help us remember to trust You like Joseph did. In Jesus' name, amen.

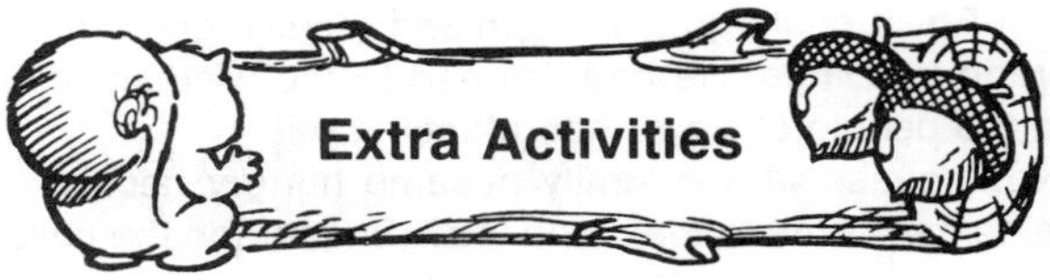

To Egypt and Back: Have two stacks of newspapers that will reach (when unfolded from the center fold) the destination marked across the room or yard from each team's line. Divide the class into two teams who form lines side by side and a few feet apart. Team members line up one behind the other. Give a stack of newspapers to the first person standing in each line. At the signal (blow a whistle, ring a bell, or clap your hands) the first player unfolds one paper, lays it down in front of him, steps on it and unfolds the next paper. He continues this process until he reaches the pre-marked line or boundary marked before the game began. Upon reaching that position, he must retrace his steps by backing up on the paper re-folding it, backing up to the next paper, etc. He hands the papers to the next team member who begins the race again. The first team to complete the relay, wins.

Wise Guessing: Before class, prepare forty 3 x 5 cards with the numbers 1, 2, or 3 written on each card. Divide the class into teams depending on the size of your class. Line all the teams up at least twenty-five feet from the teacher. Team members stand behind one another. Choose a captain from each team.

The teacher will shuffle the cards. Hold one up so no one in the room can see the number. The captain of the first team will guess by saying "We believe the card is a 3, and we will take one giant step." If he is wrong, the team is penalized by backing up one giant step. If he is correct, and the number the teacher is holding is a 3, his team will advance one giant step and continue guessing. Any team captain, during his team's turn, can request no more than 3 giant steps. He may state that he will take three "tiny" steps, or two or one. Whatever he asks for, his team will be granted . . . *if* the number the teacher is holding is guessed correctly. A team may continue guessing as long as they guess correctly. Then it is the next team's turn to guess.

Lesson 5

Praise God for His Provision

Scripture: Exodus 15:22-25a; Exodus 16:1-36; Exodus 17:15

Psalm References: Psalm 23:107:4-9; Psalm 150:3a (Pause-to-Praise verse)

Memory Verse: He is your praise; he is your God, who performed for you those great and awesome wonders you saw with your own eyes.—Deuteronomy 10:21 (NIV)

Lesson Aim: As a result of studying this lesson, the children should:

1) Know that God provided for bread, meat and manna as the Israelites wandered in the wilderness.
2) Feel the security of depending on a God who will provide.
3) Feel loved by God as they recognize all He has done.
4) Name three items the Israelites needed and how God provided those needs.
5) Thank God for providing food and clothing for us today.
6) Praise God for being our provider.
7) Sing or say the memory verse, Deuteronomy 10:21.

Materials Needed:

Pre-session. *Activi-Tree:* Use the suggestions given below and add your own ideas as you write activities on slips of paper and attach them to the Activi-Tree before class. Encourage each child to read and follow the directions on the slip chosen.

- Look up Exodus 15:22, 23 to see what the people were complaining about.
- Look up Exodus 16:1-3 to see what the people were complaining about.
- Look up Exodus 16:11 to see what the people were complaining about.
- Look up the Pause-to-Praise Verse, Psalm 150:3a, and be ready to read it aloud during the Pause-to-Praise activity center.
- Be the leader as we line up for the restroom break
- Hold the Wonders-of-God's-World box during the Bible story.

Group Mobiles: Coat hanger, posterboard, tape, empty soup can, construction paper, chenille wires, yarn, magazine pictures, and glue.

Preparation for Pause to Praise: Bible, record player or tape with trumpet music, trumpet (if available), construction paper, glue and pattern of trumpet from page 107.

Together Time. Mobiles made during Pre-session.

Snack Time. Bread sticks, and dip, fruit juice.

Bible Story Time. Wonders-of-God's-World box containing: piece of bark or wood, puffed wheat cereal, artificial bird, picture of Israelites gathering manna, picture of a pool or lake.

Light Post on Memory Lane. Toy or real trumpet, Bibles, and chalk or posterboard.

Crafts.
5-8. *Bread-Dough Magnets:* Bread dough recipe on page; magnetic strips; oven, glue, shellac.

8-10. *All-God's-Grain Trivet:* Plastic lids from butter tub or similar containers, plaster of paris, colored seeds or beans, spray sealer or shellac.

Extra Activities.
Gather the Manna: Bean Bag or small pillow.
Wandering in the Wilderness: Fifty to a hundred pennies.

Welcome the Children

Be sure to speak to each child as they arrive. Guide them toward the Activi-Tree and encourage them to join one of the activity centers. Explain that today we will be talking about how God provides for all of our needs.

Pre-session Activities

Activi-Tree. Use the activites suggested in Materials Needed. You may think of more. Be sure the Bible and reference books are available. Encourage each child to read the slip chosen from the tree and provide any assistance younger children might require. Help the children to know you are confident they will be able to successfully complete the responsibility on the slip chosen.

Group Mobiles. Allow the children to work in teams of three or four in this center to make several mobiles. Talk to the children about God's provisions. Ask them where their clothes and food have come from. Ask if they can think of anything else God provides. Allow them to draw around soup cans to make circles of different colors of construction paper. You will need eight or nine circles per mobile.

Choose pictures from magazines that show items God provides. (Sun, grain field, food on table, clothing, parents, Bible, etc.) Allow each group to choose eight items each. Cut out the pictures and glue them to the circles. Punch a hole in the top of each picture and tie a 9″ piece of yarn to each hole.

Cut two strips from the poster board. These strips should

be 2″ wide and fit along the bottom wire of the coat hanger. Make 4 holes in the center of each strip. Two at one end of the strip and two at the other spaced as in the diagram provided. Place holes in both of the strips in exactly the same area.

Push the free end of each piece of yarn through the holes and tie a knot to keep the yarn from slipping back through. Attach one strip to the bottom wire of the coat hanger by placing the strips over the inside portion of the wire and taping across the wire under the strip. Crisscross this strip with the remaining strip (Fold it slightly down the center to make it stronger because there will be no wire for support.) and wrap tape around the crisscross area and under the coat hanger wire to bind the two strips together.

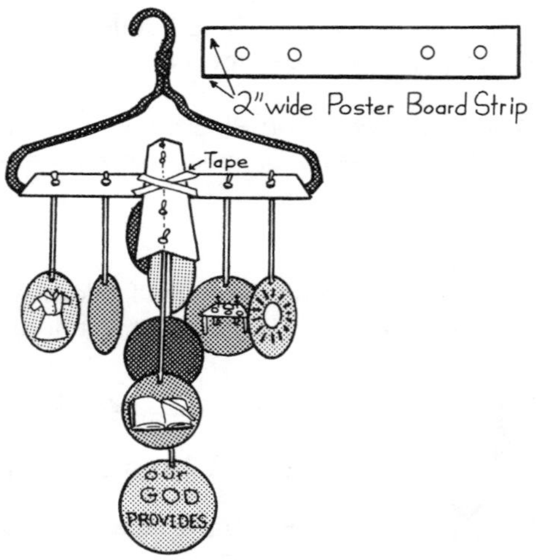

One larger circle made from the construction paper and bearing the words, "Our God Provides" should be suspended from the exact center where the two strips cross each other. This will give balance to the mobile.

Hang the coat hangers in the room where the air can move the pieces freely. Save the mobiles to share with the entire class during Together Time.

Preparation for Pause to Praise: Have the child who chose this responsibility from the Activi-Tree read Psalm 150:3a to the group.

Have the children sit in a circle around the tape recorder or record player. Play the music that includes trumpet sounds and encourage the children to listen carefully. When they hear the sound of the trumpet, they should raise one hand.

If you have access to a real trumpet or know someone who would be willing to visit your class today, ask him or her to bring the trumpet and play a short tune for the group. (Encourage this person to stay and play during the **Pause to Praise** segment also. To do this, you will need to schedule today's **Pause to Praise** around this individuals availability.)

Using a music book or catalog, cut out pictures of trumpets and glue them to the next page of the scrapbook. Allow one child to draw around the pattern on page 107 to make a large trumpet for the center of this page. Be sure to write, "Praise Him with the Sounding of the Trumpet" on the page. (This will be the fourth page of the scrapbook.)

Pause to Praise: Have one child read Psalm 150:3a. Have the children from the activity center tell about the trumpet and the sound they hear as it is blown. Ask if anyone in the group can think of any Bible stories where God's people might have or actually did use trumpets. (Answer: Gideon, Judges 7:19-22, blew trumpets and broke pitchers and the soldiers fled; Joshua, Joshua 6:16, blew trumpets and shouted as walls of Jericho fell. It is believed they used the trumpets to call the people together as they wandered in the wilderness. When Jesus returns, the Bible tells us a trumpet will sound, Matthew 24:31.)

Listen to the sound of the trumpet music on the recorder or ask the visiting trumpet player to play again for the class.

Instructions: The class will say, "We praise You, God" and the trumpeter will respond with four identical notes that match the rhythm of the children's voices. The class will then respond to the trumpet by saying, "with trumpet sounds". The trumpet will repeat the four notes in response. Then the children will say the next words as the trumpeter plays with them, "We praise Your holy name!"

You may need to repeat this exercise several times before everyone understands. Close this session by allowing one child to read Psalm 150:1-3a from the scrapbook.

Together Time: Have the children bring the mobiles to the large group. talk with the children about the items shown on the mobiles and how God is so good to provide these things for our use. Have as many children who are willing, to bow their heads and praise God for one thing He has provided. Close this session by clapping your hands together and saying, "We praise You, God, for providing our needs. We praise Your holy name."

Now let's get ready for another ride to Critter County. We've already had some special opportunities to praise God for providing so many good things for us. I wonder what we're going to learn as we visit Grandmother Mouse and Sydney. I hear Sydney is feeling "down" today and only Grandmother Mouse can cheer him up.

Let's all get in the Shuttlebug. I can't wait to see what happens. (Talk about special events happening in today's class as you ride.) There is Critter County up ahead. Are you all ready to find out what Sydney and Grandmother Mouse will do in today's story? Everyone out of the Shuttlebug! Let's go listen.

Have you ever had a terrible, awful, bad, horrible, mixed-up day? That is a day when only a close friend or special loved-one can cheer you up. Grandmother Mouse is the best cheerer-upper around! Listen as she finds a way to help Sydney.

The Broken Truck That Healed a Heart

It had been cloudy and rainy for days in Critter County. It had rained so much, that Lester had given serious thought to building an ark . . . well, it was as serious as any of Lester's thoughts can be. The creek was ready to spill over its banks. The constant rain had dampened everyone's spirits. Even Sydney was walking around with what seemed like a cloud of sadness.

It was most unusual for the little squirrel to let anything get him down. He always seemed to have a smile on his face, and a song in his heart. Something was terribly different now.

What am I going to do? thought Sydney as he walked down Memory Lane. *I prayed this morning and even spent extra time reading the Psalms. But I still feel down in the dumps. Even Lester couldn't cheer me up when he came to my house with that acorn milk shake for me.*

Just as Sydney was ending his walk, he spotted Grandmother Mouse across the street. She smiled the biggest smile for a little mouse and waved her hand.

"Hey, there Sydney," she yelled. "How are you doing?"

"Oh, I've been better, I guess," Sydney replied.

Grandmother Mouse was always able to understand the way people feel. So she crossed the street, put her arm around her friend, and invited little Sydney to her mouse house for dinner. Sydney said he would love to spend the evening with her. So off they went.

After a delicious meal, they sat down in the living room to relax. Sydney sat in the big blue velvet chair and propped his tired feet up on the footstool. Grandmother Mouse got comfortable in her rocker and carefully placed her tail across her lap, so that it wouldn't fall under her chair.

"Sydney, you just haven't seemed yourself lately. Is there anything troubling you that I can help you with?" said the tiny grandmother.

"Oh, thanks for taking such an interest in me, Grandmother Mouse. It was so special to be able to share dinner with you. I loved the acorn soup! I'm really not sure what's bothering me. I just feel so tired," said the little squirrel.

"Well, as a nurse, I know a lot of things can make us feel tired. Are you getting enough rest?" she asked.

Sydney nodded and said, "Oh, yes, I'm getting plenty of sleep. I just bought a new waterbed so I'd drift off to sleep easily. It works! I guess I am just getting really worried about my supply of food for the winter. You see, all this rain has really set me behind in my search for nuts. I mean, it's getting BAD. Can you picture me a poor, starving squirrel?"

"Oh, Sydney, I really don't think you'll starve. In fact, I'm quite sure of it for two reasons. First, God has promised to take care of you and to meet your needs. And secondly, why you have many friends! We would certainly help your little tummy stay full," said the little mouse tenderly.

Grandmother Mouse sat back in her chair and began to sip her cheese-flavored tea. She said, "Sydney, I'd like to tell you a true story . . . something that happened to me years ago when Grandfather Mouse was still living."

"We were much younger then, in fact, our children were young. Times were very hard back then, and we had trouble knowing where our next pound of cheese would come from. My husband had trouble keeping a job. So I had trouble keeping any peace of mind."

Sydney interrupted, "Why, Grandmother Mouse, I didn't know you ever had those kinds of problems. What happened?"

Grandmother Mouse answered, "It was pretty rough back then, In fact, I remember one January. It was the coldest winter we had ever had here in Critter County. Food was really hard to find. My husband was out of a job, and we had no money. The time finally came, one cold Saturday night. We ate our last piece of dried cheese for dinner and gave the baby the last of the milk at bedtime. There was no more money left in the cheeseball jar. I began to cry, and my husband heard me from the living room. He came into the bedroom and put his paw on my shoulder. He honestly tried everything to make me feel better because he was sure that God would take care of us. All I could think of was the fact that the baby would be waking up in a couple of hours, and I had nothing to give her. It seemed hopeless."

"Oh, Grandmother, you must've felt terrible," said Sydney as he was trying to imaging how Grandmother felt.

Grandmother Mouse continued, "Well, yes, it was a very sad time. My husband suggested that we pray again and really trust God. I had almost given up, but I did pray with him. We knelt down beside our bed. My husband told God of our need and that we were trusting in Him. Suddenly, there was a loud knock at the door. 'Get up quick, Homer,' I said to my husband, 'You must get the door before it wakes the baby.' And Sydney, the most amazing thing I've ever experienced was about to happen."

Sydney sat right up in his chair and leaned forward. "I can't imagine, Grandmother Mouse, what happened?"

"Well, when my husband opened the door, there stood a truck driver. He was a little goat named Gomer. The two men had so much fun laughing at how their names sounded so much alike—Gomer and Homer. Anyway, don't you know that his dairy truck had broken down right outside our house. He asked if we needed any milk and cheese. It was all going to go to waste if it wasn't put into an icebox. He wanted us to help him out by taking all this food off of his truck—for FREE. We loaded up on cheese, ice cream, even yogurt. Um, what a feast! And the very next day, my husband got a new job.

Sydney wiped a little tear from his eye as he said, "You always seem to know just what to say, Grandmother Mouse. I'm sure I won't have to worry about having an empty tummy when my heart is so full with the love that you and God show to me."

After a good-bye hug, Grandmother Mouse closed the door as Sydney walked down her front steps whistling a happy tune. Both Grandmother Mouse and Sydney went to sleep with a smile that night. They had been reminded of the warm and tender way our heavenly Father cares for us.

Have the children go to the tables and give them page 11 from the activity book.

5-8. *Make a Story Viewer:* Follow the directions on the activity page to make the story viewer. Some children will need help cutting. After drawing the missing pictures, slide the picture strip inside the viewer. Retell the story a picture at a time.

8-10. *Finish the Story:* Read the story, "Help for Mrs. Owl," carefully. Now write an ending to the story on the lines provided. Let the children share their endings if time allows.

When all have finished with the activity sheets, have the children go to the Critter County radio Station and sit in front of it. You will need someone to be Sydney and someone to read the part of Lester during today's radio program.

Critter County Radio Station

Sydney: **WWCC** wants you to be informed. We'll bring you weather, sports, personal interviews with your favorite critters. We'll let you know when, where, and how it happened. If you're looking for what's happening in Critter County, look for **WWCC** on your dial! And here's Lester with the weather.

Lester: Rain, rain, go away! Well, sports fans, it's another day inside. It's raining cats and dogs!

Sydney: Lester, Lester, excuse me. Did you say that it's raining cats and dogs?

Lester: Cats and dogs!

Sydney: That's frightening!

Lester: Sydney! It's not really raining cats and dogs. That's just the way that we creative weathermen say it's raining buckets!

Sydney: Buckets?

Lester: Hard, Sydney. It's raining hard.

Sydney: Oh, I see. Well, I know a time a long time ago when it rained food!

Lester: Food? That's my kind of storm! Tell me about it, Sydney!

Sydney: No need to Mr. Lester. Our **WWCC** listeners are going to hear all about it in their Bible Story today. Stay tuned, boys and girls! This is Sydney,

Lester: And Lester!

Sydney: Signing off for **WWCC**—the Wonderful World of Critter County.

Snack Time

Allow the children who chose this responsibility from the Activi-Tree to help with the snack.

Bread sticks, peanut butter or cheese dips, and fruit juice are suggested as the snack today. Talk with the children about the people who left Egypt. We will be learning about how they complained because they didn't think they would have enough to eat. But God provided everything they needed.

If you have a book that shows how bread is made, you might want to share it during snack time. The children will enjoy the bread sticks. Ask them to tell what their favorite bread treat is. (French toast, cinnamon toast, grilled cheese sandwiches, etc.)

After clean up, have the children return to the story area.

Songs of Praise

Play the song "Sing Praise to Him," page 140, as the children assemble in the story area. When all have gathered, sing the song together.

Sing familiar songs as well as new ones. "Praise Ye the Lord Forever," page 142; "My God Will Meet All Your Needs," page 128; "He Hath Done Great things," page 118; "Sing and Shout It," page 136; and "Great Is Our Lord," page 115.

Prayer Song: "Hear Us as We Pray," page 143.

Prayer: Ask the children to praise God for taking care of them and providing their needs. Ask God to help the children listen as they learn of the love and care He showed to the Israelites as they wandered in the wilderness.

Bible Story Time

(Have the Wonders-of-God's-World box prepared with the items mentioned. Remember to have the child who chose this Activi-Tree responsibility to hold the box and sit close to you as you tell the story.)

Today our lesson will take us to the desert. What is a desert like? (Allow a child to answer with descriptions like, very little or no water, not many animals, no food or trees.)

The Bible tells us the Israelites made quite a journey through the desert as they left Egypt. Now, how did they get in the desert in the first place? (Allow time for any child to answer.)

Do you remember that Joseph's family had come to Egypt to get grain and food? Well, many years went by, and Joseph's family grew and grew. Joseph died, and new rulers who did not know Joseph made slaves of the people who had come to Egypt to live. Three hundred years after Joseph lived in Egypt, the ruler named Pharoah was forcing the people to work very hard to build two cities in his honor. The Pharoah commanded the people to make bricks out of straw and clay, and he ordered his servants to beat many of the slaves to make them work. It was a very hard life that Joseph's great, great, great grandchildren had to live. But, God knew what was happening to these people, and He sent Moses to lead them from Egypt to a land far away. In the new land they did not have to be slaves anymore. But to get to the new land they had to cross the desert. God chose the route they would take, and Moses led the people where God told him to go. They walked right into the desert. Let's see what happened.

God Provides

Exodus 15:22-25; 16:1-36; 17:15

"Oh, we're so hungry", the people said. "It's true that life was very hard for us in Egypt. But, at least we had food to eat and water to drink. You have brought us out here in the desert to die, Moses."

The people complained and complained. They had forgotten how very bad life was when they were slaves in the land of Egypt. Many of the people had forgotten to trust God to provide what they would need. Open your Bible to Exodus.

Who looked up Exodus 15:22, 23 after visiting the Activi-Tree today? (Allow this child to tell the class what he found the people to be complaining about—water.)

The Bible tells us the people had been walking for three days in the desert after watching Pharoah's army drown in the Red Sea. They had spent all three days looking for water and had found none. When they finally came to some water on the third day, they found it was bitter and not good to drink.

I want you to listen carefully because I want you to see how God provided for the people of Israel.

The Bible says Moses cried to God, and God showed him a piece of wood. (Take the wood from the box.) Moses threw the wood into the water, and the water became fresh. The people were able to drink it. They were not thirsty anymore.

Now you would think the people would stop complaining about needing things because God had provided for them, but the Bible says they complained again.

Ask the child who chose the slip from the Activi-Tree instructing him to look up Exodus 16:1-3 to tell what the people complained about this time. (The answer is meat and food.) Allow the child with Exodus 16:11 tell the class what God promised the people. (That at twilight they would eat meat, and in the morning they would be filled with bread.)

It is very exciting to hear how God provided these things for the people. The Bible says that when it was evening (Take the artificial bird or picture of a quail from the box.), quail came and covered the whole camp where the israelites were staying. The birds became the meat for the people. God provided for their needs. And, not only did God provide the meat, but the Bible says the next morning there was dew all over the ground. (Take the picture of Israelites gathering manna and the puffed-wheat cereal from the box.)

After the dew was gone, thin flakes like frost covered the ground. The people asked Moses what it was, and the Bible says Moses told them, "It is the bread the Lord has given you to eat."

God had again provided what the people needed. Let's praise God now for all that He provided. Clap your hands together and say, "We praise You, God, for providing water. We praise You, God, for providing meat. We praise You, God, for providing bread. We praise Your holy name".

God knew how quickly the Israelites would forget what He had done if He gave them enough food for their whole journey. So, God did something very wise. He gave them just enough food for each day. Everyday the families would have to gather just enough for that day's needs. If they gathered too much and tried to save it for the next day, it would spoil and taste very bad. The people had to trust God *EVERYDAY* to provide exactly what they needed.

Application: God wants us to obey Him and trust Him to provide for us, too. I want you to do something special for me the rest of today and until we meet for class again. I want you to start thinking about all the things God has provided. When you wake up in the morning and put on your clothes, think about where they came from and praise God for them. Think about who provides the job for your mother and daddy to work so they can buy your shoes. Think about who made the sheep whose coat gave the wool to make the material in your shirts and dresses. Think about who provides the rain that makes water come to your faucet when you are thirsty. Every time you think of something God provided, stop and praise Him. Just take one or two seconds before you put on that shirt, or eat that ice-cream cone, or play with that special toy, to say in your heart or right out loud, "I praise You, God, for providing this for me."

Have the children go to the tables and give them page 12 from the activity book.

5-8. *What is Different?* Put an **X** on the items that are different in these pictures. In the boxes below, draw a picture of some of your favorite things God has provided for you.

8-10. *The Shepherd Psalm:* Draw pictures for the missing words. Look up Psalm 23 in your bible as you make your picture story.

When the children have finished the activity papers, have them go to the Light Post on Memory Lane.

The Sounding of the Trumpet. Allow the children to see the trumpet before you begin. Have the children turn to the memory verse while you write it on the board. Tell them only you know when the trumpet will sound. They are to try as hard as they can to memorize the scripture before the trumpet blows. Give the class two minutes to memorize. Blow the trumpet and ask if anyone thinks he or she can say the verse. The first one to say the verse takes his or her stand at the trumpet. This time wait forty-five seconds. Allow the student who said the verse correctly to blow the trumpet, and choose someone to say the verse. Shorten the memorization time each round. Try to allow enough time for each student to have a chance to say the verse.

Sing "He Hath Done Great Things," on page 118.

5-8. Bread-Dough Magnets: Have the dough made ahead of time so the children will spend this time molding their magnets. You may choose to make and cook two or three magnets per child before class so the children may shellac the pre-made magnets while their hand-made magnets are in the over.

Recipe for Bread Dough

¼ C. Salt ¾ C. Hot water 2 Cups flour	Combine the water and salt and add one cup of flour until well blended. Add the remaining flour a little at a time until the dough is no longer sticky. Bake molded objects at 300° until golden brown. Allow to cool completely before applying paints or shellac.

Have the children to make four or five magnets each. Let them roll the dough into small loaf shapes. Be sure the finished product is large enough to conceal the magnet strip which will be applied to the back of each loaf or roll. Use a plastic knife to slant small cuts in the loaves to give them a "french bread" effect. make dinner rolls or hot cross buns using your imagination to make magnets that resemble bread. Place the finished pieces in the oven. The dough will puff slightly as it bakes.

When the loaves have completely cooled, shellac them with a thin coat of real shellac or coat them with a mixture of two parts glue to one part water. This will give a glazed effect to the magnets and will allow them to last longer. You might want to use a blow dryer to help the shellac or glaze dry faster. Attach the magnets to the back of molded pieces, and they are ready for Mother's refrigerator.

8-10. Mosaic-Seed Trivet: Have various colors and shapes of grains and seeds for this project. Provide each student with a butter tub lid. (Clear lids work best) encourage the children to make a design in the inside of the lid. When they are pleased with the design, pour a thin layer of plaster of paris around the seeds. The students may wish to add a few grains where too much space is left open. The more seeds and grain, the more colorful the finished trivet will be.

Allow the trivet to dry until the plaster of paris is cool and no longer damp. After completely dry, you may choose to spray it with a Krylon spray available in most craft stores. This will seal the trivet and give it a shiny appearance.

***Important:** Remember to spray or shellac any project in a well-ventilated area. Taking the projects outside for spraying is best.

Well, boys and girls, we have come to the end of another visit in Critter County. It is time to get in the Shuttlebug and ride home. Shall we take the Shuttlebug ride today or . . . would you like to pretend we are walking with Moses across the wilderness to a new home? (Allow the children to choose.) Let one child drive the Shuttlebug as he takes those who chose to ride. Allow the other children to line up behind you and weave in and out around the room on a pretend journey through the wilderness. When both groups have arrived at their destination, bow your heads for prayer. If it is a nice day, it would be fun to take the children outside for this journey home.)

We praise You, God, for giving us all that we need as we live in your beautiful world. We praise You for providing our food and clothing; for giving us water to drink and for making so many different fruits and vegetables that help our bodies grow strong. Help us to always think about You being our provider. We love You, God, and praise You for all you have given. In Jesus' name, amen.

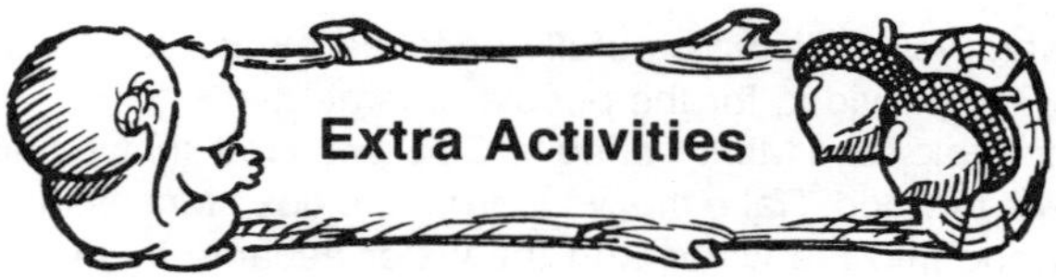

Gather the Manna: Divide the class into two teams. Have the children line up with one team facing the other (team members standing side by side). Allow four or five yards between the lines and place the beanbag or pillow in the center of the playing field between the two teams. Choose one line and number the players. Begin at the OPPOSITE end of the other line and follow the same procedure. Tell the children it is important to remember their numbers.

The teacher will call a number. Each of the players on both sides having that number must run to the center and grab the "manna" trying to successfully take it back with them to their place in line. The player who missed gathering the "manna" is to chase the player who took it. If the chaser catches the player with the "manna," the "manna" is returned to the center and two more numbers are called. If the "manna" successfully makes it to the capturer's position, that team is given five points. The "manna" is placed in the center, and the game begins again.

Wander Through the Wilderness: Before class or during the bathroom break, hide fifty to a hundred pennies around the room. (The number of pennies depends on the size of your class.) Divide the class into two teams. Two members from each team wander around the room looking for the pennies. When they have found three pennies each, they must take the pennies to their team and tag the next two players who will wander around looking for their three pennies. The play will move rapidly at first, but the fewer the pennies, the harder they will be to find.

The first team who decides to give up sits down. The other team is given sixty seconds to end their search. When time is up, count the pennies. The team with the most pennies is the winning team. Take the children out of the room for a few minutes and hide the pennies to play again.

Lesson 6

Praise God for He Deserves Praise

Scripture: Background of David's life: 1 Samuel 17; 18:1-16; 20; 2 Samuel 5:1-4; 7:8-16

Psalm References: Psalm 18; 47:1, 2; 96:1-6; Psalm 150:3b (Pause-to-Praise verse)

Memory Verse: Clap your hands, all you nations; shout to God with cries of joy.—Psalm 47:1 (NIV)

Lesson Aim: As a result of studying this lesson, the children should

1) Know that David praised God for specific reasons and in many circumstances.
2) Know that God deserves our praise.
3) Feel the desire to praise God for Who He is and all He has done.
4) Praise God by singing and repeating statements of praise.
5) Sing or say the memory verse, Psalm 47:1.

Materials Needed:
Pre-session. *Activi-Tree:* See the following list of suggestions for the papers to be placed on today's Activi-Tree. Be sure to choose responsibilities appropriate for the age of your students.

- Be the announcer during Critter County on radio.
- Pick up all the napkins and cups after snack time. (2)
- Look up Psalm 150:3b and see which instrument is mentioned after the trumpet. Tell the students in the **Pause-to-Praise** center.
- Read Psalm 18:1-3 during Bible Story time.
- Read Psalm 18:16-19 during Bible Story time.
- Read Psalm 18:46-50 during Bible Story time.
- Help prepare the pudding for snack time. (2)
- Drive the Shuttlebug to Critter County.

Expressions of Praise: Large piece of white butcher paper, taped or recorded music (various tempos), string, poster paint, marker.

Pause to Praise: Bible, posterboard, string, construction paper, pattern of harp from page, autoharp or piano.

Together Time. Expressions-of-Praise poster made during Pre-session.

Snack Time. Instant pudding, milk, juice, wire wisk.

Bible Story Time. Pictures of David and Goliath, David as King, and David with Jonathan; Wonders-of-God's-World box containing: stone, sling shot, crown, heart, and harp.

Light Post on Memory Lane. Poster board, construction paper.

Crafts.
5-8. *Musical Shakers:* Scissors, glue, paper-towel tubes, construction paper, self-sticking shelf paper, popcorn kernels or rice.

8-10. *Wooden Tambourine:* 1″ x 2″ x 10″ piece of wood, four 2″ nails, sixteen bottlecaps, sand paper, paint or shellac, hammer, one 5″ nail.

Extra Activities.
Musical Squares: Carpet squares or squares of posterboard.

Welcome the Children
Greet cheerfully each child as he or she arrives. Praise God for each by name and explain that today we will be praising God just because He deserves our praise. Encourage each child toward the Activi-Tree, and, after he or she chooses a responsibility, decide which learning center interests him or her. Be sure all of the activity leaders know the names of visitors.

Pre-session Activities
Activi-Tree. Be sure the papers containing the responsibilities given at the beginning of the lesson have been attached to the tree. Add any responsibilities that are of special value to your class. Be ready to help new readers to understand the directions they have chosen. Be sure all reference materials are available.

Expressions of Praise. Tear a sheet of white butcher paper long enough to cover an entire table. Have 4 colors of poster paint (pre-mixed) ready to place in the center of the table. Place one piece of yarn cut 12″ in length in each of the colors of paint. The string should be within reach of the children's hands. Explain to the students that you will be using four of the five senses God has given us as we work at the center today. We will praise God as we work for He deserves our praise for making our bodies to enjoy this activity.

Play music and show the children how to paint with the strings as you follow the rhythm of the beat. Allow the children to choose one string at a time as they stand around the table painting with the different colors.

The paper will be covered with colorful, abstract lines and the children will enjoy moving the strings to the motion of the music.

Be sure the children clearly understand the guidelines you give to make this a "splatter-free" but fun experience.

1) Only four children are to be at the center at one time.
2) Each child may paint with one string at a time during his time at the table. He may choose several different colors, but only the string belonging to that color may be used.
3) Hold the string above its bowl or cup to let excess paint drip back into the container before placing the string on the paper.
4) The dry end of the string should never get wet with paint. Be careful as you return it to the bowl or pan.

Everyone who obeys the guidelines may stay at this center as long as he or she wishes. While the children paint, help them to understand we should praise God that we can see the beautiful colors. We praise Him that we can hear the music. And, we can praise Him that we are able to feel the string in our hands as we move it to the rhythm of each song. All of these special senses cause us to praise God for making us so that we are able to enjoy this activity. He deserves our praise.

When each group of children have shared their time at the table, clap your hands and say, "We praise You, God, for You deserve praise. We praise Your holy name".

Complete the activity by printing the words "Praise God" in bold letters with the marker across the center of the dry painting. Save the banner to share during Together Time.

Preparation for Pause to Praise. Have one child read Psalm 150:3b, "Praise Him with the harp," to the children in the center. Use the pattern from page 108 to draw the harp on the poster board. (Decide if you will make one large harp as a group or if each child participating will make his own. If you prefer each child to make his or her own, you might want to cut out the harps before class and give them to the children at the beginning of this session. Follow the pattern to add the harp strings. Tie a knot on the back side of the harp after threading the yarn through the hole at the top. Draw the string to the hole at the opposite end of the harp and push the yarn through to the back tying another knot to keep the string in place. Follow this procedure for each of the strings.

Select one child to prepare the next page of the scrapbook by drawing a harp in the center of a piece of construction paper that will be added to the book. Remember to write, "Praise Him with the Harp," on the page.

Talk with the children as they work explaining that the harp was often used in Bible times. The Scriptures tell us David played his harp as a shepherd boy and later in the palace of the king. Introduce the children to the idea that David wrote many songs and poems recorded in our Bible. These songs are found in the book of Psalms.

Pause to Praise: have one child read "Praise Him with the harp . . ." from Psalm 150:3b and explain what he or she knows about the instrument.

Using the autoharp (if available), allow the children to strum across the strings to hear the sound that is made. Turn to Psalm 136 and tell the children we will praise God together as we enjoy this special song called a litany. The litany has a phrase that is repeated each time a new thought from the writer is introduced. In this Psalm, David mentions many reasons why God deserves David's praise. Each time David mentions a reason to praise God, the class will respond with the phrase, "His love endures forever."

Allow one student to strum the autoharp as you read Psalm 136:1. Continue from Psalm 136:1-16 then skip to verses 23-26.

David felt God deserved praise for many things. As we read this Psalm, we remember how great God is, and we praise Him too.

Close this session by allowing one student to read the verse from the scrapbook. Clap your hands together after the reading and say, "We praise You, God, oh Holy God, Your love endures forever!"

Together Time: Have the children who attended this session explain the work accomplished in their center. Display the banner and ask each child to think of one thing to praise God for. Allow the class to choose some appropriate place to hang the banner. Encourage the children to remember to praise God each time they see the banner.

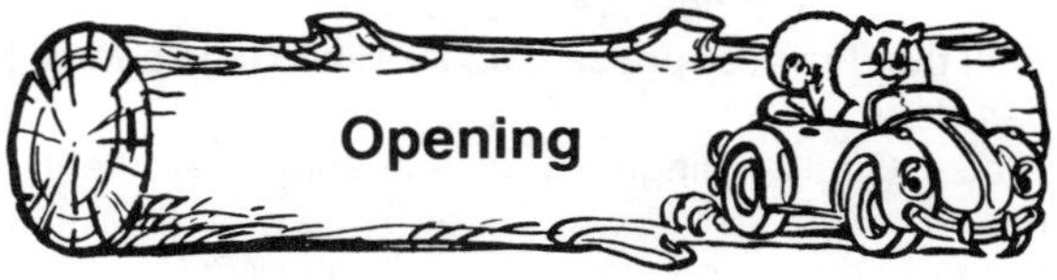

I think God deserves our praise today for bringing us all safely to class. I am so anxious to find out what will happen during our visit to Critter County. Let's all hop in the Shuttlebug. Who chose the slip from the Activi-Tree and will be our driver today? (Allow this student to identify himself.) Everyone, get set. Here we go. Talk about special activities planned during class time. When you have ridden far enough, say, "There is Grandmother Mouse's house. Let's go find out what she is eager to teach us today.

Have you ever had a day when you felt so happy you wanted to hug everybody you saw? On those kind of days, the air smells fresh, people smile, and it feels so good to be alive in God's world. Well, Beautiful Bunny is going to have one of those days. Let's listen to the story.

Grandmother Mouse's Rainbow

Grandmother Mouse stood by her kitchen sink. She was just finishing wiping the cheese crumbs off the counter.

Boy, I'm so full I can't even wiggle, she thought to herself. *I need to invite someone over tonight. Now, whom should I invite? Um, I know who needs a friend!*

The little mouse walked over to the phone and began to dial. Soon, there was an answer on the other end.

"Hello," said Beautiful.

This adorable little bunny is a favorite of almost everyone in Critter County. She's special! She's not like all the other bunnies because she has what's called a "handicap." She has to use crutches so she can walk. And Beautiful has trouble seeing clearly, so she always wears eyeglasses.

It's hard to be different from everyone else, but Beautiful handles it very well. She is beautiful on the inside because she truly loves the other critters.

Grandmother Mouse invited the furry little bunny over for the evening. Beautiful was so pleased at the invitation that she hopped right over and knocked excitedly on Grandmother Mouse's door.

"Come in," said the dear grandmother as she opened the door. The little bunny followed Grandmother Mouse into the kitchen. They enjoyed some freshly baked chocolate-chip cookies. They were still so warm that Beautiful had to hold them with a napkin to keep from burning her paw.

"These cookies are wonderful, Grandmother Mouse. Thank you so much for baking them for me," said Beautiful with a big smile on her face.

"Oh, you're quite welcome, my dear. Now, I have an idea I'd like to share with you. I've been asked to teach the children's Sunday school lesson this week because Pastor Penguin wants the children to know about my Rainbow of Promises. And tonight, I thought you might enjoy helping me make a rainbow to show the class."

Beautiful laid her cookie down on the table and began clapping her paws together.

"Oh, Grandmother Mouse, that sounds like so much fun. You always come up with the best stories and ideas. Can we do it now?"

Grandmother Mouse smiled and patted her on the shoulder. "Well, now, just a minute, Sweetheart. I'll get the things we'll need then well see what we can do."

Grandmother Mouse got some paper, glue, some coloring pencils, and her Bible. She said to Beautiful. "Now, dear, I'll draw the pattern on the paper, and you can cut it out.

For almost an hour, the two friends cut and colored together. While they worked, they enjoyed spending time getting to know each other better.

Grandmother Mouse learned that Beautiful sometimes feels like she's not as good as everyone else because she's different. Of course, this makes Beautiful sad sometimes.

Grandmother asked the little bunny, "What bothers you the most?"

Beautiful looked down at the floor. She finally said, "Sometimes it's hard to know who your friends really are. A few times the critters have made fun of me because I can't do everything like the others. They were afraid the critters wouldn't like them if they were friends with me.

Grandmother Mouse said tenderly, "That must really make you very sad. I think I understand how you feel. Beautiful, now that we almost have the rainbow finished, I'd like for you to help me find some verses in my Bible. Would you please read, Matthew 21:22?"

Beautiful turned through the pages of the worn Bible until she found the verse that says, "If you believe, you will receive whatever you ask for in prayer."

"That's a beautiful verse," said the bunny after she read it out loud.

"I call that the bottom verse," answered Grandmother Mouse.

"What does that mean," asked Beautiful.

"Watch this," said Grandmother Mouse as she took the rainbow they had just made. Very carefully she printed the words of this verse across the bottom of the rainbow.

"I call this the bottom verse on my Rainbow of Promises because it always reminds me that my heavenly Father has promised to take care of me and meet my needs. Now, honey I'd like you to look up my blue verse, please. It's John 16:33."

Beautiful looked it up and read, "I have told you these things, so that in me you may have peace. In this world you will have trouble. But take heart! I have overcome the world."

"I like that verse too, Grandmother Mouse. Why do you call it your blue verse?"

"I gave it that name because whenever I feel sad or 'blue' as they say, I remember my heavenly Father loves me and I love Him. Whatever problems I'm facing here are going to be gone some day, and I'll be in Heaven. When I think about THAT promise, I'm not 'blue' anymore. Now, would you please write this verse on the blue color of our rainbow?"

"Next is one of my favorites because it is my yellow verse," said the little mouse with a big smile on her face.

"Why is it your yellow verse?" asked Beautiful.

"Well, some days are just happy days. You know the kind I mean. the sun is shining and the birds are singing from the trees. On that kind of day, I think about my yellow verse which is Philippians 4:13. It reads, "I can do everything through him who gives me strength."

Beautiful sat up straight in her chair and said, "This is really neat having a verse for the colors in the rainbow. How did you think of this, Grandmother Mouse?"

"Well, Sweetheart, if you'll remember the story of Noah and the flood, then you'll remember the rainbow itself is God's promise to us that He will never flood the whole earth again. One day, I was thinking about God's promises and decided to make a list of some of the promises from the Bible that mean the most to me. I knew it would be easier and more fun if I used colors!

"This is really fun. I'm going to go home and make one of these to hang on my dresser, then every time I look at it, I can think of MY rainbow of promises."

Grandmother Mouse smiled and looked at her little friend. "Beautiful, I asked you to come over here to help me with this project because I want you to have THIS rainbow. I need to keep it until Sunday. Then I plan to tell the class that you came over to my house and helped me make it. I'm going to give it to you, then when your friends are giving you a hard time, and you feel sad, you can remember God's special promises that He made to you."

So after adding more promises to the rainbow and having some more milk and warm cookies, Beautiful went back home.

But she was different. From that day on, she has always remembered that she IS special. And she has her very own rainbow to prove it.

Have the children go to the tables and give them page 13 of the Critter County activity book.

5-8. *Which Direction?* Look carefully at each row of objects in the four squares on your sheet. Draw circles around the objects that are going in the same direction.

8-10. *Words That Rhyme:* Color the objects that rhyme with the picture in the box. Then use the words to fill in the blanks for the Psalm below. (Answers: knee, sea, bee, me.)

When all have finished, have them go to the Critter County Radio Station and sit in front of it.

Sydney: You're tuned to **WWCC**—the Wonderful World of critter County! Our program today is being brought to you by Fitter Critters, makers of Power Pellets, those nifty vitamins that help all the critters grow big and strong. We take you now to the Critter County Sports Arena where Lester the Lion is about to run the 100 yard dash. The crowd is going wild. Lester, excuse me. I realize that this is rather a big moment for you. Can you tell us how you feel?

Lester: NERVOUS! Sydney, I've worked long and hard. I really appreciate the support from my fans.

Sydney: Boys and girls, you should see all of the posters and hear all of the cheers. They sure do love ya, Lester!

Lester: It means so much, Sydney, so very, very much.

Sydney: It's always nice to be applauded, to be thanked, to be praised, especially when we deserve it. The Bible tells us that God is worthy to be praised. That means that He *deserves* it.

Lester: Oh, Sydney, the race is about to begin!

Sydney: That's our interview, folks. Thanks for joining **WWCC,** Lester. This is Sydney, signing off, and wishing Lester the very best.

Today we will make a snack before we eat it together. Have the children who chose these slips from the Activi-Tree be special assistants to pour the pudding and milk in the bowl and help stir. While the pudding is setting, take time to praise God by asking the children what they want to praise Him for today. Sing one of their favorite songs and remember to praise Him for providing good things to eat. Two or three serving spoons of pudding in a styrofoam cup, a napkin, and plastic spoon will make this a "tidy" and "tasty" snack time. After clean up, everyone should return to the story area.

Play the song, "Sing Praise to Him," page 140, as the children assemble in the story area. When all have gathered, sing the song together.

Sing familiar songs as well as new ones: "Give Glory to the Lord," page 137; "O Give Thanks," page 128; "Praise Ye the Lord Forever;" page 142; "Clap Your Hands," page 119; and "He Hath Done Great Things," page 118.

Prayer Song: "Hear Us as We Pray," page 143.

Prayer. Ask God to help the children to listen as we learn about praising Him. Ask for Him to guide their lives that they might always desire to praise Him for all things.

(Have Bibles marked for the four children who will be reading the special Psalms of David during the Bible story time. Be sure to have the Wonders-of-God's-World box and/or the pictures ready as you begin.)

We have learned so much about God during the class times we have spent together. We have praised Him for being so powerful. We have learned about His knowledge and wisdom. We have seen how He kept His promise to Noah and how He provided for His people as they wandered in the wilderness. Our God is a great God Who deserves our praise! Sometimes it is good to just stop everything we're doing and just praise Him because He is there. Let's praise Him together before we listen to our story. Clap your hands and repeat, "We praise You, God, oh mighty God. We praise Your holy Name!"

That kind of praise is the praise the Bible person we'll talk about today often felt. Can anyone guess who the Bible person is? (Allow time for an answer.) Tell the boys and girls there is a clue to the name of the Bible person in the Wonders-of-God's-World box. Take the slingshot (tree twig with rubber band or string) and stone from the box. This should help you remember. (The Bible person is David.)

David's life can teach us so many things. He loved and praised God constantly. God was with David, and David loved and obeyed God in good times and bad. David praised God because he knew God deserved His praise.

David's special praise of God is found in the book of Psalms in our Bible. He wrote many songs. We can still read those songs today. If you have a Bible with both the Old Testament and New Testament, you can open it to the very middle, and you will almost always find the Psalms. Let's listen to what the Bible says about David's life that would make him want to write songs which bring praise to God.

David's God Deserves His Praise

1 Samuel 17; 18:1-16; 20

The slingshot and stone should remind us of the time God was with David as he faced the giant, Goliath. David was so small. He was only a boy and the giant was over 9 feet tall. (Look around to see if you can see something tall enough to explain this height to the children.) He would not even by able to stand up in this room. (Most teachers will have rooms with 8′ ceilings.)

All the men in the army were afraid of the terrible giant. But, the Bible says David stood before Goliath and said, "You come against me with sword and spear and javelin, but I come against you in the name of the Lord Almighty . . . the battle is the Lord's!" And, David put the tiny stone in his slingshot, ran out to meet the giant who was coming to attack him, hurled the stone into the air hitting Goliath in the forehead . . . and, the Bible says the giant fell face down on the ground. David killed Goliath.

Now, listen to the words David wrote in the Psalm. See if you can understand how David felt as he wrote this Psalm praising God. (Allow the child who has Psalm 18:1-3 to read the words David wrote.)

David knew it was God who had saved him from the giant. He remembered to give God the praise He deserved. There was one more reason for David to praise God. (Take the heart from the box.) David's very best friend was the son of king Saul. His name was Jonathan. Jonathan's father became very angry at David because David won so many battles, and the people would give David more praise than they would give their king. Saul didn't like that. He wanted more praise from the people. Saul planned to kill David. Jonathan made a plan to help David escape.

Jonathan told David to go into a field one day until he could talk with the king. Jonathan promised to send a signal to David if he found out the king would not change his heart. Jonathan talked to his father and realized he would have to send David far away. He was very sad that his father wanted to kill David. Jonathan sent the signal he had promised.

After David saw the signal, he and Jonathan met in the field and cried together because they were such good friends and did not want to part. Then, David went far away so Jonathan's father would not kill him.

David loved Jonathan for caring so much for him, but David knew someone besides Jonathan deserved the praise for taking care of his life. Listen to this song and see if you can understand why David would write these words of praise to God. (Allow the child who has Psalm 18:16-19 to read.)

After many years, David became king. (Remove the crown from the box.) He won the victory in many battles. He led the people closer to God because the people listened when David gave God praise. David made mistakes, but when he was wrong, he asked God to forgive him. He became determined to live a better life.

The Bible says God loved David very much. God promised He would love David forever, and He would bless his sons and grandsons and great-grandsons. He even promised that the Savior of the world would come through someone of David's family. God kept that promise when Jesus came because the Bible tells us Joseph, Jesus' earthly father, was of the family of David.

Now, listen to these words written by David, the great king. Remember he was a righteous man who loved God. See if you can understand why David would feel God deserved this praise. (Have the child who has Psalm 18:46-50 read it to the class.)

Application: Take the harp from the box. David had a very special life for us to remember. Think of all the things that happened to him. In everything David did, he praised God.

We need to think of our lives. When we are hurt or lonely or afraid, we need to talk to God and trust him like David. When we enjoy happy times and special warm feelings, we need to be thankful to the people who are a part of those feelings, but we also need to remember to give praise to God. It is God who deserves our praise.

Close this lesson time by clapping your hands and repeating, "We praise You, God, oh mighty God. We praise Your holy name!"

Have the children go to the tables. Give them page 14 from the Critter County activity books.

5-8. *David's Musical Instrument:* Begin with number 1 and follow the dots to complete the picture. It is a harp. Color the picture.

8-10. *David's Life of Praise:* Start at the top and help David make the right choices that will lead to the box that gives God praise.

When all have finished with the activity papers, have them go to the Light Post on Memory Lane.

Have a large sheet of poster board prepared with the outline of a heart. Squares drawn inside the heart contain the words to the memory verse. Each square is covered with a square of construction paper fastened at the top so the paper can be lifted to reveal the phrase of the memory verse listed below. Allow the children to see behind each of the squares until they have read the complete memory verse several times. (Pattern is on page 111.)

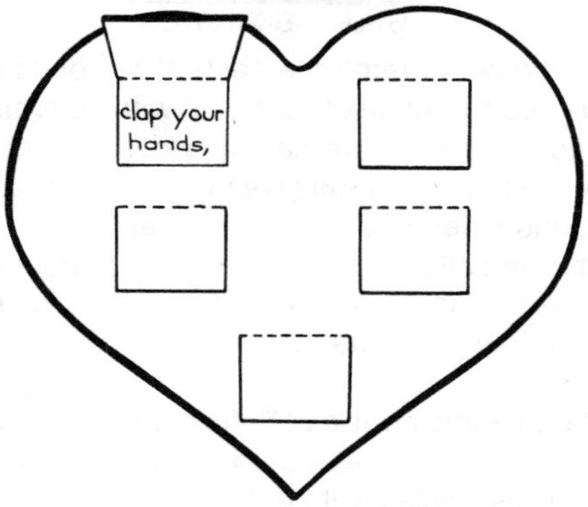

Close the construction paper flaps so the verse is concealed. Ask questions about the heart. Which square contains the reference? Which square has the phrase "all you nations"? Try lifting half of the windows to see if the children can complete the verse. Continue experimenting with the questions about the heart until one student volunteers to say the entire verse. That student may choose a classmate to repeat the verse.

Close this session by singing, "Clap Your Hands," on page 119.

Craft Time

5-8. Musical Shakers: Give each child a cardboard roll from the center of paper towels. Cut the length of the roll in half for each shaker. Prepare circles of paper as shown in the diagram. Have the children cut on the lines indicated being careful to stop where the lines stop. The circle at the end of the cuts should be just large enough to cover the opening at each end of the tube. Draw a circle with glue around one of the ends of the tube and about 1/4" down. Place the construction paper circle over the end of the tube and fold the paper slits around the tube. Press firmly to smooth the glue evenly around the papers. Hold this end for a few moments. Turn the other end up and follow the same procedure. This time, however, place 1/4 cup of popcorn or rice inside the tube before covering the end. Gently peel the backing from the piece of self sticking shelf paper that has been pre-measured to fit around the circumference of the tube. Lay your shaker at the edge of the sticky paper and roll the shaker across the paper covering the shaker and the fluted edges of the paper ends.

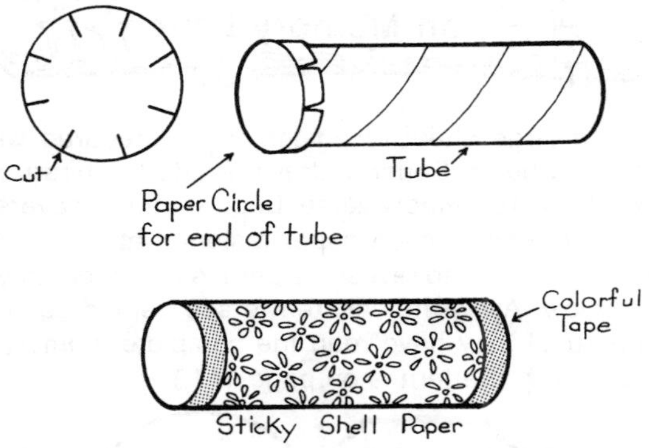

You may choose to reinforce each of the ends by taping around the circumference of each end with colorful tape. Be sure to keep any tape from covering over the hollow covered end of the tube. This will give the rice or popcorn inside a louder sound when you use the shaker.

Play music and allow the children to keep rhythm with the shakers. Use the shakers the next time you recite praise instead of clapping your hands.

8-10. Wooden tambourines: Before class, tap four small holes at 2" intervals at one end of the board leaving 3" for the handle. These holes will be the guidelines the students will use to pound the nails into place when making the tambourine.

Using a 5" nail, prepare twelve bottlecaps for each tambourine by hammering the nail through the center of the caps.

Use the sand paper to sand all the edges and top and bottom of the board until smooth. (Paint the board, if you choose, but remember to plan some activity for the class while they wait for the paint to dry.) Thread 3 bottlecaps on each 2" nail. Place the nail in one of the pre-marked holes and hammer the nail at least 1/4" into the wood. Follow this procedure with the remaining nails and bottlecaps. When all have finished, play some music and encourage the class to keep rhythm with the wooden tambourines. The tambourines can be held in one hand and clapped against the other hand or hit against the leg to make the rhythm sound.

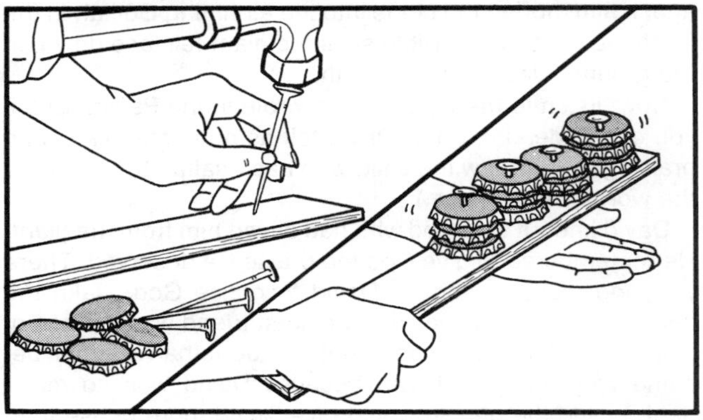

Shuttlebug Ride Home

Have everyone bring their shakers or tambourines, and sing and keep the rhythm as we praise God. Choose some favorite choruses and allow the children to sing as you take the pretend ride home. After singing, talk with the children about today's class.

Hasn't it been a special day in Critter County? We visited Grandmother Mouse, and we learned about David and how he praised God because God deserved his praise.

I'm glad God gave us His word to study so we could remember men like David. Here we come to the end of our ride. Let's praise God together just because He deserves our praise. (Use the instruments made during craft time.) Say to the rhythm, "We praise You, God, Oh mighty God. We praise Your holy name."

Closing Prayer

Oh, God, how we praise You for being our mighty, wonderful, God. You created all things, and You have taken care of Your people since You made the world. We praise You for all you have given us. Help us, like David, to live our lives obeying Your commands so that others might see how much we desire to praise You. In Jesus' name, amen.

Extra Activities

Musical Squares: Allow the children to choose a partner. If one is left without someone as a partner, allow this student to start and stop the music. Form a circle with the squares allowing one square for each couple except one.

Have the couples stand beside the squares. When the music begins, the children move around the circle. When the music stops, the couple must stand together on the square next to them. The couple which does not find a square must sit out until the game is played again. (Each couple eliminated could get their instruments and keep time with the music until they play another round.) Play musical squares until one couple is declared the winner.

For added fun, try walking around the squares backwards to the music.

Charades of Praise: Explain that each Bible story on the slips of paper should cause someone in the story to praise God. Each team will guess the story and tell who should have praised God.

Write the following suggestions on slips of paper. Divide the class into two or three teams. Allow each team to choose a charade from the papers provided. Give all teams five minutes to work out their Bible charade.

One team acts out the Bible story while the other teams guess. Give one point to each team with the correct guess. The team with the most points when all the charades have been completed, wins.

Suggested Charades

Noah lands on Mt. Ararat and comes from the ark.
Abraham helps Lot to escape from the burning city.
Abraham offers Isaac as a sacrifice.
The Princess finds Moses in the basket.
Elijah builds the altar that God burns.
Jonathan warns David that he will be killed and sends David away.
Moses receives the Ten Commandments.
The Israelites cross the Red Sea.
Jonah is swallowed by a great fish.
Moses makes the bitter water sweet to drink.
David kills Goliath.

Lesson 7

Praise God for Childhood

Scripture: Matthew 19:13,14; Luke 2:52; Mark 10:13-16; Luke 18:15-17

Psalm References: Psalm 127:3, 119:9-12; Psalm 150:3b (Pause-to-Praise verse)

Memory Verse: Unless the Lord builds the house, its builders labor in vain.—Psalm 127:1 (NIV)

Lesson Aim As a result of studying this lesson, the children should be able to:

1) Know that God made them children intentionally and that He enjoys watching them grow.
2) Feel increased self-worth because they are valued by God.
3) Praise God for making them.
4) State two specific things they like about themselves.
5) Choose three specific goals they can accomplish as children.
6) Sing or say the memory verse, Psalm 127:1.

Materials Needed:
Pre-session. *Activi-Tree:* Write the following instructions on the slips of paper you will fasten to the Activi-Tree before class. Be sure reference books and Bibles are on hand. Encourage each class member to choose a responsibility from the Activi-Tree before visiting one of the activity centers.

- Be Sydney during Critter County on Radio.
- Help the teacher during snack time.
- Be the leader as we line up for restroom break.
- Hold the Wonders-of-God's-World box during **Together Time.**
- Look up the story in Luke 2:40-52 and be ready to share during Bible story time.
- Look up the word *lyre* in the dictionary. Be ready to tell what it means.
- Look up Psalm 127:3 and be ready to read it later in class.
- See if you can find how many times the story of Jesus and the children is found in the New Testament. Write the references. (You may need to assist in the use of a concordance for this responsibility.)

Creative Kids: Sugar-cookie batter, people-shaped cookie cutters, evaporated milk and food coloring, clean paint brushes and oven.

Preparation for Pause-to-Praise: Encyclopedia, construction paper, pattern of lyre from page, string, marker

Together Time. Wonders-of-God's-World box containing pictures of animals and their offspring, pictures of a mother, daddy and baby.

Snack time. Cookies made during Pre-session, fruit juice

Bible Story Time. Wonders-of-God's-World box prepared with: picture of Jesus with children, magazine pictures of boys and girls with different expressions (happy, sad, hurt, laughing), construction-paper heart that opens (pattern on page 111; phrases listed under Bible lesson page; Pictures of children interacting with adults.

Light Post on Memory Lane. Posterboard or chalkboard, construction-paper triangle

Crafts.
5-8. *"All About Me" Book:* Posterboard, colorful material, paper, sticker of Jesus, markers, yarn, glue, magazine pictures or actual family pictures, scissors (pinking shears if available)

8-10. *Picture Frame:* Posterboard, material, scissors, glue, instant camera and film optional, ribbon.

Extra Activities.
Memory Masters: Bell or handkerchief.
Hit the Sack: Two grocery sacks, two posterboards, two markers, two sets of clues from page 53.

Welcome the Children
Greet each child by name as you direct them toward the Activi-Tree. Tell the children you have many things to learn about being children, and you are excited about being together today because the whole class is centered around them. Tell each child we will praise God for making us children who will grow up to be adults. Be ready to give assistance to early readers as they choose activities from the Activi-Tree, and then guide the student to an activity center.

Pre-session Activities
Activi-Tree. Have the slips attached to the tree and be sure each child chooses one responsibility. Introduce new children to the teachers or leaders as you guide the children toward an activity center.

Creative Kids: Make a basic sugar-cookie-dough recipe or buy sugar cookie dough from the grocery. Cut the cookie figures with the cookie cutters provided. When each child has his own cookie, place small bowls of different color "paint" (made from food coloring and 1/8 cup of evaporated milk for every color). Using clean paint brushes, allow the kids to paint clothes (jeans and shirt; skirt and blouse; blue or green eyes; hair) on the cookies before baking them. You may want to write the names of your students on a sheet of paper in the order cookies are placed on the cookie sheet. After baking, you will be able to give each student his or her personal cookie. Be sure to paint several extra in case some children remain in the other center during this time. Surprise these children with personal cookies at snack time.

As the children work, talk with them about how special it is to be a child. Ask them if they can tell you why they are glad they don't have to be a grown up yet. What is their favorite thing to do? What do they think will be different about them when they grow up. Why did God design life so we would be babies first, then children, then grown-ups? Why didn't He choose to make us all grown up when we were born?

Try to challenge their thinking with these questions and listen carefully to their answers. Activity centers should prepare minds for the learning opportunities that follow. Remember to bake the cookies before snack time today.

Preparation for Pause to Praise.

Have one student read Psalm 150:3b "... and lyre". Have the child who looked up *lyre* in the dictionary tell what it is. (Be sure to have a picture of a lyre.)

Using the pattern on page 108, draw around the lyre on poster board. You may choose to make one pattern for the scrapbook page or each student may make and decorate his own. Cut out the lyre. Use the markers or cut out patterns from wallpaper books to decorate the lyre. Place strings in the positions you see in the picture just as you did for the harp in Lesson 6.

Write the definition of the lyre on the scrapbook page and be sure to add the words, "... and lyre".

Pause to Praise: Have one child read the Scripture verse. have one child describe the lyre. One child may share how the lyre was made at the activity center. If a tape recorder or record player is available, allow the children to listen again to how the harp or strumming of an autoharp sounds. Strum the instrument and say, "We praise You, God, with instruments of praise. We praise Your holy name."

Close this session by allowing one child to read the entire Psalm 150 from the scrapbook as another child turns the pages.

Together Time: Have the children come together to talk about the activity center they chose to attend. Have the Wonders-of-God's-World box prepared with pictures of animals and their babies. Talk about how God made every creature to be small and then grow to be bigger like its parents. Encourage them to discuss why this plan for life and growth is important. See the questions under Creative Kids" activity for more discussion ideas. Close this session by reading or allowing a child to read, Psalm 127;3. Say together, "We praise You, God, for making us children. We praise Your holy name".

We should have a good time together, boys and girls, as we talk about being children. Let's all climb into the Shuttlebug and get ready for our ride to Critter County. Grandmother Mouse is going to be in our Critter County story. We'll study about Jesus during our Bible lesson. We'll see that He enjoyed having children near Him and told His disciples how special children are to God. We'll make some crafts to take home to remind us of today's lesson. We will eat the cookies you painted during pre-session. We have so much to do. We'd better get to Critter County soon so we can let the fun begin. Oh! There it is just over that next hill. Here we go!

How many of you have special, precious gifts you wouldn't want to loose or give away? (Allow time for response) We all have things that are very special to us because they bring us good memories of people and events. Lester and Sydney are going to visit Grandmother Mouse today. She has some precious memories to share. Let's listen.

Grandmother Mouse's Wall of Memories

"Well, hello, Lester and Sydney. Won't you come in?" said Grandmother Mouse as she opened the door of her little mouse house. "How are you boys doing?"

"Oh, I guess we're hanging in there," said the brown-eyed squirrel with the big brown eyes. "Lester and I have just finished jogging, and we just wanted to stop by and give you something."

"That's right, Grandmother Mouse," said Lester as he handed her a small white box. "Here's a little something my wife made for you. Liona Lou knows how much you like to hang things on the wall. She made this for you."

"I can't believe this! Why it's not even my birthday or Christmas. Gifts always seem extra special when you get them as a total surprise! Please come in and have a seat. I'll fix you boys some lunch. How about acorn soup and lion chow?" asked the little mouse.

Sydney spoke right up, "Well, the acorn soup gets my vote. But I'll pass on the lion chow. Those big pieces keep getting caught in my throat."

"Oh, Sydney! Be a man!" said Lester in his teasing voice.

"It has nothing to do with being a man ... or in my case a SQUIRREL, that lion chow is BIG. I mean we're talking big. Why, one piece is bigger than my whole head!" Sydney was quick to reply.

Everyone giggled as Grandmother Mouse left the room to begin to fix lunch. While she was gone. Sydney and Lester were looking around her living room.

"Boy, she really has some beautiful things," said Sydney as he picked up a rose colored flower vase.

Lester walked out into the hall.
"Hey, Sydney, what are all of these things hanging on her wall?"

"Beats me," Sydney answered. "We'll have to ask her."

About that time, Grandmother Mouse returned to the room with a tray of delicious treats.

"Well, this should keep you boys from starving!"

Sydney and Lester began to eat like they hadn't eaten for a week.

Sydney spoke up, "Oh, this is truly wonderful. UM, UM. Tell us, Grandmother Mouse, we were wondering what those things mean that are hanging on your wall in the hall."

Grandmother Mouse perked right up and said, "Oh, you mean my Memory Wall. Oh, I'd just love to tell you all about that. Come, let's go in, and I'll show you."

So they finished their snacks and joined her for the tour. Grandmother Mouse began to explain, "These all have significance to me."

Lester chimed right in. "Well, what in the world does signifalglance mean?"

Grandmother Mouse explained, "Lester, significance means that something is special . . . that it means something important. Anyway, as I was saying, everything on this wall is significant or special to me for one reason or another. Ah, here's the very first Mother's-Day card my little boy made for me. See how he colored the flowers black? Now who else would think of such a thing?"

Lester laughed his deep belly laugh and said, "Ho, ho, black flowers. That's pretty funny, but that's not as bad as what Lunchbox did for Liona Lou and me. Last week, he decided to fix us breakfast in bed. It was a cold morning, and he wanted to give us hot cereal. So he warmed up some milk and put it on my corn flakes!! Oh, honey, we're talking gross."

Sydney and Grandmother Mouse laughed out loud as they imagined Lester and Liona Lou enjoying this not-so-tasty treat. Finally, Sydney stopped laughing long enough to say, "Tell us what do the rest of these things stand for, Grandmother Mouse."

"Why, I'd be glad to," she said smiling. "See these dried flowers? These are from my wedding bouquet. This ribbon hanging here was the ribbon my little girl had in her hair the first time we took her to church.

Over here is a card that my best friend sent me when I graduated from nursing school. Her name is Elizabeth, and she's a beautiful gray elephant."

"Grandmother Mouse, I think this is a great idea. Why I'm going to suggest to Liona Lou that we do this at our house. We already have things we could hang that are special to us because Lunchbox made them," said Lester.

Sydney suggested, "Hey, Lester, are you going to hang your warm corn flakes up on your wall for the world to see?"

"Very funny," was Lester's answer.

Grandmother Mouse interrupted, "Lester, I think you and Liona Lou would really enjoy a Memory Wall. Of course you already have a lot of things to hang now and with the new baby coming . . . oh, I almost forgot. Where is the gift you brought me from Liona Lou?"

Lester went to the living room and got the small box for Grandmother Mouse. She opened the lid and saw a beautiful plaque all wrapped in pink tissue paper. As she took it out of the box, she read these words out loud: "A friend loves at all times."

"Oh, Lester, this is beautiful. I truly love it. I think so much of you, Liona Lou and little Lunchbox! You're such a fine family. In fact, I have a place right here on my Memory Wall to hang this. I'll see it often. My heart will be warm and happy when I see it and think of you," said Grandmother.

Lester smiled and said, "Oh, that's really sweet, Grandmother Mouse. I'll tell Liona Lou when I get home what you've done. Um, could I just ask one favor? If Liona Lou doesn't start a memory wall at our house, could I bring over Lunchbox's warm corn flakes to hang on your wall?"

Everyone laughed at Lester, as usual.

Have the children go to the tables and give them page 19 from the Critter County activity books.

5-8. *My Wall of Memories:* In the blank picture frames draw pictures of things that mean a lot to you. Color your pictures.

8-10. *Grandmother Mouse's Wall of Memories:* Draw pictures in the blank picture frames. Color all the pictures. Be ready to explain the pictures you draw.

When all have finished, have the children go to the Critter County Radio Station and sit in front of it. (Let the child who is to be Sydney take his place. Be ready to assist if help is needed.) You will need someone to be Poncho for today's radio station.

Sydney: Boys and girls you're tuned to **WWCC,** where we bring you music, news, sports, weather, personal interviews, and game shows! And speaking of game shows! It's time for . . . "Name the Game!"

Poncho: Game? you mean like baseball, football, or soccer?

Sydney: No, Poncho. Game can also refer to animals, and that's what we want our players to do—name the animal!

Poncho: I'll play! I guess animals are some of my favorite people!

Sydney: OK, Poncho, here we go. What is a cow before it's a cow?

Poncho: A calf.

Sydney: That's right! And what is a dog before it's a dog?

Poncho: A puppy!

Sydney: And a cat before it's a cat?

Poncho: A kitten!

Sydney: That's great! And a frog before it's a frog!

Poncho: A tadpole!

Sydney: Oh, Poncho, way to go! That can be a hard one to remember! And what is a goat before it's a goat?

Poncho: Wow! I guess it's a . . . goaty.

Sydney: Poncho! No! It's a kid!

Poncho: Sydney, that's what you call a little "people". Before they're adults. They're kids!

Sydney: The point is Poncho, that in God's great wisdom,

He made us little before He made us big. That's great!

Poncho: I don't know, Sydney, I've always been pretty big.

Sydney: Poncho, you were a piglet before you were a pig! And you know, God loves us little guys very much. We may be little to the eyes of those around us, but there just aren't any "little" people to God.

Poncho: We're all winners, game or no game.

Sydney: You got that one right, Poncho. This is Sydney, signing off, for "Name the Game," and **WWCC.**

Allow the children who chose this responsibility to assist with the preparation of the snack area. Give each child the cookie he or she painted during Pre-session (or the one painted by a special friend or teacher for the students who chose to remain in the other pre-session activity and did not paint their own).

Talk about favorite things we do as children (trips to the park to play on swings, ride the kiddie rides at the carnival or amusement park, or sit on daddy's shoulders to watch a parade). Discuss how things are changing as we grow. What are some of the things the children enjoy doing now that they know adults don't do? What will they look forward to doing as grown-ups (drive a car, have children, not go to school)?

Be sure to use this time to listen to what the children are saying. You can discover many special needs and attitudes as you listen to the children's answers and comments during discussion.

After clean up, have the children return to the story area.

Play the song "Sing Praise to Him," page 140, as the children assemble in the story area. After all have gathered, sing the song together.

Sing familiar songs as well as new ones. "Forever Will I Praise Your Name," page 138; "How Much Do You Love?," page 134; "Even a Child", page 133; "The Builder," page 120; and "Clap Your Hands," page 119.

Prayer Song: "Hear Us as We Pray," page 143.

Prayer. Ask God to bless the children as they listen to the story that shows how much Jesus loves them.

(Have several pictures of children on hand. The pictures should show children in different circumstances (happy with friends, loving parents, lonely, being left out, sad, hurt, surprised, anxious to open gift).

Take a few minutes to discuss how each of the children feel in each picture and why they are feeling that emotion. Ask the children if there are times when they have felt like any of the children in the pictures. Guide their thinking toward understanding that everyone goes through times when they feel good and bad. When we feel bad it is wonderful to know we have a special friend in Jesus. He knows how we feel because He was once a child and remembers what childhood is like. (Have the child who looked up Luke 2:40-52 tell what he learned about this story of Jesus during childhood.)

Jesus and the Children

Matthew 19:13, 14; Mark 10:13-16; Luke 18:15-17

We know Jesus was born as a tiny baby. He lived in Nazareth as a boy, and he grew.... just like we grow. *(Child's Name)* has told us about one event in Jesus's life that occurred when he was twelve years old. But, when Jesus became a man, did He remember how it felt to be a child? Did He take time for children? Today's story will give us the answer to the question. I believe, the answer will make us feel good inside, and we will want to praise God because Jesus is our special friend. Ask the child who discovered how many times this story was found in the New Testament, give the number. (Allow child to answer three times, in Matthew 19:13, 14; Mark 10:13-16; and Luke 18:15-17.)

Three times this story is mentioned! Oh, boys and girls ... it must be very important. If someone tells you about a special event just once, they want you to know about it and what happened. If they tell you two times, they want to be sure you remember. But, if they tell you three times, it is SO special, and they want it to mean something special to you, too. We should realize that God wants us to be sure we understand how much children mean to Him. He had this story included in the Scriptures three times.

The Bible tells us Jesus was teaching people in the country of Judea. (Show Judea on a map if available.) He was very busy answering many questions and teaching adults about the kingdom of God. Some people stepped out of the crowd and brought their children to Jesus so he would talk to them and touch them.

Have any of you ever waited after a concert or special event like a ball game or a play to meet with the people you had gone to see? Maybe you wanted their autograph or just wanted to say, "Thank you", to them for being there. (Allow the children time to answer.) Well, this is exactly what these people did. After Jesus finished teaching, they took their children to see Him.

The disciples who were standing near by thought Jesus was too busy to talk with the children. The disciples felt he had more important things to do than stop His conversations with the adults in the crowd. They tried to send the children away. Imagine how this must have made the children feel! (Very Sad!) But, Jesus stopped them. Jesus said to his disciples (Show the picture of Jesus and the children.), "Let the children come to me and do not hinder them, for the kingdom of God belongs to such as these."

I can just see smiles on the faces of all those children

when Jesus said He wanted to see them. The story in Luke tells us Jesus picked the children up in his arms, put His hands on them and blessed them. What a special day it was for these boys and girls when Jesus showed them how important they were to Him.

Let's praise God together for Jesus' love. Clap your hands together and say, "We praise You, God, for Jesus' love. We praise Your holy name".

Can you imagine how special it would feel to have Jesus pick you up and show you He loves you?

Jesus taught the people standing around Him a lesson. He said, unless grown-up people become like little children, they cannot enter into Heaven. I wonder what Jesus meant by that. (Allow time for children to try to answer.)

Children trust grown ups to take care of them. They ask adults for answers and depend on grown ups to help them. Look at these pictures of kids and grown ups from the Wonders-of-God's-World box. (Allow the children to discuss how the grown ups and children are sharing with each other.)

Application: The best way to become a grown up who trusts God and depends on Him is to look to God and depend on him all the time you are growing. God knows that children are always ready to trust Him and depend on Him. Children believe Jesus will do everything he says. God wants grown ups to learn to trust in Him with the same special feelings that children have.

The Bible says some pretty special things about being a child and growing. Let's listen to this verse in Psalm 127:3. (Allow the child to read who had this assignment from the Activi-Tree.)

That verse sounds like you are VERY special. You have been given as a reward from God. Always remember how special you are to Him. Show Him how much you appreciate His love for you by living like He has asked you to live.

Listen to this verse. It will give us a clue as to how we can please God as a child. It will tell us what we can do with our lives that will help us to grow and depend on God. I'll read the verse. When you hear something you can do to please God, raise your hand.

Read Psalm 119:9-12. See how many clues from the verse the children hear. You may have to read the passage more than once.

Take the heart that opens from the Wonder's-of-God's-World box and as the children hear the clues, insert the phrase inside the heart.

Phrases for the heart:

1) Live according to God's Word.
2) Seek God with all your heart.
3) Do not stray from God's commands.
4) Hide His Word in your heart to keep you from sin.

Let's praise God together by reading verse 12 again. I will read it to you, and then you repeat it with me. (Read the verse, "Praise be to You, Oh Lord, teach me Your decrees.") Close the lesson by clapping your hands and saying the verse together one more time.

Have the children go to the tables and give them page 20 of the activity book.

5-8. *Jesus and the Children:* Color the picture of Jesus and the children. Read the praise verse together.

8-10. *As We Grow:* Follow the mixed up lines that lead to the items used by each person pictured. What do each one use?

Korean Kid's Memorization:

Explain to the children that in America we are taught to read from left to right and across the page. Korean children read differently, and their Bible looks very different from ours. Korean children read from right to left and up and down the page. Today we will think of the Korean children God made as we memorize the verse.

Write each word from the verse on the posterboard or chalkboard following the illustration. Ask if anyone can read the verse before the teacher reads it to the class. (Allow any who would like to try, to answer.) Move your finger up and down to follow the words from right to left as you encourage the class to read the verse several times together. Use a construction-paper triangle to cover some of the words. Allow any student to move the triangle across the words after successfully repeating the entire verse. The students take turns covering the words as each successfully quotes the verse. Keep saying the verse as long as time permits or until each member of the class has taken his turn at the board.

Illustration: start here

	R						
	E	F					
	F	A			V		W
L	E	S	T		E	T	R
A	R	H	H	I	R	H	I
S	E	I	I	N	S	E	T
T	N	O	S		E		E
	C	N					
	E						

Close this session by singing the "The Builder," on page 120.

5-8. "All About Me" Book: Cut a piece of posterboard in a 9″ x 4″ rectangle. Cut a piece of material a little longer and wider than this posterboard piece. (Cutting this material with pinking shears will give the book a decorative edge. Cut a window in the upper portion of the material. Make the window large enough to frame the words "All About me". Glue the material to the posterboard and write these words in the window. Cut four blank pieces of white paper 8¾″ x 3¾″. Fold these sheets and insert them inside the cover. Wrap the piece of yarn around the inside center fold and tie a bow on the outside of the booklet to hold the papers in place. Each page of the booklet will tell something about the child who owns the book.

Have the children draw their own pictures or glue magazine pictures that refer to the captions given on each page. If you are planning ahead, you might encourage the children to bring a recent picture of themselves for the first page of the booklet.

Suggested captions:

1. This is "Me."
2. When I was born, I was so small (actual baby picture).
3. Then, I began to grow (actual or magazine picture).
4. These are my brothers and sisters (or parents if only child in the family).
5. My favorite foods are (magazine pictures or draw).
6. My favorite sport is (draw).
7. My favorite subject at school is (write).
8. Special people in my life (draw or list—autographs).
9. My favorite friend in Critter County is (draw).
10. My church building looks like this (draw).
11. The Bible verse I want to remember is (write).
12. Praise God for making children (pictures of kids).
13. I praise you God for making "ME."

Encourage the children to share their books with one another. you might want to include a blank page for autographs of friends in the class. In the center of this page place a sticker or picture of Jesus.

8-10. *Picture Me Perfectly:* You will need to choose the instant camera and film you will use to take pictures of the children before you prepare the materials for this craft. The dimensions of the picture frame will be determined by the size of the photo. Be sure to take an individual shot of each student in the class.

Use posterboard to cut a square that will border the four sides of your picture. The border area around your picture should be ¾" wide. Cut two of these pieces to be identical. Cover one of the squares with material that completely wraps around the entire boarder. (Calico material is suggested.) Glue the material in place and fasten the other square to the back of the covered square concealing the material edges.

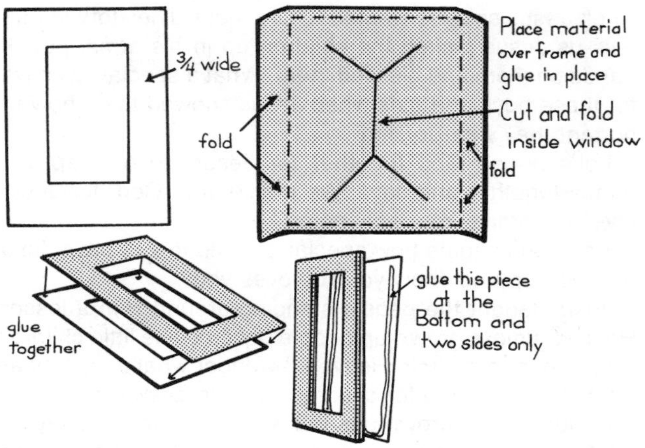

Cut a piece of posterboard to fit the size of the frame. (This time, the center is solid.) Glue this piece at the *bottom* and *two sides only.* Leave the top open to insert the picture. The picture should slide easily between the frame and this square back. Attach a stand cut from posterboard using the pattern on page 98. The picture should stand alone. (To insure longer life of the frame, you may choose to run a strip of hot glue around all the outside edges and apply a ribbon to conceal the glue, attaching a bow at the center top of the picture.)

Encourage the children to look at the picture and see the child God has created. Then think about the grown up he or she would like to become.

What a good time we have shared today in Critter County! Didn't we learn a lot as we worked together? Let's get into the Shuttlebug now and rest a little as we drive home. Ask the children to pretend that Jesus will be there to meet them. How do you think He will look when He sees you? What do you think He would do? Guide their conversation toward the understanding that Jesus would take time for them and make them feel special. He would be glad to see them. Praise God again for treating them as children who can grow to love Jesus.

Closing Prayer

We thank You and praise You, Father for making us. We thank You for allowing us to be children who can grow like Jesus grew. Help us to learn the things we'll need to know that will allow us to become grownups who will follow Jesus everyday of our lives. Thank You for Your Word that teaches us how to be like Him. We praise You for allowing us to know how much Jesus loves children. help us to serve Him in all we do and say. We praise you Father, our Heavenly Father. In Jesus' name, amen.

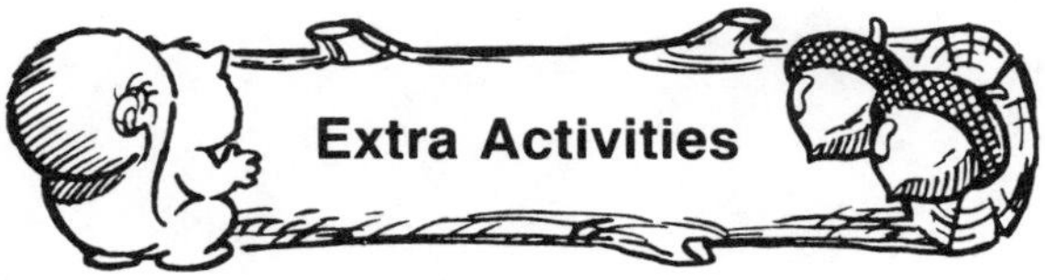

Extra Activities

Memory Masters: Have the students sit in a circle. Have every child decide what he or she would like to be when he or she grows up. Each child should tell out loud what occupation he or she has chosen as the others listen and try to remember. The teacher starts the game by walking around the outside of the circle. She drops the handkerchief on a child's lap or rings a bell overhead. Any student in the circle who remembers this student's occupation, stands. This student must tell the chosen's student's occupation AND the occupation of one student on either side of the chosen student. If the guess is correct, the student who is guessing walks around the circle an chooses the next student to be guessed. If incorrect, the chosen student takes the position of finding another classmate and the play continues. Allow play to continue until all have had a turn on the outside of the circle.

Hit the Sack: Divide the class into two teams. Each team is given a paper sack, two beanbags, posterboard, a marker. The teacher (or child who would make the number of children on one team uneven) keeps two separate bowls of clues marked with the name of each team.

The first player from each team comes forward and is given two bean bags. The paper sacks have been placed ten feet ahead of the players and side-by-side. Each player throws each of the bean bags hoping to hit his team's sack. A "hit" occurs when the beanbag goes in the IN sack. (Place something heavy in the bottom of the sacks to keep them from falling over each time they are hit.) If successful, the teacher draws a clue from his teams bowl, and he is permitted to draw that body part on the posterboard. (If he hits the sack both times, he draws two body parts.) If he accidentally hits his opponent's sack, he is forced to draw the body part on his opponent's board giving that team an advantage. The first team to draw the complete person wins the game.

For extra fun: Change the figure drawn (but clues do not change) Draw a baby, a mother, a boy or girl, grandfather.

Put the same number of blank papers in each bowl as body parts. If someone hits the sack but a blank is drawn no body part can be added to the picture. (This will add excitement if someone hits the wrong sack. They still may not have to add a body part to their opponent's board.)

Clues to include: head, neck, right arm, left arm, body, right leg, left leg, right foot, left foot.

Lesson 8

Praise God for His Healing

Scripture: Luke 7:1-10; Matthew 8:5-13

Psalm References: Psalm 119:9-12; 103:1-3; 121; Psalm 150:4a (Pause-to-Praise verse)

Memory Verse: Praise the Lord. How good it is to sing praises to our God, how pleasant and fitting to praise him!—Psalm 147:1 (NIV)

Lesson Aim: As a result of studying this lesson, the children should be able to

1) Know that God made our bodies with the ability to heal when we get hurt or become sick.
2) Know that God cares about our condition of health.
3) Feel secure in the knowledge that God is with us when we are ill.
4) Praise God for His healing power.
5) Name three things they can do to take care of their bodies.
6) Pray for one person who is sick or injured.
7) Sing or say the memory verse, 147:1.

Materials Needed:

Pre-session. *Activi-Tree:* Have reference books on hand for the assignments given that require reference information. Attach the following slips containing learning and helping activities to the Activi-Tree and encourage each student to choose a slip before joining an activity center.

- Help prepare the snack today. (2)
- Drive the Shuttlebug to Critter County.
- Drive the Shuttlebug home from Critter County.
- Look up the word *centurion* and remember it's meaning.
- Look up Matthew 8:6 and find out what was wrong with the servant.
- Be the leader in line.
- Look up and be ready to read Psalm 103:1-3 during Bible story time.
- Be Sydney, the announcer, during the Critter County Radio program.

Diorama Drama: Four or more (depending on the size of your class) shoe boxes, chenille wires, construction paper, glue, clay, cottonballs, material scraps, reference Scriptures.

Preparation for Pause to Praise: Two aluminum pie tins, string or yarn, nail, fifteen bottle caps, Bible, picture of tambourine, music, construction paper and glue.

Snack Time. Slices of various fruit or fruit salad and juice. Exercise record or music.

Bible Story Time. Wonders-of-God's-World box containing: empty cough syrup bottle, empty aspirin bottle, Dr.'s stethoscope, blood-pressure cup, band aids, picture of Jesus; and a picture of a synagogue.

Light Post on Memory Lane. Scrap paper, Bible.

Crafts.
5-8. *Get-Well card:* Vegetables (potato, carrot), poster paint, construction paper, typed verse on page 59.

8-10. *Planter:* 15″ soup or vegetable can, colored twine, glue, paint brushes, shellac or spray sealer.

Extra Activities. *Concentration:* Thirty-six cards, eighteen matching pictures. *The Doctor Is "In":* Basket, slips of paper, rope or tape, chairs

Welcome the Children

Greet the students with a smile as you call each by name. Encourage them to choose an activity paper from the Activi-Tree. Be ready to assist new readers if they choose a reference activity. After each has accepted the responsibility from the Activi-Tree, guide them to one of the activity centers. Remind them they may choose either center, but they must complete the project they begin in any center they select. Introduce new students to at least one classmate and to the teacher working at the center.

Pre-session Activities

Activi-Tree. Have the slips prepared and attached to the tree before class. (See suggested activity slips at the beginning of this lesson.) Be sure there is a responsibility on the tree for each student.

Diorama Drama. Allow the students to work in teams of three or four per diorama. Give each group a story assignment from the references listed below. Notice that all the references show an account of Jesus healing someone. Each group will look up the reference in the Bible provided , and then work together to make a scene depicting that story inside the box. The scenes may be as elaborate as time will allow.

Let the children use their imagination and the materials provided to make the scene. Remind them that they will be sharing their diorama during **Together Time.** At least one person per group should be ready to tell the story in their box to the class.

Suggested References

Matthew 8:14, 15—Peter's Mother-in-law
Mark 2:1-5, 11, 12—Paralytic
Mark 3:1-5—Man with withered hand

John 9:1-7—Blind man
Luke 17:11-19—Ten lepers
John 5:1-9—Lame man

Preparation for Pause to Praise. Have one student read Psalm 150:4a "Praise Him with Tambourine." Talk with the students about how the tambourine was used in Bible days when the people sang and danced before God. If you have a real tambourine on hand, you will want to encourage the children to tap it to the beat of music as you listen on a record player or recorder.

Allow two or three children in your center to work as a team to make a tambourine to keep in class while two or three other children add the seventh page to the scrapbook. *Directions for making tambourines:* Put the pie tins together rim to rim. With a small nail, punch nine holes around the circumference of the tins. Weave a long piece of string in and out of the holes to tie the pie pans together. Tie with a simple knot as you complete the last hole. The teacher makes holes in the center of the pop bottlecaps by using the hammer and nail. Weave enough string through three bottlecaps and tie them to one hole so they hang loosely from the side of the pie tins. Follow this same procedure with the next four holes. Allow the other holes to remain empty so you will have space to hold the tambourine.

Play music from a tape recorder or recorder player and let the children keep the rhythm by twisting the tambourine back and forth in the air or hitting it against their hand or leg.

On the seventh page of the scrapbook let the children draw tambourines or find pictures of the tambourines to glue to the construction-paper page. Write the words, "Praise Him with Tambourine," on the page.

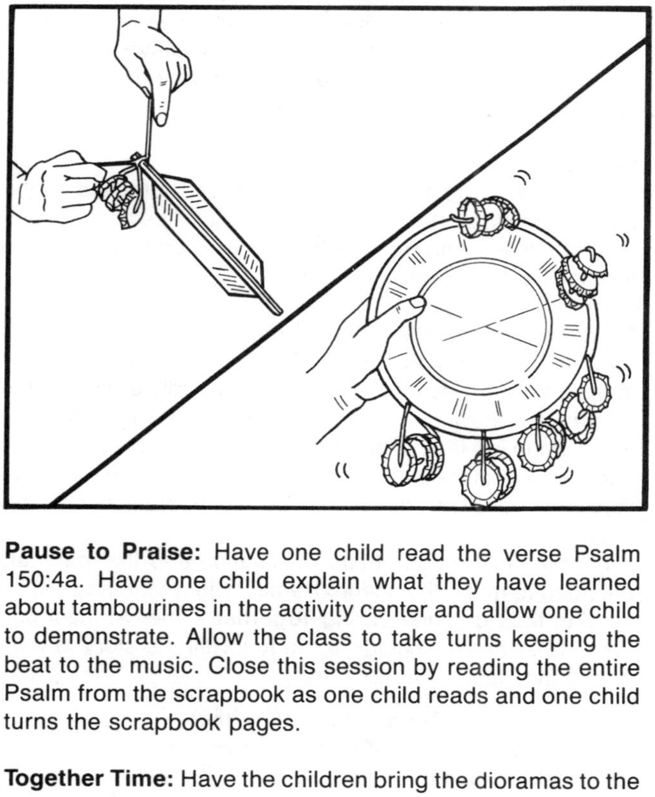

Pause to Praise: Have one child read the verse Psalm 150:4a. Have one child explain what they have learned about tambourines in the activity center and allow one child to demonstrate. Allow the class to take turns keeping the beat to the music. Close this session by reading the entire Psalm from the scrapbook as one child reads and one child turns the scrapbook pages.

Together Time: Have the children bring the dioramas to the story area. Allow each group to explain the diorama they worked on by telling the story in their own words and displaying the diorama before the group. Talk with the children about Jesus' power to heal. Praise Him for His power of healing by clapping your hands together and saying, "We praise You, God, for Your healing power. We praise Your Holy Name."

How many of you can remember being sick when you were little? Maybe you had the chicken pox or a very bad cold or the flu. (Allow the children a short time of discussion.) Look at you now. You feel strong and healthy. You aren't sick anymore. You are all feeling well enough to take a bumpy ride to Critter County. Let's get in the Shuttlebug and talk about what makes us healthy and strong as we ride to Critter County. (Allow the child who chose this activity from the Activi-Tree to drive the Shuttlebug.) We will visit Dr. Duck's office today. His office is usually filled with sick critters. He does all he can do to make them well again. Here's his office now. Let's stop and see what is happening.

When you are sick, mother takes care of you. She knows what to do to make you feel better. But there are times when she needs help. That's when she calls the doctor and makes an appointment for him to see you and treat you so you will get well.

Sometimes an accident happens and you have to have immediate medical care. We call this an emergency. Sometimes this means a rush trip to the hospital of the doctor's office.

Mrs. Bunny's baby has had an accident. She rushes her baby to Dr. Duck's office. Dr. Duck, Grandmother Mouse, and Mrs. Bunny's friends help the baby rabbit and Mrs. Bunny in many ways. Listen to find out what each critter did to help them.

Friends to the Rescue

It was an unusually warm Saturday afternoon in early May. Many of the residents of Critter County were cleaning up their yards and cars after spending the long winter months indoors. Kites were flying up high where usually only birds dare to sail and the trees were blowing in the breeze as though they were keeping time to silent music.

Dr. Duck's office was almost empty after months of coughs and colds. Grandmother Mouse looked so clean and crisp in her starched uniform and nurse's cap. She was busy filling the jar with cotton balls for Dr. Duck when suddenly the front door flew open. It was Mrs. Bunny carrying her baby in her arms.

"Oh, Grandmother Mouse, please help me ... my baby wandered away from our nest because she was chasing a butterfly and she fell into a deep hole. I think she's really hurt," cried Mrs. Bunny as she placed the baby in Grandmother Mouse's arms.

Grandmother Mouse used her most soothing tone of voice as she spoke, "Now, my dear, you just be seated here in the waiting room for a few minutes. I'll take this little one in to see the doctor. Where is your husband?"

"Oh, of all times, he was called out of town on business. He was asked to speak to the National Hare Dresser's Convention, and won't be home until Saturday. And one of my boys is home sick with rabbit pox.... Oh, I don't know what I'm going to do," the sad mother cried.

Grandmother Mouse spoke again, "Now you just sit here for a few moments while we take a look at the baby. I'll be back as soon as the doctor has seen her."

Grandmother Mouse had just closed the door behind her when the front door to the office opened wide and in walked Mrs. Skunk. "Hello, dear. I just heard about the accident with your baby and I wanted to see if there is anything you need or anything I can do to help you," said Mrs. Skunk as she put her paw around Mrs. Bunny.

"Well, thank you so much for coming here. Yes, I do need help. When the baby got hurt, I grabbed her and hopped over here as fast as I could, leaving her brother at home in his crib. He'll be waking up anytime," said Mrs. Bunny.

"Don't you worry another minute. I'll go and pick him up and take him to my place. I know he has the rabbit pox, and is running a fever. I'll keep him quiet and happy by reading books to him until you get home. Just give me a call then, and I'll bring him home." Without another word, Mrs. Skunk was out the door—and on her way to take care of Mrs. Bunny's sick child.

Quick as butterfly kisses, the front door opened again, and in walked Poncho the pig.

"Please excuse the grease on my hands; I was working on my car when I heard about the accident. Is Bernie still at the Hare Convention?" asked the pig.

"Yes, and he won't be home until Saturday," replied Mrs. Bunny.

"Well, I came right over to see how I could help you," offered Poncho.

"Oh, that is so sweet of you, Poncho. The only thing I can think of is that I need some milk and clover from the store. I was going there after my boy woke up from his nap. But I'm sure I can do it on my way back home," said Mrs. Bunny.

"Consider it done, my dear. On your kitchen table when you arrive at home will be the freshest of clover that the deli has to offer, and enough milk to keep those kids happy for days." And with that, Poncho disappeared through the door.

The pretty receptionist walked over to Mrs. Bunny and handed her a piece of folded paper. She opened it and read the following message: "We just heard about the accident because Pastor Penguin called us. Please know we are on our knees right now praying for you and your family. Love, Lester and Liona Lou."

Soon after Mrs. Bunny read the note, Grandmother Mouse walked over and sat down beside her. She put her paw on the bunny's shoulder and said, "Well, it looks like your little girl will be O.K. However, she hurt her eyes when a stick scratched it and her right leg is also hurt. She'll need to use crutches for a while.... God was obviously there taking care of her because it could have been much worse."

Mrs. Bunny smiled and said, "I'm so thankful, she's going to be OK. When can I see her?"

"In just a few moments, Dr. Duck will be finished bandaging her leg, and you may take her home. I can stay for awhile and fix your dinner so you can hold and rock her. She's been through quite a scary afternoon, and I know she will feel much better if you hold her."

As the two ladies walked home together, Mrs. Bunny said, "You know when I first realized that the baby had fallen and was hurt so badly, I got really scared. Bernie is out of town, and I didn't know how I was going to be able to handle all of this. Then my heavenly Father reminded me of the verse in Psalms that says, "What time I am afraid, I will trust in Thee." And as always, my God has taken very good care of me. Mrs. Skunk came and picked up our little boy, and Poncho went to the store for me and now you're going home with me to help with dinner. Grandmother Mouse, God has always met my needs and takes such good care of me. Why was I afraid?"

"Well, my dear, no matter how old we get, there's still a part of us that's like a child. We still get afraid when we think we might get hurt. But you're right, our strong heavenly Father knows all about it. He just loves to hold us and take care of us," shared the sweet grandmother.

"And I love the way He takes care of me," said Mrs. Bunny.

"Me too," added Grandmother Mouse as the two walked around the bend of the road called Memory Lane which is located in the heart of Critter County.

Have the children go to the tables and give them page 21 from the Critter County activity book.

5-8. *Critter Finger Puppets:* Color the critters and then cut out both of them. Have fun making up stories about them.

8-10. *Critter County Puppets:* Follow these simple instructions to make a puppet. Then use this one for a pattern to make more. Use your puppets to tell your own Critter County stories.

When all have finished, have the children go to the Critter County Radio Station and sit in front of it. Let the child who will be Sydney take his or her place.

Sydney: Sydney, here. I've been joined by my co-host, Rascal, the raccoon. Thanks for tuning into **WWCC.** Rascal, I have a rather novel idea for our program, today.

Rascal: Novel idea, Sydney? You're going to write a big book?

Sydney: No, silly. Novel can also mean new and interesting. I have a new and interesting idea for our show.
Rascal: Lay it on me little buddy!
Sydney: Well, **WWCC** always tries to be the first to bring you the news and sports.
Rascal: Yes.
Sydney: But I know something that happened a long, long time ago, that would have made one exciting radio program, but they didn't have radios!
Rascal: That's a shame! But what can we do about it now?
Sydney: Let's ask all of our **WWCC** listeners to pretend that we're going back over two thousand years ago in time. We'll be the reporters!
Rascal: I'm all for it! You start.
Sydney: This is **WWCC**—coming to you live from Capernaum.
Rascal: Capernaum??
Sydney: Capernaum. We've received word today that Jesus has gone to the side of the sick, sick, very sick servant of one of the centurions.
Rascal: Well, that's great, what happened?
Sydney: That's the news for tonight. We now return to our regular program. "Cowboys in Capernaum."
Rascal: Sydney, you can't do that! What happened to the sick, sick, very sick servant of the centurion?
Sydney: Rascal, our listeners are going to hear all about in their Bible story. Stay tuned.

Various kinds of fruit or fruit salad is suggested for today's snack. Talk with the children about how nutritious fruit is for the body. (Explain the word "nutrition" or see if any child can explain it.) Be creative and play some music to exercise during snack time today. The children will enjoy watching the teachers exercise. They will probably be able to show the teacher some exercises, too. Emphasize taking care of the body God has given us.

Play the song, "Sing Praise to Him," page 140, as the children assemble in the story area. After all have gathered, sing the song together.

Sing familiar songs as well as new ones: "Sing and Shout It," page 136; "Praise Ye the Lord Forever," page 142; "What Time I Am Afraid," page 132; "He Hath Done Great Things," page 118; and "Clap Your Hands," page 119.

Prayer Song: "Hear Us as We Pray," page 143.

Prayer Ask God to help the children listen carefully to the Bible lesson to learn of His healing power. Help the children praise God for His concern for the sick.

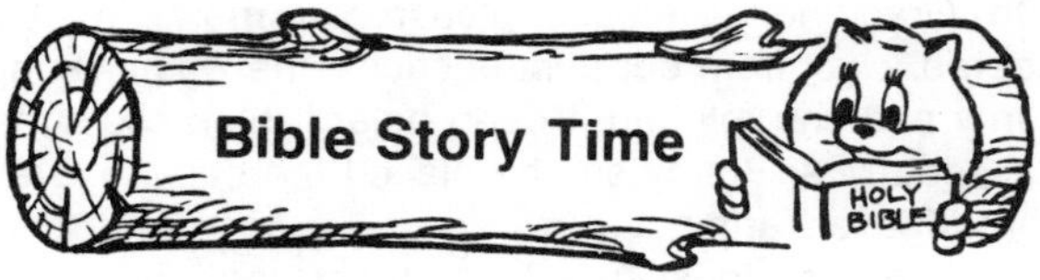

(Prepare the **Wonders-of-God's-World"** box with the items mentioned under **Materials Needed** at the beginning of this lesson. Give the children several hints referring to the contents of the box and let them try to guess the items inside. As each item is guessed, allow the child who guessed to hold that item throughout the lesson period.)

All of the things in the box have to do with our body as it works to get well after we have been sick. We should praise God for making our bodies so they will heal. Wouldn't it be terrible if every time we fell down and skinned our knee or scratched our elbow, the scratch would not heal? We would have a lot of scratches and bruises on our bodies by the time we grew up. But, God made our bodies so they would get better when they hurt. Our cuts heal and our bruises go away. Sometimes we need special medicine to help our bodies do the work of healing. I praise God that He has allowed men to discover medicines that make us feel better.

Today, our Bible lesson will tell us about someone who was so sick, he almost died. But, it didn't take any medicine or any doctor to help him. Listen as I share the story.

The Centurion's Servant Is Healed
Matthew 8:5-13; Luke 7:1-10

The Bible tells us about a man who was called a centurion. Someone looked up the word "centurion" because you chose that slip from the Activi-Tree. Tell us what a centurion is. (Allow the child to explain that a centurion was a soldier who was the leader of one hundred men.) The centurion had so much to do and so many responsibilities taking care of his one hundred soldiers that he had servants to help him with his work. The Bible says one of his servants was very sick. This was a servant the centurion loved very much. He wanted to see him get well. What was wrong with the servant? (Allow the child who had this assignment to tell the group the servant was paralyzed.)

His servant could not move. It was very sad for the centurion to see his servant in this condition. He could not help his servant move his arms or legs. The servant's muscles were completely still, and the Bible tells us the servant was about to die.

The centurion heard that Jesus had come to Capernaum, and he sent Jewish elders to meet Jesus. The elders asked Jesus to come to the centurion's house and heal his servant. They told Jesus that the centurion was a good man and had built the synagogue. (If you have a picture of a Jewish synagogue, show it now.) This was the building where the Jews went to worship God.

Jesus went with the elders to see the centurion and his servant, but before Jesus even got to the house, some of the centurion's friends came to meet Jesus. They told Jesus the centurion did not feel worthy to have Jesus come to his house. The centurion did not want to trouble Jesus or take His time. The friends told Jesus that the centurion believed in Jesus and knew if Jesus would just say the word, his servant would be well. Jesus was so pleased with the faith. He turned to all the people who were with Him and told them He had not seen anyone in all of Israel with as much faith as the centurion.

Jesus said the servant would be healed, and when the people went to the centurion's house, the servant was completely well. He was healed the very hour Jesus had said he would be.

Clap your hands together and say, "We praise You, God for Your healing power. We praise Your holy name."

Application: I want you to notice something about this story. Look at the articles you have in your hands. I will pass the box around our class, and if you know the servant wasn't healed or treated with the article you have, put it back in the box. Pass the **Wonders-of-God's-World** box around our class, and watch the children return the articles one by one.) Talk to them as the box circulates. Explain that no doctor's instruments touched the servant. No bandages were used, no shots, no machines, and no pills. Jesus was there. All Jesus had to do was say the servant was healed and the man was made well.

Jesus healed many people when He was on the earth. We can't see Him or touch Him today, but the Bible says He is with us. We should praise God that we can trust Jesus when we are hurt or feel sick. We can tell Him how we feel, and we can ask Him to be with us and help our bodies get better.

Listen to this verse in Psalm 103:1-3. (Read the verse or allow a child to read.) Close this session by clapping hands and saying, "We praise You, God, for Your healing power. We praise Your holy name."

Have the children go to the tables and give them page 22 from the Critter County activity books.

5-8. *Psalm 121:* Listen as your teacher reads Psalm 121, then draw a line to the word picture that best fits in the blank. (Answers: hills, earth, foot, and sleep)

8-10. *My Puzzle Message:* Use the words in the **Word Box** to discover a special message. (Answers: 1. paralyzed; 2. servant; 3. healed; 4. faith; 5. soldiers; 6. Centurion; 7. Synagogue: 8. word; 9. servant.) The special message is "Praise God."

When all have finished, have them go to the Light Post on Memory Lane.

Great Physician's Prescription: Write each word of the memory verse on separate slips of paper. You will need to make two sets of each. In the upper right-hand corner of one set write the symbol Rx. On the upper right hand corner of the other set, make the doctor's symbol.

Mix all the papers together and put them in a large bowl in the center of the room. Blow a whistle or give some starting signal for the class to take the papers from the bowl and match the groups by looking at the symbol. When all have found the set of words belonging to one group. allow the group to try to form the memory verse by putting the words in proper order. After 5 minutes, allow the teams to look up the verse. How close did they come to getting the right sequence of words? Spend the rest of the time seeing how many team members can memorize the verse and say it before craft time.

Close this session by singing "Praise Ye the Lord," on page 116.

5-8. Get-Well Card: Let the children make a Get-well card for a relative or friend. If there is someone in the church who is ill and has worked with children, you might encourage several children to make an extra card for him or her. (Include a picture of the class to make this card really special.)

Begin by cutting vegetables in half and carving a design which can be dipped in poster paint and pressed onto construction paper. (Potatoes and large carrots work best.) Easy designs are stars, heart shapes, half moons and smiling faces. You may also provide materials for the children to be creative as they decorate the card. (Example: sponges, stencils, string, bottlecaps,)

Provide a 6″ x 8″ sheet of construction paper that will fold to card size. Dip the vegetable stamp in poster paint and allow excess paint to drip into the bowl or container before applying the object to the paper.

On the outside of the card write the words, "Thinking of You." Have the following message printed for the inside of the card.

> This card comes to say
> "I'm, thinking of you,"
> And it is sent with a prayer
> That you'll feel better too!

Allow each child to sign his or her greeting and encourage the children to personally deliver the card. Perhaps the minister would enjoy some cards to take with him on hospital visits in the week ahead.

When the craft is complete, include a special prayer time when the class can pray for the health of each person receiving the card. Close by praising God.

8-10. From the Heart: Give each student a clean, empty soup or vegetable can that has had the wrapper removed. Cut enough colored twine to wrap tightly around the size can you have chosen. The twine will cover the can from top to bottom. Allow the children to paint glue (Caution them to make a thin layer.) on the can, 1/2″ of space at a time, starting at the bottom. Wrap the twine around the can being sure each round of twine is sticking to the glue AND fitting close to the layer of twine below it. Continue adding glue and wrapping the can until you reach the top. The teacher may help cut a tail from the left-over twine. Use a pencil or similar object to push the tail under the four or five rows of twine at the top. Press the twine firmly for a few minutes and set the can aside to dry.

Take the planter outside and coat it with a layer of shellac or spray varnish to make it shine and seal the twine. (Be sure to do this outside for better ventilation.)

Put a layer of gravel or small stones about 1/2″ deep in the bottom of the can. Cover the gravel with dirt or potting soil to a depth of 1″ from the top of the can. Allow each child to plant the flower or sprig of greenery you have chosen for the project.

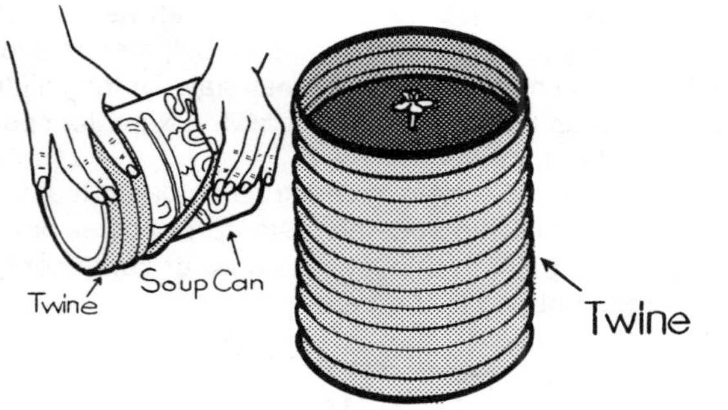

Talk with the children about giving the planter to someone who does not feel well. Encourage the children to share one of the verses about healing and/or God's special care when they take the planter to the person they have chosen.

Shuttlebug Ride Home

I can hardly wait for the people to see what you have made to cheer them up and let them know you are praying for them to feel better. Let's get in the Shuttlebug and head for home. When you return to class, you can share with us how your friend or relative felt about your card or planter. Talk with the children as you ride. Remember special events that took place in class today. Direct their thoughts toward God's healing. As you arrive home from your pretend journey, praise God one more time together by clapping your hands and saying, "We praise You, God, for Your healing power. We praise Your holy name."

Closing Prayer

Thank You, God, for giving us so many lessons from Your word about Jesus as He healed the people. Help us to remember that You are with us when we hurt and when our bodies need special care. We praise You for making our bodies capable of recovering from scrapes and bruises. We thank You for giving doctors the medicine we take when our bodies need help to get better. Help us to trust in You for all things. We praise You for Your healing power and Your love. In Jesus' name, amen.

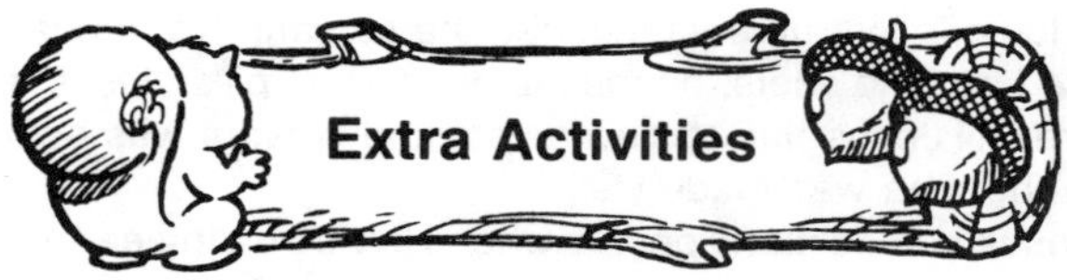

Extra Activities

Concentration: Before class prepare thirty-six blank 3 x 5 cards with pictures or words about good health or medical supplies. You will need two sets of eighteen identical pictures or words. Use magazines or draw your own pictures. Lay the cards down six across and six face down in a square.

Divide the class into two teams. Each team takes a turn turning over two cards. (Allow a new team member to do this each turn.) If a match is made, the team keeps the match and takes another turn. If no match is found, the cards are turned over in the same spot, and the team members concentrate on remembering which card held which picture. At the end of the playing time, the team with the most matches in their possession, wins. Mix up the cards, place them face down and play again.

The Doctor Is "In": Arrange six chairs (or fewer, depending on the size of your class) in a row at one end of the playing area. Approximately thirty-feet away, rope off or tape off a square area on the floor. All but the six class members seated in the chairs will stand here. The chairs are the "waiting room." The square area is the Dr.'s office. Halfway between the chairs and the roped area, place a basket containing one hundred slips of paper. (Fifty 3 x 5 cards torn in two make the best size.)

The object of the game is to get a seat in the waiting room. When the teacher says, "The Doctor is in," both groups scramble toward the basket, pick up a slip and try to claim a vacant seat in the waiting room. Only the patients successful at claiming a seat with the slip in their hand are permitted to keep the slip. All other slips go back to the basket and students without a seat return to the office area. Any student sitting in the seat with no slip is escorted to the office area and his seat is available to any alert classmate.

Play out this action six times. After the six rounds of play, the student seated with the most number of slips is declared the winner and the game begins again.

Lesson 9

Praise God for Being Our Father

Scripture: Luke 15:11-24

Memory Verse: To our God and Father be glory for ever and ever. Amen.—Philippians 4:20 (NIV)

Psalm References: Psalm 89:26; Psalm 119:76; Psalm 5:11; Psalm 103:13-22; Psalm 150:4 (Pause-to-Praise verse)

Lesson Aim: As a result of studying this lesson about God our Father, the children should be able to

1) Know that God is their heavenly Father.
2) Feel the love their heavenly Father wants to give.
3) Talk to God through prayer.
4) Sing or say the memory verse, Philippians 4:20.

Materials Needed:

Pre-session. *Activi-Tree:* Write special duties for the children to accomplish during class time. Roll the papers containing the duties and fasten them to the tree.

- Be the "father" and drive the Shuttlebug today.
- Look up the memory verse and mark it in your Bible.
- Look up the word *inheritance* in the dictionary and find out its meaning.
- Pick up all the pictures after **Together Time.** Tell its meaning.
- Look up the word *famine* in the dictionary. What does it mean?
- Look up the **Pause-to-Praise** verse, Psalm 150:4 and read it out loud.
- Be Sydney, the announcer, during the Critter County Radio Time.

My Father: Construction paper, magazine pictures, glue, scissors, crayons.

Preparation for Pause to Praise: Picture of Bible people dancing and singing, Bible, construction paper, glue, and magazines (preferably shoe catalog).

Together Time. "My Father" pictures from pre-session. **Wonders-of-God's-World** box containing pictures of fathers and sons.

Critter County Story Time. Baseball cap, baseball bat, a Band-aid.

Snack Time. Popcorn and fruit punch. (Optional: Bring a popcorn popper and make the popcorn in class.)

Bible Story Time: Bible, picture of a modern-day father and son, picture of Bible-time father and son.

Light Post on Memory Lane: String or yarn, posterboard circle with memory verse printed on one side.

Crafts.

5-8. *Stained Glass Window:* Wax paper, old crayons, scissors, glue, construction paper, yarn, and newspapers; cool iron.

8-10. *Prayer Reminder:* Babyfood jar for each child; 1½" praying hands (plastic type found at local Christian bookstore); moth crystals; water; felt circle, rick rack or ribbon. (A hot glue gun would be most helpful for the teacher to use.) Water resistant glue is a must.

Extra Activities. Blindfold

Welcome the Children

Make the children feel special as they arrive today. Tell them we will be talking about fathers and ask each child to think about what his or her father is doing during class time. (Later, each child can share with the class.) Involve the children in the Pre-session activities.

Pre-session Activities

Activi-Tree. Instruct the children to pick an assignment from the slips of paper placed on the tree before class. Allow them to make preparations for completing the assignment chosen. Let each child know you are confident of his or her ability to complete the assignment.

My Father. Give each child a piece of construction paper. From a box of pre-cut pictures (for younger children) or from an old mail-order catalog (for older children), have the children choose a picture of a man who reminds them of their father. (Be sensitive to the possibility of having a child in your class who does not know his or her father (through death or a divided-home situation). Help this child by saying, "Let's pretend you could choose your father. What would he look like. What work would he do, and what things would he enjoy?" Encourage this child to talk to one of the teachers or assistants as he or she works. Valuable information the child may give will help you meet special needs.)

Glue the picture of the father in the center of the page. Encourage the children to find the pictures in the magazines that show their father's interests, favorite articles, or his occupation. (Example: a brief case, books and papers, uniforms, eye glasses, wallet, sports equipment, etc.) Allow them to choose as many pictures as time will permit. Glue the items around the central picture of the father and draw lines with crayons from each item to the father. Tell the children they will be sharing their papers during **Together Time.**

Preparation for Pause to Praise. (Have the child who picked this assignment from the Activi-Tree read Psalm 150:4 out loud.) Tell the children that today's word taken from the Psalm is "dancing." There are not many people who praise God by dancing today, but in Bible times it was common for the people to enjoy this form of praise. Write the words ... "and dancing" on the picture you may have found in old curriculum materials. Allow the children to add this picture to the scrapbook to be shared during the **Pause to Praise.** Choose a record or tape to play for the children that talks about praising God. (If no record player or tape recorder is available, sing one of the class' favorite songs of praise). Have the children form a circle and keep time to the music. Take several steps to the right and then clap hands, and then take the same number of steps to the left. Clap hands as you sing and continue to add basic motions. (Suggestions: bending knees, raising arms in the air, and turning in a circle.)

Allow the children to be creative but not undisciplined. Remind them to think of God and pattern their motions in the form of praise. If they are able to establish a routine, be sure the students share it during Pause to Praise.

Pause to Praise: Have one student from your group read Psalm 150 out loud to the entire class. Have another child explain how boys and girls and men and women used the dance to praise God. Share the routine learned during Pre-session with the rest of the group. If the routine is easy to learn, you might allow the children who know it to teach the others. Close this session by allowing one child to share the entire scrapbook. Read together one page at a time until all four verses of Psalm 150 are completed.

Together Time: Be sure each child has the paper made during the Pre-session activity. Have the children sit in a circle as you talk about fathers. Encourage the children to share what their fathers are doing as you are having class. Allow them to take turns showing their papers and explaining their father's occupation or interests. Close this session by praising God for our fathers. Clap your hands together as you say, "We praise You God for making our fathers. We praise Your holy name." Emphasize to the children that God is our heavenly Father.

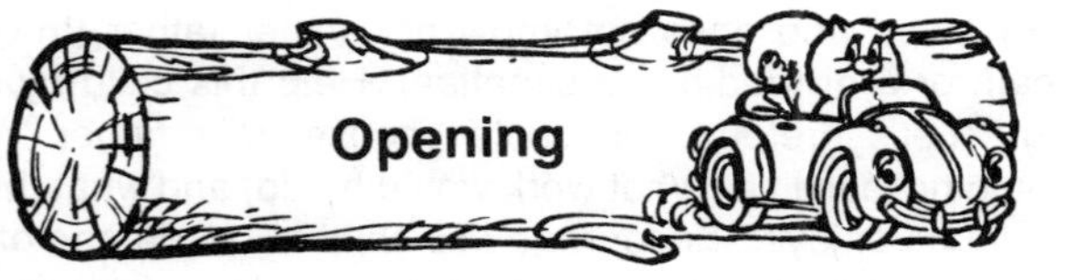

Boys and girls, it is time for all of us to climb in the Shuttlebug and fasten our seatbelts so we can ride to Critter County. Who is going to be the father who will drive us? (Let the child who chose this assignment from the Activi-Tree take the driver's place in the Shuttlebug.)

We have so much to learn today. We will be listening to the Critter County story first. Then, we will make a quick stop at the radio station before our snack time. We will listen to a Bible story about a very special father, and we will work on our activity books and make a craft to take home. Everybody in! We're off to Critter County!

All of us can remember times when we have been hurt or lonely or afraid or sick. Who do you want to be with you most when you feel this way? (Allow time for the students to answer,) Most of us just want our mother or daddy. Well, Lunchbox, the little lion cub, felt that way too. Listen to today's Critter County story.

A Heart That Hurt

It was the bottom of the ninth inning in one of the most exciting games ever played in Critter County. The Bears were beating the Lions by a score of four to two. The game was almost over.

Mildew the mouse was on second base and Rascal the raccoon stood on first. Lunchbox came up to the plate and picked up the bat.

Sydney was pitching for the Bears. He was having a particularly fine game. He looked in at the plate as Lunchbox stood nervously waiting for the ball to come his way.

"C'mon, Lunchbox, hit a good one," his teammates yelled from the bench.

Boy, I'd sure like to get a hit, the little lion cub thought to himself. *We could win if I would just get a hit!*

Sydney took the ball into his hand and studied the way Lunchbox was standing. Then he leaned back and threw the ball.

"Strike one," called Dr. Fluoride the giraffe. He always umpires the games because his long neck allows him to see the ball so well.

Quickly, Sydney prepared to throw the ball again.

I'm going to try and strike out Lunchbox, thought the little squirrel with the big brown eyes.

"Get ready, Lunchbox," called Rascal from first base.

Then Sydney threw the ball hard and fast.

"Strike two," yelled Dr. Fluoride at the top of his lungs.

Oh, no, thought Little Lunchbox. *One more strike, and I'm out. We'll lose the game. I just have to get a hit.*

Sydney leaned back and threw the ball as hard as he could. He was sure that Lunchbox would never be able to hit it. But good ol' Sydney was wrong!

Lunchbox saw the ball coming, and he swung the bat as hard as he could.

WHACK! The ball sailed high over second base, high over center field, and high over the fence. All of Lunchbox's teammates jumped to their paws and feet and cheered as the happy lion cub rounded the bases.

The celebration continued in the locker room as all the critters got ready to go home. Each one congratulated Lunchbox and said how happy he was that Lunchbox had helped the Lions win the game.

Finally, everyone left the locker room and began to walk home. It was on this walk back to the den that Lunchbox's right paw *really* started to hurt.

Oh, my paw hurts so much, Lunchbox thought as he looked down. *No wonder it hurts! I've got a big splinter in it. It* must've happened when I hit the homerun. Oh, it hurts so much. The lion cub started to pout. Then tears poured down his face because it hurt *so* much.

He was crying so hard that he could hardly see where he was walking. Soon, Cream Puff came along on her way home and saw Lunchbox crying.

"What's the matter, Lunchbox?" she asked.

"When I hit the homerun, I got this *big* splinter in my paw. It hurts *really* bad," Lunchbox cried.

Cream Puff looked at his paw and said with a mean sound to her voice, "Oh, Lunchbox, it doesn't look very bad. Grow up and stop crying like a baby." And she walked away.

Lunchbox cried even harder.

Soon Rascal came strolling down Memory Lane and saw his friend Lunchbox.

"Hi, where you headed?" he asked.

Lunchbox said, "I'm going home because I've got a *big* splinter in my paw. It is really hurting." Lunchbox waited for his friend to show some concern for his problem. Instead, Rascal shrugged his shoulders and said, "That's too bad." Then he walked away.

Poor Lunchbox cried even harder and ran all the way home . . . hoping he wouldn't see anymore of his friends. As he ran into the den, he saw his father. Lester was reading the paper.

"Daddy, Daddy. I need to talk to you," cried Lunchbox.

Lester immediately put down his paper and said tenderly, "Why, what's the matter, son? Climb up here on my lap and tell Daddy what's wrong."

Lunchbox began to tell his story almost as fast as the tears ran down his cheeks.

"Daddy I'm hurt, and I was coming home, and I was crying because it hurts so much. When I told Cream Puff, she made fun of me. Then she told me to stop crying like a baby. Then I saw Rascal. I thought for sure he'd help me feel better. But he didn't care at all that I was hurt. He just walked away," sobbed the little lion.

Ol', wise Lester had heard enough. He took his big, strong arms and wrapped them around his son.

"Here, my boy, you can cry right here whenever you want. I'm so sorry you've had such a hard day. We'll take that splinter out in a couple of minutes, then your paw will be much better by tomorrow. But I'm more concerned about the hurt in your heart caused by your friends," said Lester.

"You see, son, no friendship is ever perfect. We all fail each other . . . even those we love the most. It makes me *very* happy that you came home to Daddy," continued Lester.

"That's because you always make everything all right, Daddy," said the little lion.

"Well, I love you so very much, that I always try to be what you need. But even I can fail you . . . even though I love you so very much. There's only one Father who can love you perfectly. He'll never let you down. He'll never leave you alone. Your heavenly Father loves you even more than I do. And that's a lot of love, my little one!" said Lester.

"Just remember, son, one of the ways that you honor and praise your Father is to share your feelings with him. Then he can take better care of you. That makes everyone happy,' said Lester lovingly.

And with that, the little boy snuggled in close to his daddy's chest. They both enjoyed feeling close and loved.

Have the children go to the tables and give them page 23 from the Critter County activity book.

5-8. *Help Lunchbox Find His Father:* Help Lunchbox as he looks for his father. Color all the stepping stones with the letter **F** on them. Then he can find his way.

8-10. *A Picture Story:* Color the six pictures and then cut them apart. Now put them in order so they will tell the story of Lunchbox and his father.

When all have finished with the activity sheets, have the children go to the Critter County Radio Station and sit on the floor in front of it. (Let the child who is to be the announcer go to his or her place.) You will need someone to be Lunchbox in today's radio broadcast.

Sydney: **WWCC**—the Wonderful World of Critter County, is bringing you a personal interview with Lunchbox, the star of the Bear/Lion baseball game today. Lunchbox, you must be very excited.

Lunchbox: It was *great,* Sydney!

Sydney: I do understand, Lunchbox, that there was a small injury after the game.

Lunchbox: A small in-ju-y? Do you mean, did I get a splinter in my paw? I sure did! But my *Dad* took care of it. He made it all better!

Sydney: That's some Dad you have Lunchbox!

Lunchbox: I know it! He's the greatest! I think he can do just about everything, and I can tell him anything. He keeps secrets real well.

Sydney: You know, Lunchbox, God our heavenly Father, wants to be that kind of friend to us. He can do everything, and we can tell Him anything. He never fails.

Lunchbox: I know that, Sydney, cause my big Dad, Lester, told me so.

Sydney: That's great, Lunchbox! It looks like this has been an "all-star" day for you. This is Sydney signing off.

Lunchbox: And this is Lunchbox wishing you a fine farewell too.

The snack suggestion for today is popcorn. If you have a large bowl, allow one of the children to walk around the class, stopping by each student long enough for the child to reach in for as much as his or her hand will hold. Talk about fun times when you remember eating popcorn with your father (T.V., carnival, movies, camping) Popcorn is a nutritious snack the children might enjoy making it in the room if time permits. Serve the popcorn with fruit juice or punch. After clean-up have the children return to the story area.

Play the song "Sing Praise to Him," page 140, as the children assemble in the story area. After all have gathered, sing the song together.

Sing familiar songs as well as new ones: "Clap Your Hands," page 119; "Be Kind and Compassionate," page 126; "Our God and Father," page 115; "Even a Child," page 133; and "Praise Ye the Lord Forever," page 142.

Prayer Song: "Hear Us as We Pray," page 143.

Prayer. Ask God to help the children listen as we learn of God's love for us, for we are His children. Ask Him to help them understand He is their loving heavenly Father.

(Be sure to have your Bible open to today's story. Look at the children as you talk with them.)

Boys and girls, we have been talking about fathers today. Before our lesson, let's just take one minute to praise God for the father He has given. Close your eyes and think of your father. See his face in your mind and praise God by thanking Him for that special face that means so much to you. Now, open your eyes and tell me some of the things you think about when you think of your father. (Allow the children enough time to answer.)

All the things we have mentioned have to do with the father we see everyday . . . the one who lives at home. But, do you know you also have a special father you cannot see? God is our heavenly Father. We praise Him for being the good Father He is. He knows when we are hurt or lonely or sick. He knows when we are happy or excited. He wants us to know how much He cares for us. He gave us the Bible to tell us how much He loves us.

Listen carefully as I share this Bible story with you and see if you recognize times when this boy's father is like our heavenly Father, God.

The Prodigal Son
Luke 15:11-22

Jesus told this story: There was a man who had two sons. The youngest son knew he and his brother would receive part of everything their father owned after their father's death. (Ask the child who looked up "inheritance" to share the definition with the group.) The money this boy knew he would receive from his father was his inheritance. Promising an inheritance is a way of giving what you have to your children so your possessions can stay in your family always.

Some of you may sleep in a bed or have a toy that has been given to you by your grandma or grandpa. If so, you have received an inheritance.

The youngest son decided he would like to have his portion of everything his father planned to give him. He asked his father for everything that was being saved for him, and his father decided to divide his possessions between the two brothers.

The young son was very foolish! The Bible tells us after he received the wealth, he went to a far away country and spent everything he had. The Bible says he used the money for "wild" living. He wasted everything his father had given him until there was nothing left. And then . . . a famine came to the land. (Allow the child who looked up "famine" to explain its meaning.) Yes, a famine means there was no food. All the crops in the fields died and there was nothing to harvest. The animals could not get enough to eat, and they starved. People became frightened because it was very hard to find enough food to keep from being hungry.

The young boy tried hard to find a job. His money was gone and he needed to make money to buy any food he could find. The only job he found was a job feeding pigs. He became so hungry; he wanted to eat what the pigs were eating.

One day he thought to himself, "Even the servants who work for my father have food to eat. I will go home to my father. I will tell him I have been foolish. I will ask if he will let me live in our house as a servant." And so he began his journey home.

He was still far away from his house when his father saw him. Can any of you guess what happened? (Allow time for the children to answer.)

The father ran to meet his son. He threw his arms around his son and kissed him. He was so happy to see him.

The son asked if he could come home to be a servant, but the father didn't listen. He sent for the nicest robe and put it on him. He put a ring on his finger and sandals on his feet. He even ordered his servants to fix a big feast for a special celebration.

Application: Tell me what made the boy's father so special. (Allow time for the children to answer.) If you're thinking he loved his son very much, you are right. Even though his son did some very foolish things, his father still loved him as his son. He welcomed him home and would not let him be a servant.

Think about our heavenly Father, boys and girls. How was this father like our Father, God? (Wait for a response.) God loves us so much. When we have done things that do not please Him, we know He still loves us and wants us to do better. He always wants what is best for us.

Let's praise God for being our loving heavenly Father. Clap your hands together and say, "We praise You, God, our heavenly Father. We praise Your holy name."

Have the children return to the tables and give them page 24 from the Critter County Activity book.

5-8. *A Father Forgives:* Look at each picture and number them in 1, 2, 3, and 4 order. Check Luke 15:11-12 in your

Bible for the correct order. Now tell the story in your own words.

8-10. *The Prodigal Son:* Look closely at the pictures. Color and cut the picture apart. See if you can put them in correct order.

When all have finished their activity sheets, have the children go to the Light Post on Memory Lane.

Write the memory verse on a piece of paper that can be hidden behind your hand. Attach the paper to a string that is long enough to measure around the circle made by the class. If you have a large class, you may choose to do this activity with several circles. However, this activity will work well with everyone playing at the same time.

Be sure the string has the memory verse attached before you tie the ends of the string together. Have the children slide the verse around the circle to be sure everything is in order. Choose one student to be the Father in the center of the circle. Have the students slide the verse from one to another trying to keep the Father from seeing who has the Scripture circle concealed behind his or her hand. The Father guesses when he thinks he sees who has the verse. He asks, "My son, do you have the verse?" If he guesses correctly, the student with the verse must try to say it with no mistakes. The entire class repeats the verse. When a student repeats the verse successfully, that student becomes the Father. Play continues until each class member has taken a turn being Father or recited the verse.

Say the verse together and then sing, "Our God and Father," on page 115.

5-8. Stained Glass Window: Before you begin, cover the tables with newspaper to protect the tables from the crayon shavings. Give each child two pieces of 6″ x 4½″ wax paper. Have plenty of old crayons on hand and be sure many bright colors are included. Have the children peel all the paper off the crayons. Show the children how to use the edge of scissors to shave the crayons onto one piece of the wax paper. Have a teacher standing by ready to use the cool iron. (This teacher should practice making a window before class to determine the right setting for the iron.) When each child has shaved the colors chosen for his window, place the second piece of wax paper over the shavings. Place a towel over the paper to keep it from sticking to the iron and run the iron over the towel. The shavings should melt between the two pieces of paper.

Give the children two construction-paper frames made from the pattern provided on page 112. (Older children might cut their own.) Glue the wax paper between the two frame pieces. Write the words "Our Father Which Art in Heaven" across the top of the window as shown. Cut the excess wax paper from the top of the frame to give the appearance of a window. Attach a string or piece of yarn to the top of the window, and it is ready to hang in the sunlight.

Help the children understand this is a prayer reminder. If they hang it somewhere in their room, they can remember to praise God each time they see it.

8-10. Prayer Reminder: Provide each child with a baby-food jar and lid, a three by three inch square of felt, a small pair of plastic praying hands and some water-resistant glue. Have water and moth crystals close by.

Let the children draw around the rim of the jar as it is placed upside down on the felt. Cut out the circle and glue to the outside of the lid. Let the teacher place a small strip of hot glue inside the lid and assist the child as he presses the plastic praying hands into the glue. Let the child measure 1 tsp. of moth crystals and place them inside the jar. Fill the jar with water to within ¼″ from the top. Put the lid containing the praying hands on the jar and twist to be sure it is secure. Let a teacher run a band of hot glue around the lid to seal it. Cover the glue with ribbon or rick rack. Encourage the children to gently shake the jar and watch the crystals float in the water.

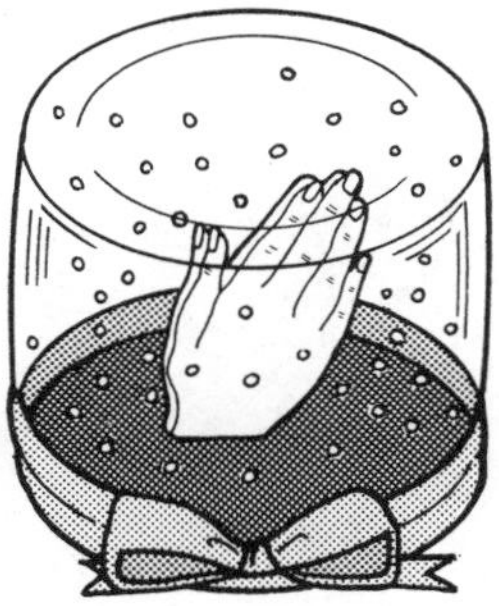

This prayer reminder can help the students to think of praising their heavenly Father in prayer.

It's time to climb in the Shuttlebug for one more ride home. We have had a very special time together. I am happy to drive you back to the place where you will meet your mother and father. As we are riding, tell me some of your favorite things you did at Critter County. (Allow time for the children to answer.) I am so glad God is our heavenly Father. Let's praise Him together one more time as we say the memory verse from His Word. Repeat the memory verse together.

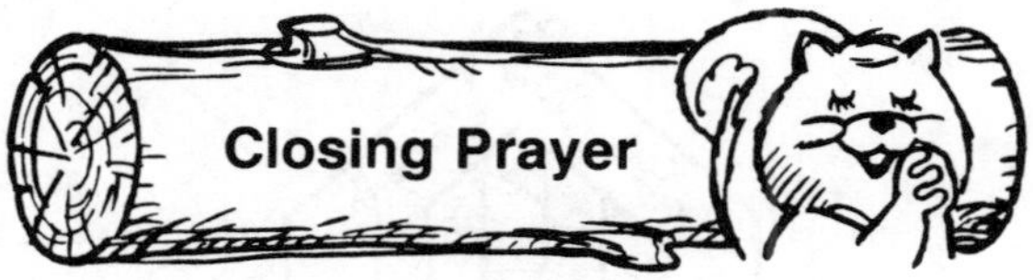

Closing Prayer

Our Father in Heaven, we thank You and praise You for this special day we have shared together. Thank You for the lesson of the boy and his father. Help us to grow up knowing You love us more than anyone. Thank You for giving us so much. We trust You to take care of us. We love You and praise You for being our Father. In Jesus' name, amen.

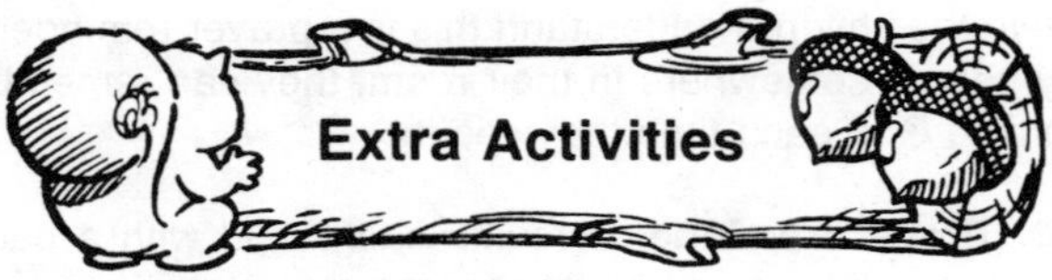

Extra Activities

Father to Child: Have all of the children sit in a circle with one who is chosen to be the father standing in the center. The father begins the game by choosing a child in his mind. He asks anyone in the circle, "Have you seen my child?." The classmate spoken to replies, "What does your child look like?" The father begins to describe his child by giving clues to the person's identity that he has in his mind. He might say, "He has brown hair and is wearing a red shirt." When the person he is describing catches on, he or she gets up and begins to run around the circle trying to get back to his or her seat before being caught by the person the father has been talking with. The father sits in the seat of the one answering the questions. If the child returns to his or her seat without being caught, the one who answered the questions becomes the father. If the child is caught, the seat is given to the other player, and the child becomes the father.

Guess the Child: Blindfold one child who will stand in the center of the circle. Let the child move around pointing to his friends. When he stops, the friend he is pointing to may disguise his or her voice to sound like a father, and the child in the center must guess the name of the friend speaking. When the child guesses correctly, he trades places with the father, and the game begins again. To make the game more interesting, allow the children to move around in the circle after the child is blindfolded.

Lesson 10

Praise God for His Power Over Death

Scripture: John 11:1-45

Psalm References: Psalm 56:3, 4, 11, 13; 103:13-27; 118:4-7a; Psalm 150-4b (Pause-to-Praise verse)

Memory Verse: But thanks be to God! He gives us the victory through our Lord Jesus Christ.—1 Corinthians 15:57 (NIV)

Lesson Aim: As a result of studying this lesson the children should be able to

1) Know that Jesus raised Lazarus from the dead.
2) Feel confident that God will provide for all of our needs now and after death.
3) Be assured that God is able to help us through the hurt we feel when someone dies.
4) Praise and thank God for providing life beyond this world.
5) Sing or say the memory verse, 1 Corinthians 15:57.

Materials Needed:
Pre-session. *Activi-Tree:* Write the following suggestions on slips of paper and attach them to the Activi-Tree before class. You may want to add some others. Be sure that there is a slip for every student.

- Be the leader as we line up for restroom break.
- Drive the Shuttlebug today.
- Be Sydney for the Critter County on Radio.
- Look up the story of Lazarus in John 11:1-45. Find the name of Lazarus' sisters.
- Look up Psalm 150:46, and be ready to read it.

Bible Drama: Paper, pencil, or marker; towels and robes, or large pieces of cloth, hair pins, safety pins, and Bible-time costumes. Bible should be opened to Matthew 9:18-26.

Preparation for Pause to Praise: Bible, sturdy box, varied sizes of rubber bands.

Snack Time: Popcorn

Bible Story Time: Fig leaf, picture of Lazarus' two sisters, white gauze, handkerchief, picture of tomb, picture of Jesus.

Light Post on Memory Lane: Posterboard and marking pens

Crafts:
5-8. *Jesus Brings Life Banner:* Burlap or solid color felt, pencil or fine point markers, multi-color felt, scissors, glue, yarn.

8-10. *Son Visors:* White or multi-color file folders. Clear adhesive shelf paper, bright color markers, scissors, pattern on page, stencils, paper punch, and elastic string or yarn.

Extra Activities: *Balloon Volleyball:* balloon, masking tape. *Lazarus, Come Forth:* Sheet

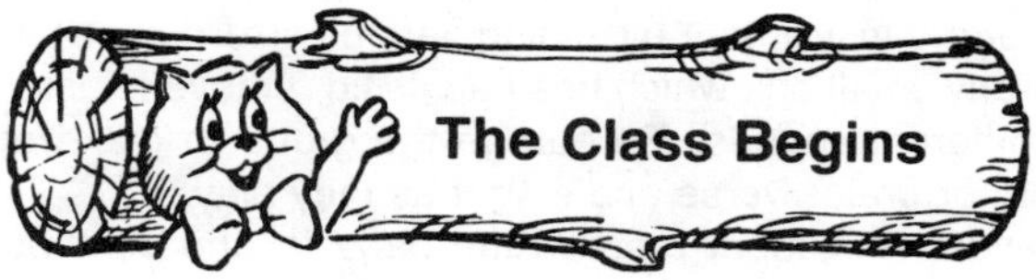

Welcome the Children

Encourage all assistants and teachers to be with class and prepare all centers before the children arrive. Greet each child by name. Guide each toward the Activi-Tree as you tell them that we will be praising God for a very special reason today. Encourage each child to watch and listen as they work in their chosen activity centers. See if they can guess what we will praise God for in the lesson time. Be ready to assist any new readers if they have selected a reading responsibility from the Activi-Tree.

Pre-session Activities

Activi-Tree. Help each child understand the responsibility he or she has chosen from the tree and give assistance when needed. Remember the names of those you will call on during the Bible story time for answers to questions found on the tree.

Bible Drama. Look up the story of Jesus raising the ruler's daughter from the dead (Matthew 9:18-26). Read the story slowly (Or allow an older class member to read the story aloud to the group.) If time permits, allow the students in the group to re-tell the story in their own words as you write down what they say. This writing can be used later as the script for the Bible Drama.

Allow the children to choose costumes for as many characters as your materials will allow. Appoint specific characters to play the Bible roles. Let one child read the "script" or the Bible account as the others act out the story from their imagination. The teacher should be the director or guide who encourages the children to participate. (You may find this activity more meaningful if you remove these students from the room as they practice. They will produce the Bible Drama during **Together Time.** They will enjoy practicing in a "non-threatening" environment the first few times they act out the story.) Be sure to guide their conversation toward the understanding that Jesus had power over death and used that power to restore the girl's life.

Praise God for His power over death by clapping your hands and saying together, "We praise You, God, for Your power over death. We praise Your holy name."

Preparation for Pause to Praise. If there is a piano near by in an empty classroom or auditorium, this would be an excellent time to take the students in this center, and allow them to see inside the instrument. Play several of the keys and allow the children to watch the mallets hit the strings.

Have the child who got this activity read Psalm 150:4b, "Praise Him with the strings." Allow the children to examine an autoharp, guitar, or violin. Explain that all the instruments are considered "string" instruments because you must hit the strings to make them vibrate and make the musical sound. Ask the students to recall any other string instruments that could be used to praise God (the harp and lyre). Encourage the students to work as a group to make their own string instrument by sliding various size rubber bands over any small box which has had its lid removed. Listen to the different sounds. Encourage the group to make up a Psalm or praise verse and sing it as they play.

Have one student prepare the page for the scrapbook. Glue various pictures of stringed instruments to the construction paper and write, "Praise Him with the Strings" on the page.

During Pause to Praise: Have the same child read Psalm 150:4b to the entire class, and the other children share what they have learned about string instruments. Have one student to demonstrate the different sounds from the string instruments that they have made with rubber bands. If time permits, take the entire class to observe the piano.

Sing one of the student's favorite choruses as the teacher or a classmate plays one of the instruments. Close the session by clapping your hands and saying, "We praise You, God, on instruments of string. We praise Your holy name!" Have one child read the scrapbook from the beginning.

Together Time: Have the students who prepared the Bible drama during pre-session present it to the class. Talk with the children about what they have learned. Tell them that we will be talking about Jesus' power over death as we share during our class-time. Be sure to praise the Bible Drama people for a job well done.

Boys and girls, we need to gather at the Shuttlebug. (Allow the student who is today's driver to take his or her place.) We will be taking a trip to downtown Critter County where all the critters are shopping for their new spring clothes. We have so much to talk about and some very important things to learn about God's power over death. Be thinking about questions you've always wanted to ask. But, first, let's make a stop at the Fur and Feather Clothing Store. I do hope Rascal will tell us about his new friends. Let's see.

We'll be talking about Jesus' power over death in our Bible lesson today, But, Rascal has a special lesson to learn, first. He will be sad when a little bunny dies, and Rascal does not have the power to help him.

The Tale of Two Bunnies

Springtime in Critter County always finds the mother critters taking their children to the Fur and Feather Clothing Store to buy new outfits for the kids. A typical afternoon would find an ostrich family buying new jeans for junior or a young giraffe being fitted for a new turtle neck sweater.

Directly behind the store stands a large oak tree that has sheltered the ground beneath it for generations. In fact, springtime always finds several squirrel families making new homes in the strong arms of this mighty tree. Underneath the branches, bunnies and little field mice make their nests out of soft grass. Some use brightly colored quilts that Grandmother Mouse has made.

It was one warm, Saturday afternoon in April that Rascal went with his mother to the store to get new soccer shoes. He always enjoyed getting new athletic shoes because they allowed him to run even faster. After he tried on several pairs, he finally chose the one that felt and looked the best. As his mother was going to the cash register to pay for them, Rascal said, "Mother may I go out back and play on the swing?"

"Yes, you may go," she said.

The old oak tree looked so tall as the young raccoon would swing from the branch. The air would blow through his fur as he would try to make his toes touch the sky. After several minutes, his mother came out.

"Rascal, I have to go to the bakery to get some bread for dinner. You may stay here and play, if you'd like," she said.

"OK," said Rascal as he climbed out of the swing. He thought to himself, *I'm going to pick some of these wild flowers for Mother. Boy, she'll be surprised.*

As Rascal was picking a bouquet of yellow and white daisies, Poncho the pig walked up to him.

"Hey, Rascal, what's happening?" Poncho asked.

"Oh, nothing much. I'm just pickin' a little surprise for my mother. She's been up late at night with my sister who's sick. This'll make her day!"

Poncho smiled at Rascal and said, "Sounds good to me. I'm sure she'll by happy and proud of you."

"Hey, can you help me for a minute? I need to find a nest of bunnies that are here under the oak tree. I've just learned that these babies don't have a mother and daddy any more and need someone to take care of them," Poncho asked.

"Sure, I'll help you look," Rascal said happily.

After a few minutes, Poncho said, "Hey, buddy, here are the little fellows . . . two of 'em."

Both Poncho and Rascal knelt down by the simple little home as the bunnies slept peacefully.

"Well, they'll be waking up soon, and they'll be hungry. Better figure out now what to do with them," said Poncho.

Rascal perked up his ears an said excitedly, "I'll take them home with me. I can feed them with an eye dropper and keep them by my bed. Oh, please let me take care of them until they can make it on their own!"

Poncho thought this was a great idea because Rascal

seemed old enough to handle this responsibility with ease.

When Rascal and his mother got back home, they made a bed for the bunnies. They put some cotton balls inside the shoe box that Rascal's new soccer shoes came in.

"I'll go and make their milk and honey formula while you get the eye dropper out of the medicine chest," Mother said to Rascal.

For three days, the little raccoon was faithful in feeding and caring for the furry babies. Every three or four hours, he'd warm the milk in the microwave until it was just the right temperature. He'd know it was just right when the babies would perk right up and drink the milk as fast as they could. Often, they seemed to smile as they took their "bottle". Then when each tummy was full, the little fellows would sit right up and burp! Then Rascal would know it was time to take their bibs off and put them back in their bed.

On Wednesday morning, Rascal awoke to the smell of bacon frying in the kitchen. He pulled himself out of bed and went over to say, "Good morning" to his little friends. Suddenly, he burst into tears and ran to his mother in the kitchen.

"Mother, Mother, one of my bunnies is dead!" he cried.

While Rascal sobbed with his head on the kitchen table, his mother went into the bedroom and discovered that Rascal's fear was true. Only one of the bunnies was alive. She returned to the kitchen and found her son crying.

"It's all my fault. I didn't take good enough care of the bunny. That's why he died. I didn't feed him right. It's all my fault. Maybe he didn't like his bed. Oh, I wish I had never been born," sobbed the little raccoon.

The wise mother sat down and gently put her paw around the raccoon's shoulders, "Rascal, I understand why you're so upset. You've worked hard to feed and care for the bunnies. I know how much you've loved them. But because one didn't live, you can't blame yourself. You did everything you could so he could live."

"Sweetheart, maybe there was something wrong with the bunny. Maybe he was sick and that's why he couldn't live," said Rascal's mother.

"Mother, I really did try to take good care of them," said Rascal.

"I know you did, son. I am proud of the job you did. You see, as long as you always do your best, you can be proud. And even though we do our best, sometimes we fail. In other words, sometimes the bunny lives, but sometimes it dies," Mrs. Raccoon explained.

Several days passed, and Rascal's bunny grew and grew,. He was soon able to eat clover. On Monday afternoon, Rascal decided to let his little friend free in the woods.

"I'm taking the bunny back to the oak tree, Mother," he said as he closed the kitchen door.

As the raccoon held the bunny in his paws for the last time, kneeling under the mighty oak, he said, "Well, here you go, little fellow. I'm glad I could take care of you until you could be on your own. Sorry, about your brother, but I want you to know, I did the very best I could."

Rascal gave the little bunny a kiss, put him on the ground and watched him hop into the yellow and white daises. When he was almost out of sight, Rascal spoke softly, "I love you." It is sad that the little bunny did not live. But, this story should help us to know how very powerful God is when He shows his power over death. Nothing Rascal or you or I could do would help the little bunny . . . but Jesus could! Later we will have a story with a happy ending when our Bible story tells us about two sisters who were happy when Jesus brought their brother back to life.

Have the children gather at the tables, and give them page 25 from the Critter County activity books.

5-8. *Rascal Sets the Bunny Free:* Complete the picture by cutting out the objects at the bottom of the page. Glue them on the picture where they belong. Color the picture.

8-10. *Rascal Sets the Bunny Free:* Color the picture of Rascal setting the bunny free. Retell the story.

When all have finished, have the children go to the Critter County Radio Station and sit in front of it. You will need someone to be Sydney and someone to be Rascal in today's Critter County Radio program.

Sydney: We now interrupt our regular broadcasting for a special announcement. **WWCC** has just received word that today's Bible story teaches that Jesus raised his good friend Lazarus from the dead! After being in the grave for three days, Jesus brought Lazarus back to life. We go to Rascal, our news correspondent for an up-date.

Rascal: Well, Sydney, we have to imagine the excitement and joy of the crowd that day. Everyone was so upset when Lazarus died, and then they were so excited when Jesus brought him back to life. **WWCC** hopes to have an interview with some of the boys and girls who hear the story. We'd like to get their reaction! Back to you, Sydney.

Sydney: Boys and girls, I am sure that all of you have had someone that you loved very much to die—maybe a pet, or a grandparent, or a friend. And, as much as we love them and want them to be with us again, there is nothing we can do. But you know God has the power over life and death. He can do anything. Nothing is too hard for God. Today's Bible story is going to show us that. Be sure to share your feelings about this story with your teachers and friends today. **WWCC** thanks you for joining us. There is so much we can learn together!

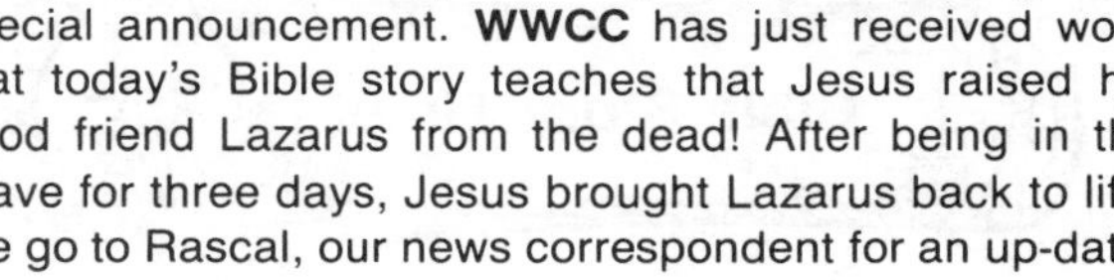

A popcorn snack and fruit juice is suggested for today's treat. Popcorn balls could be made before class, or popcorn could be popped during the class period.

Choose the treat that best suits your class. During the

snack time, talk with the children about the popcorn. Help them to understand that the popcorn is really a seed that could grow more popcorn if it were planted in the ground and watered. Just like all seeds, the popcorn kernels have died. It doesn't look like there is any life in a kernel. However if the plan for new life is followed, the seeds will begin to grow to live again. After clean up, have the children return to the story area.

Play the song "Sing Praise to Him," page 140, as the children assemble in the story area. When all have gathered, sing the song together.

Sing familiar songs, as well as new ones: "Forever Will I Praise Your Name," page 138; "Victory," page 121; "Clap your Hands," page 119; "Praise Ye the Lord," page 116; and "He Hath Done Great things," page 118.

Prayer Song: "Hear Us as We Pray," page 143.

Prayer: Ask God to help the children understand that He has the power to overcome all things . . . even death. Ask Him to help them listen as we hear the story of Jesus who brings his friend back to life.

Have the Wonders-of-God's-World box ready with the items found under Materials Needed at the beginning of this lesson.

Tell the children that today's lesson is very special. It will tell how very powerful Jesus is, and how He used His special power to bring someone back to life. (Be serious, yet cautious, with the students as you tell them that today's lesson will deal with death.) Death is not easy to talk about. It sometimes gives us memories of people we love who are not with us anymore. Even grown ups do not want to talk about death very often. It makes us sad. However, in today's lesson, it is a time of praise. We want to think about how God has made it possible for everyone to live. He has power over death. Take the fig leaf from the Wonder's-of-God's-World box. Ask the children to remember back to the first lesson learned during the first visit to Critter County. Do you remember about how God made man and woman? (Allow the children to answer, and if any child does not remember, have one student explain.)

When God made Adam and Eve, He put them in a beautiful garden. He told them to take care of the garden, and all of the animals. They were to enjoy all that God had made for them. He let them walk everywhere in the garden, and He told them that they could do anything . . . except touch one certain tree. He told Adam and Eve they were not to touch this tree, or to eat of its fruit.

He said that if they disobeyed His command, something terrible would happen. Who can tell me what would happen? (Allow time for the answer that Adam and Eve would die.)

The Bible tells us that both Eve and Adam chose to disobey God's command. They ate the fruit. And because God keeps His Word, what He said came true. Adam and Eve lived for awhile on the earth, but their bodies grew old, and then eventually they died.

Since that time, people have continued to be born, and they have continued to die. Death was a very terrible thing before Jesus came. People didn't realize that Jesus would help us to understand that we will live again.

Listen to this Bible Story and see if you can remember another special time when someone came back to life.

Lazarus, Come Forth
John 11:1-45

Our Bible lesson tells us about a man named Lazarus. He lived in a city very close to Jerusalem. One person in our class knows were Lazarus lived because he or she looked it up as his or her assignment from the Activi-Tree. Tell us what city Lazarus lived in. (Allow the child to answer Bethany.)

Lazarus and Jesus were good friends. The Bible tells us that Jesus loved him.

Lazarus was not alone in his family. (Take the pictures of two sisters from the box.) He had two sisters who loved him too. (Allow the child who looked up their names tell the class about Mary and Martha.)

The Bible tells us Lazarus became very sick. Mary and Martha sent word to Jesus. He was two miles away in Jerusalem when the message arrived about Lazarus, and Jesus decided to stay a few days longer before leaving to see Lazarus. Before Jesus arrived at Bethany, Lazarus died.

Jesus knew Lazarus had died. He told His disciples that He was going to Bethany anyway so they might have a stronger belief in God. He knew the miracle that the disciples were about to see.

When Jesus and his disciples arrived at Bethany, they were told that Lazarus had been in the tomb for four days. (Show the picture of a tomb, and explain how the body was laid inside a cave. A stone was usually rolled in front of it.)

Mary and Martha heard that Jesus was coming, and Martha went to meet him. When she saw Jesus she told Him if He had come earlier, Lazarus would not have died. She then added something very important. She showed how much she believed in Jesus' power over death when she said, "But I know that even now, God will give You whatever You ask."

After she said this, Jesus told her that her brother would rise again.

Martha sent for Mary, and they all went together to the tomb. (Take the handkerchief from the box.)

The Bible tells us that when Jesus saw Mary crying because she was so sad about her brother, he began to cry too. He cried so much that the people around talked about how much he loved Lazarus. They could not understand why Jesus did not come earlier and heal Lazarus. They did not know they were going to see something greater than any healing.

Jesus asked for the stone to be taken away from the front of the tomb. Martha knew that the tomb would have a terrible smell, and she reminded Jesus that Lazarus had been dead for four days.

Jesus reminded Martha that she was about to see the glory of God. The stone was taken away, and Jesus began to talk to God. He said, "Father, I thank You that You have loved Me. . . . I said (these things) for the benefit of the people standing here that they might believe that You sent Me."

Then Jesus spoke in a very loud voice. (Take the strips of gauze from the box.) He called, "Lazarus, come out! And Lazarus, the man who had been dead for four days, came out of the tomb. He still had the strips of cloth on him, and the people had to unwrap him to let him go.

Application: Boys and girls, what does this story tell us? (Allow time for them to answer. Encourage them to share that Jesus has power over death.)

Lazarus had been dead for four days. Mary wanted him to be alive. Martha wanted him to be alive. All of his friends were very sorry that he had died . . . but they could do nothing. Yet, when Jesus called to Lazarus, he came out of the tomb.

Jesus knows that God has power over death. God is the one who created man. He told man not to sin. Because man disobeyed, God had to allow man to die. Only God can have the power to overcome death, and make men live again.

Can you think of anyone else who died and then came back to life? (Encourage the children to think of Jesus.)

Jesus did. Jesus came back to life and told us that if we will believe in Him, and obey His commandments, we can live forever. We will be alive while we live on earth, and when we die, we can be alive where Jesus is. It is so good to know Jesus came back to life, and He promises us life if we obey Him.

Let's praise God for His power over death. Clap your hands and say, "We praise You God for Your power over death. We praise Your holy name."

Listen carefully to the children's conversations during the remainder of the class period. See if any children have questions that might be able to be answered by you. Be careful to answer their questions with Scripture whenever possible. Do not dwell on frightening information about death. Try to direct the children to build their trust in God who has the power to overcome death and take away our fears.

Have the children go to the tables and give them page 26 from the Critter County activity book.

5-8. *What Belongs?* Look carefully at each set of pictures. Color the items that do belong in the set.

8-10. *Decode the Verse:* Use the code on your paper to discover the Scripture verse. Check your answer with John 3:36a. (Answer: Whoever believes in the Son has eternal life.)

When all have finished with the activity papers, have them go to the Light Post on Memory Lane.

Light Post on Memory Lane

Write the Bible verse on a large piece of paper for all to see. Have the children read the verse several times. Place the verse under a rug, or on top of a table. Have the students sit around the table. Take turns trying to say the verse. Anyone who has to peek gets five points. Go around the class giving everyone two chances. The students with the least number of points are the winners.

Craft Time

5-8. Jesus Brings Life Banner: Before class, cut the words, Jesus Brings Life from white or yellow felt for each student. Cut a piece of solid color fabric, or burlap into a 14″ x 12″ rectangle. (If you choose burlap, it will make the banner more appealing, but the teacher may have to sew a running stitch along the sides to keep the burlap from fraying. The bottom of the banner can be frayed on purpose to give added effect.) The top two inches of the material will fold over the dowel rod so the banner will hang. Use the patterns on pages 102, 109, 110, and 111 to make designs of multi-colored felt scraps that will brighten your banner. Arrange the felt pieces you choose around the words, Jesus Brings Life. When you are pleased with the design of your banner, glue the felt pieces in place on the solid rectangle. (The teacher can help with a few dots of glue from a hot glue gun to keep the pieces in place.)

Glue the top two inches of the banner over the dowel rod and attach one piece of yarn so the banner is ready to hang. Each banner will be different if you have allowed for the originality of the children as they have chosen their designs. Yet, each banner should remind the children to today's lesson.

8-10. Son Visor: Use the pattern on page 110 to cut the visor from paper that has a file-folder thickness. Give each child a square piece of clear self-sticking shelf paper that is large enough to cover the finished visor.

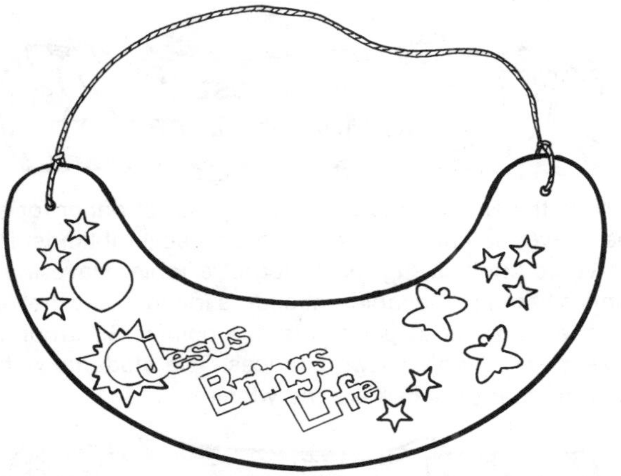

Allow the children to use markers, stickers, and patterns from pages 102, 110, and 111 to decorate the outer portion of their visor. Be sure the words "Son Visor" are centered within the design. Then, turn the visor over, and write the words, Jesus Brings Life and today's memory verse upside down on the inside. (Position these words so that when the child is wearing the visor he or she can look up and read the words clearly.) When each child has finished decorating their visor assist the students to carefully peel the paper from the clear sticky side of the shelf paper square. Lay the visor in the center of the sticky paper and press all areas of the visor firmly to cover and seal the top design. Cut around the outside of the visor. With a small paper-hole punch, center a hole at each edge of the visor. Tie one or two pieces of elastic string securely to one hole. Measure the owner's head and be sure you allow enough string to tie the elastic securely in the opposite hole. The Son Visor should fit snugly.

Allow the children to wear the Son visor during the remainder of the class period.

Shuttlebug Ride Home

Let's pretend it is a bright sunshiny day in Critter County. Everyone put on your Son Visor, and we will get in the Shuttlebug for our ride home.

Didn't we learn a lot during our visit today? Remind the children of special events and give them time to respond. As you get closer to your destination, tell the children you will be praising God one more time when you arrive at home.

Clap your hands and say, "We praise You, God, for Your power over death. We praise Your holy name."

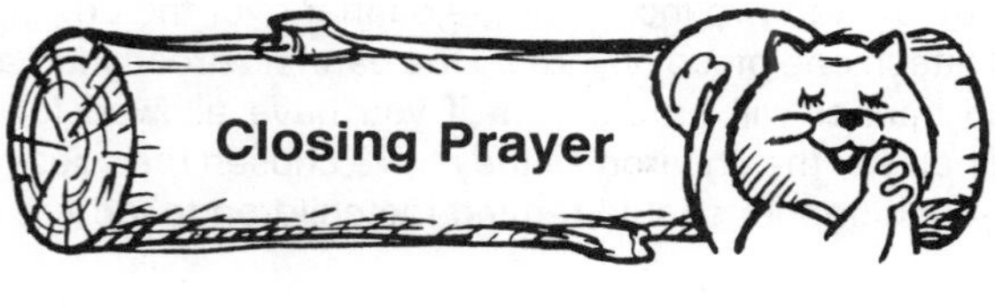

Closing Prayer

We praise You, Father, for allowing us to be together today. We give You special praise for our lesson. We know how happy Mary and Martha must have been when Lazarus came to life. Help us to remember that Jesus brought Lazarus to life to teach us about Your power, and to help us remember that we will always be able to be alive with you if we belong to Jesus and obey Your commands.

Thank You for the special feeling we have inside when we think about coming to live with You someday.

Help us to serve Jesus every day we are on earth. In His Name, amen.

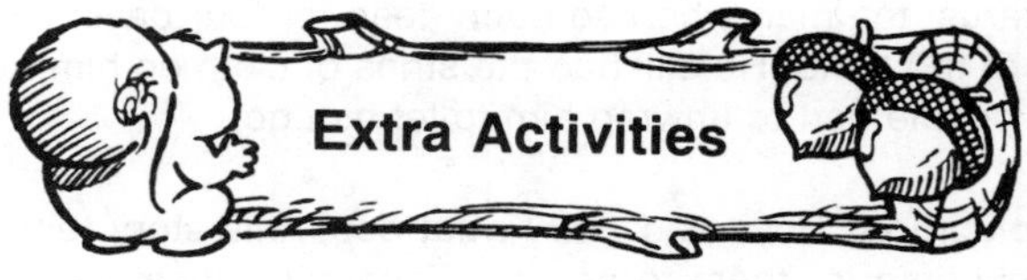

Extra Activities

Balloon Volleyball: This game is best when played outside, but if you have the space, it is a fun-filled indoor activity. Divide the class into two teams. Make an imaginary net by laying a rope or placing a piece of masking tape across the width of your playing field dividing the two sides.

Blow up a large balloon and play the game like regular volleyball. The only rules to change are that at least three, and no more than three, **must** hit the balloon each time before it crosses to the other side (even when serving). There are *no* out-of-bounds. Both teams try to keep the balloon from touching the ground, and unless you are serving, you may never hold on to the balloon. It should always be tapped with your hands or any part of your body. The first team with seven points wins.

Lazarus, Come Forth: Divide the class into two teams. Hang a sheet across the doorway to your room or from two objects that will conceal "Lazarus." Have six children (three from each group) leave the room. (You should probably select fewer if the class is small.) Draw straws among the six players to see who will be Lazarus. The children remaining in the room will take turns asking Lazarus four questions (to be answered yes or no). Two questions per team is suggested. Both teams must listen and concentrate on the answers. Lazarus must disguise his voice trying to keep the opposite team from guessing who he is. After the four questions have been answered, each team is allowed to guess who Lazarus is. After both guesses have been made, the class yells, "Lazarus, come forth." Lazarus steps from behind the sheet to reveal his identity. The team that guessed correctly gets five points. If Lazarus is a member of the team that correctly guesses him, the team is awarded the five points and a two point bonus. Lazarus joins his team members, and tries to guess the next Lazarus. Draw straws again to begin the next round. Use only four of the original six children before bringing in six more, or they will be able to guess by the process of elimination.

The team with the most points at the end of playing time wins the game.

Lesson 11

Praise God for His Forgiveness

Scripture: Acts 9; 22; 26:9-29

Psalm References: Psalm 111:9, 10; 103:1-3, 12-13; Psalm 150:4b (Pause-to-Praise verse)

Memory Verse: Praise the Lord, O my soul; all my inmost being, praise his holy name. He forgives all my sins and heals all my diseases.—Psalm 103:1, 3 (NIV)

Lesson Aim: As a result of studying this lesson the children should be able to

1) Know that God forgives their sins.
2) Know that God cares about how they live and the choices they make.
3) Know that God worked in Paul's life because Paul surrendered to Him.
4) Feel responsible to obey God.
5) Praise God for His forgiveness.
6) Name specific actions that will please God.
7) Sing or say the memory verse, Psalm 103:1, 3.

Materials Needed:
Pre-Session. *Activi-Tree:* Write the following suggestions on the slips you will attach to the tree before the children arrive.

- Drive the Shuttlebug to Critter County.
- Look up Acts 13:9 and see what Saul's name became as he traveled, teaching about Jesus.
- Look up the word *forgive* in the Bible dictionary and tell us its meaning.
- Be Sydney during Critter County on Radio.
- Be the leader in line.
- Help with the snack time preparations.
- Look up Psalm 150:4b and be ready to read it during Pause to Praise time.

To Forgive or Not Forgive: Story sequences given on pages 73, 74, paper, markers or crayons.

Preparation for Pause To Praise: Bible, construction paper, flute (if available), pop bottle, flute-a-phones (plastic type from dime store for each child), glue and scissors.

Together Time. Pictures from open-end stories shared during Pre-session, Happy Endings provided on pages 73 and 74.

Snack Time. Cookies made in the shape of a cross, fruit punch.

Bible Story Time. Wonders-of-God's-World box containing a quarter picture of a flashlight picture of Jesus.

Light Post on Memory Lane. Spinner board (directions on page).

Crafts.

5-8. *Cross Picture:* Styrofoam tray, paper punch, yarn, glue, ribbon or rick rack and trim scraps.

8-10. *Flannel Story Board:* Box with lid, flannel, felt scraps, patterns from page, felt-tip markers, scissors.

Extra Activities. *Great Game Exchange:* Several games made during the thirteen weeks of study.
Forgive Me: Sock for every player, beans and yarn.

Welcome the Children

Greet each child by name as you welcome him or her to the classroom. Encourage each child to choose a slip from the Activi-Tree. Be sure to introduce new students to the teachers and leaders in each center. Try to interest the child in one of the centers after he or she completes the assignment on the slip from the tree. Tell the children we will be talking about praising God for His forgiveness as we share in the class time today.

Pre-session Activities

Activi-Tree: One slip of paper per child has been placed on the tree before class. (See the suggestions for the slips at the beginning of this lesson.) After each child chooses a slip, he or she may become involved in an activity center. Be ready to assist with special directions or references. Be sure a Bible Dictionary is available for today's session.

To Forgive or Not Forgive: Give each child two sheets of white paper and have them number the sheets, 1, 2, 3, and 4 in the upper right-hand corner of each side of the paper.

Have the child who chose this responsibility from the Activi-Tree give the definition of "forgive". To forgive means to excuse and to stop feeling resentful toward someone.

Read the following situations one at a time. Give the children three minutes after you pose the question at the end of each story, to draw a picture describing what they believe should happen next. Have the students to explain their pictures.

Do not read the "Happy Endings" provided until Together Time. Tell the children in this center they will hear the real ending of the stories after they share their papers during Together Time. Compliment the students on the pictures they draw and help them to understand they need to find a solution to the story that will show forgiveness.

Open End Stories

1. Lisa and Jennifer are best friends. Jennifer loves cats and has raised a fluffy white pet named "Snowball" since it was a kitten.

Lisa likes cats too, but does not have one of her own.

One day, on the way home from school, Jennifer notices a tiny, thin, yellow cat following behind her and Lisa. She feels sorry for the kitten because it seems like it has no home. Jennifer decides to take the kitten home with her.

Lisa says she would like to have the kitten, but Jennifer explains that "finders are keepers". This hurts Lisa's feelings, and she doesn't know how to forgive Jennifer for taking away her chance to have the pet kitten. Lisa decides to . . .

2. Jason was a new kid in the neighborhood and to make him feel welcome, Eric invited him over to show him his baseball-card collection. It wasn't until after Jason had left Eric's house that Eric noticed his prize "1961 Hank Aaron" card was missing.

Eric knew Jason had taken the card. Eric wants the card back but he also realizes Jason does not go to church and has not learned how to please God by making the right decision when faced with the temptation to steal. Eric is sure he can get the card back AND help his friend learn to never steal again. Eric decides to . . .

3. Susie and Gretchen had been friends since kindergarten. They are now in the fifth grade and they both tried out to be cheerleaders. Gretchen was chosen but Susie did not make the cheering team. Gretchen's feelings were hurt when Susie stomped her feet and said she never liked Gretchen. Susie said she would never speak to Gretchen again. Gretchen cried because her friend hurt her this way. But Gretchen decides to. . . .

What happens next?

Happy Ending of Forgiveness

1. Lisa decides to keep treating Jennifer as her friend and forgive her for hurting her when Jennifer kept the kitten. Lisa treats her as the friend she has always been and hopes Jennifer invites her over to pet the kitten. Jennifer knows Lisa's birthday is three days away. After giving the kitten a shampoo and tying a beautiful blue bow around the kitten's neck, Jennifer gives Lisa the kitten as a birthday present. Lisa names the kitten "Jena" and cries when her friend hugs her and says "Happy Birthday". Lisa is glad she forgave Jennifer. Lisa and Jennifer will always be good friends.

2. Eric took a dollar from his savings bank and bought Jason some special plastic folders used to display baseball cards. He slipped several cards that were "doubles" on his collection into the folders. He called Jason to tell him he was coming to visit at Jason's house the next day.

Eric gave Jason the folders and explained that he wanted to say, "Welcome to the neighborhood." He told Jason he knew they would become good friends.

Jason was so surprised at Eric's kindness that he apologized for taking Eric's card. He returned it, and the boys planned a trip to the baseball-card shop together on Saturday. Sunday, Jason went with Eric for his first visit to church.

3. Gretchen finds a special card about "friends" at the shopping mall. She writes Susie a note to tell Susie she does not want to be a cheerleader without Susie's help.

Gretchen tells Susie that it was Susie who gave her the confidence to do a good job at the try-outs. Gretchen explains that no matter what Susie has said, Gretchen still wants to be friends.

Susie enjoys the card and the funny verse, but most of all, Susie feels happy that Gretchen said such special things to her.

Susie calls Gretchen to apologize for being selfish and angry, and Susie invites Gretchen to sleep over at her house on Friday so they can both make up new cheers together.

Susie becomes the best assistant to the cheerleading team the school has ever known. And . . . Susie is still Gretchen's best friend.

Preparation for Pause to Praise: Have the child who looked up this verse read Psalm 150:4b to the group. If you have a flute or have invited someone from your congregation to play the flute, allow time for the children to listen to a song played on the instrument.

Encourage the children to take turns blowing across a pop bottle to learn how they could play the flute. Fill several pop bottles with various amounts of water. Allow the children to blow across the bottles and listen to the different sounds they make.

Have one child draw a picture of a flute. (Or cut one from a magazine.) Glue this picture to the center of the construction paper making the next page for the scrapbook. Be sure to write, "Praise Him with the flute", on the page.

If you have flute-a-phones for each child in the center, practice playing together as everyone covers the same number of holes and blows one note. Half of the group covers one hole and the other half chooses a different hole to cover. Explain how they are playing in "unison" when they all play the same note. They are playing in "harmony" (hopefully) when two or more play different notes.

Pause to Praise: Have the same child read Psalm 150:4b to the class. Have one or two children explain what they have learned about the flute. Demonstrate blowing into the bottles filled with water and let any children who were not in the center try to blow a tune.

Allow the flutist time to play a familiar song for the children. Close the session by allowing one child to read the entire Psalm 150 as another class member turns the pages to the scrapbook.

Together Time: Have the children bring the pictures drawn during pre-session to the large group. Explain that we will be talking about forgiveness. Allow one child to explain what their center accomplished during Pre-Session.

Read story number one and allow one child to explain the picture he or she drew to complete the story. Ask if any other student would like to finish the story as they feel it should end.

Read the "Happy Endings of Forgiveness" provided. Allow the children time to discuss how they feel about the real ending.

Follow this procedure with stories two and three. Close this session by talking about how grateful we are to God for forgiving us for the things we have done wrong. Praise Him by clapping your hands together and saying, "We praise

You, God, for forgiving our sins. We praise Your holy name".

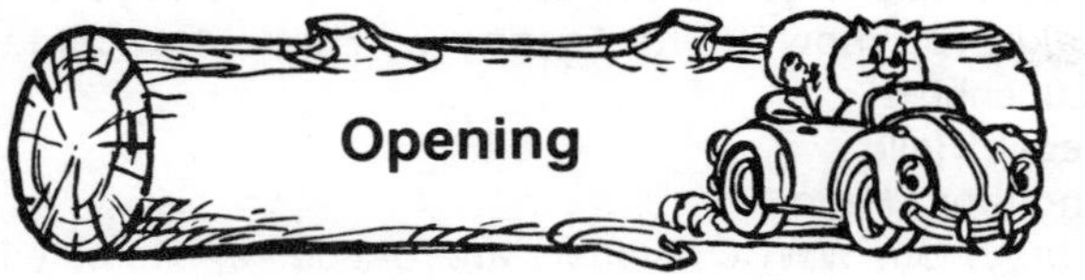

How many of you have ever done something that you are really sorry you have done, and you have had to depend on someone to forgive you? How many of you have needed to forgive someone like the children in our stories during Presession. We are going to talk more and more about forgiveness. Let's all head for the Shuttlebug. Who will be driving today? (The child who chose this from the Activi-Tree will drive.) We are going to the Critter County School and I can't wait to find out what happens when Rascal and Lunchbox get into a fight right in the middle of the school yard. I am glad we can all find out together. I see Critter County up ahead. We're almost there. Let's park here next to the swings and go to the story area to lean about Rascal and Lunchbox.

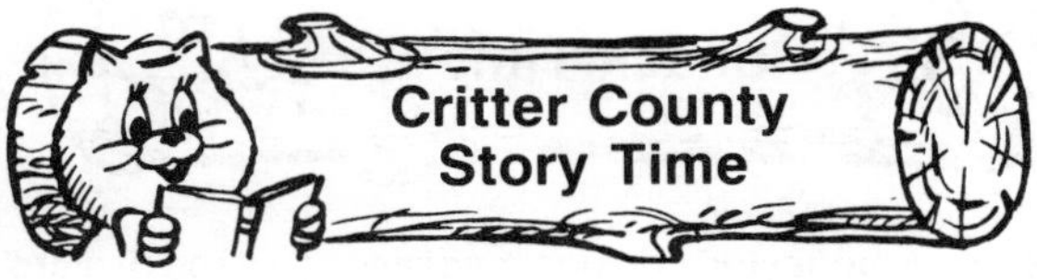

Sometimes we do things without thinking. When this happens, we might say something to hurt someone elses feelings, or we might be tempted to hurt the other person physically. Listen to what happens when Lunchbox and Rascal let their anger erase the love they feel as friends.

Rascal Says, "I'm Sorry."

Boy, I don't think this day will ever end, thought Rascal as he turned to look at the clock in his classroom. *I think everyday I go to school, it's longer until that last bell rings."*

But finally the bell did ring and the furry little raccoon hurried to get his books and jacket together.

"I can't wait to get home and fix a triple-decker-honey sandwich. Boy, I am STARVED!" he said to himself.

As quickly as he could, Rascal zipped up his red sports jacket and put on his favorite baseball cap. He was really proud of this cap because he had won it when his Little League team finished in first place last year. He wore it every day to school.

With his books under his right arm and his ball glove under his left, he scampered down the front steps and out onto the playground. Rascal saw his friend Lunchbox over by the swings. He yelled, "Hey, Lunchbox, what are you doing?"

"Oh, nothing much. Want to toss the ball around for awhile?" answered the young lion cub.

Rascal had a hard time making the decision because his mouth was already watering as he was thinking about that honey sandwich.

Finally, he said, "Sure, Lunchbox, I'd love to play ball with you for a little while. I can't stay too long though because I have to get home to do my paper route."

So the two friends began to toss the ball back and forth. Each time Rascal threw it to Lunchbox, he threw it a little harder. Lunchbox did the same thing, until both boys were throwing the ball as hard as they could. Then it happened.

Lunchbox threw the ball toward Rascal. The raccoon put up his glove to catch it, but he missed it. And the ball hit him right on the leg. It hit him *hard!*

Boy, was Rascal ever mad! He ran up to Lunchbox and screamed, "You hit me on purpose!"

As soon as he had spoken the words, his right paw went into a fist. And he punched Lunchbox right in the stomach. This took Lunchbox by surprise. He stood for a minute and then got very angry. "Hey, I never hit you on purpose with your old ball, and you can't hit me and get away with it!" yelled Lunchbox at Rascal.

Lunchbox tackled Rascal and knocked him to the ground. Round and round the two critters went. Fists, feet, and dust were flying in all directions when Sydney arrived.

Hey, guys, you stop this RIGHT NOW!" yelled Sydney as he moved in and began to separate the fighting critters.

After only a few minutes, Sydney got the fighting stopped. "Now stand up here, and tell me what is going on?" said Sydney in a stern voice.

Both critters began to speak at once as each tried to tell his side of the story.

Finally, Sydney interrupted, "OK, that's enough. Rascal, you tell me your side of the story, and then I'll hear from you, Lunchbox."

Rascal began, "Well, we were playing ball, and Lunchbox threw the ball as hard as he could, and hit me on the leg on purpose."

"No, I didn't hit you on purpose! I threw the ball, you missed it, and it hit your leg," yelled lunchbox. "And then Rascal hit me in the stomach, and I hit him back."

"Is that the way you remember what happened?" Sydney asked.

Rascal was beginning to feel uncomfortable in his stomach like he always does when he's in trouble.

"Yes, that's pretty much what happened," Rascal replied. He looked at his friend. "I'm really sorry I punched you out, Lunchbox. I guess I kinda know that you didn't mean to hit me with the ball. I just felt real dumb when I missed it, and it hit me. Guess I wanted to act like it was all your fault so I wouldn't feel so dumb."

"Well, I guess it's OK, Rascal," said Lunchbox with a little smile on his face.

It seemed like all was well once again in Critter County. The fight was over, and Rascal had told Lunchbox that he was sorry for hitting him. Nobody even had to tell him to do it this time.

But as the critters turned to start toward home, the wise little squirrel said, "Hey, wait a minute, fellows. Could I have a word with you, Lunchbox?"

The little lion brightened right up. "Sure, you can talk to me. What's up?"

"Well, Lunchbox, there's a very important lesson for you to learn here. I don't want you to miss it," said Sydney.

"Yeh, don't get in the way of Rascal's fist!" Lunchbox chuckled.

Sydney said, "It seems that Rascal made a couple of mistakes. First, he thought that you hit him on purpose, and then he slugged you in the stomach. He was wrong on both counts like he said. But Lunchbox, you were wrong too," said Sydney.

"How could I have been wrong because he punched me first?" questioned Lunchbox.

"Well, the Bible warns us against acting like that. We are to treat people the way we want to be treated. Now listen to me for just a minute. You did nothing to Rascal. You just threw the ball expecting him to catch it. It was not your fault that he missed it and then ran to you and hit you. You couldn't help any of that. We cannot control the way other people act. But we CAN help the way we react. When Rascal hit you, you should have obeyed God. You should have loved Rascal and been kind to him, even though he was being mean to you."

Lunchbox scratched his forehead above his right eye. He looked a little confused. "You mean that I can't help what other people do to me, and I'm supposed to behave even when they don't?"

"You got it!" said Sydney with a smile.

Lunchbox turned to Rascal and said, "Well, I'm sorry too. I shouldn't have hit you. Will you forgive me so we can be friends again . . . old pal, old buddy?"

Rascal got a big grin on his face as he said, "Hey, we're friends for life . . . and that's more than a thousand years."

Have the children go to the tables, and give them page 27 of the Critter county activity book.

5-8. *Friends Forever:* Color the picture of Rascal and Lunchbox. Remember to be brave enough to say, "I'm sorry," when you have hurt your friend.

8-10. *Forgive!* Look carefully at the pictures on this page. Draw a line from the picture on the left to its matching picture on the right. Remember, it pleases God when we are willing to forgive others.

When all have finished, have the children go to the Critter County Radio Station and sit in front of it. (Allow the child who chose the slip from the Activi-Tree to be Sydney.) You will need someone to be Rascal and someone to be Lunchbox today.

Sydney: **WWCC** coming at you from Critter County. The news is being brought to you by Firefly Fixtures! They brighten your nights and lighten your sights. If it's lamps you need lit, that's a job that they'll fit! They're the Firefly Fixtures!

And now for the news . . . Not too much excitement here in the County today. Harry the horse reports that the corn crops appear to be coming in right on schedule. Grandmother Mouse hosted a little luncheon for some of the critters. The food was reported to have been, as expected, scrumptuous. A little too much excitement on the playground today. It seems that Rascal and Lunchbox had a little misunderstanding over a game of toss. We take you now to the scene... Hello, Rascal and Lunchbox.

Rascal: Hello.

Lunchbox: Hello.

Sydney: Our **WWCC** listeners are, of course, interested in what happened today.

Rascal: I learned about actions. I must always try to be my very best.

Lunchbox: And I learned a whole lot about reactions. I can't do a whole lot about how Rascal acts but I can do a whole lot about how Lunchbox reacts.

Sydney: Well, boys, those are definitely exciting lessons. Thanks for joining us there on **WWCC.** Remember, listeners, Firefly Fixtures wants to light your nights.

Rascal: And our Heavenly Father wants you to stay out of all fights!

Sydney: Well, said Rascal. This is **WWCC.** Thanks for joining us.

We have suggested cookies made in the shape of a cross. They can be iced or decorated with colored sugar. The children will enjoy eating the cookies and drinking fruit punch as they talk about all the things they are learning about forgiveness. Listen carefully to their conversation. You may discover special needs or interests you can address later in the Bible lesson or craft time discussions. After clean up, have the children return to the story area.

Play the song "Sing Praise to Him," page 140, as the children assemble in the story area. When all have gathered, sing the song together.

Sing familiar songs as well as new ones: "Praise Ye the Lord Forever," page 142; "Praise the Lord for His Forgiveness," page 125; "How Much Do You Love?" page 134; "Clap Your Hands," page 119; and "Even a child," page 133.

Prayer Song: "Hear Us as We Pray," page 143.

Prayer: Ask God to help the children understand about forgiving one another as they learn how God forgave Saul.

(Place a quarter in one corner of the Wonders-of-God's-World box and tape it down. Place a picture of yourself over the quarter so it completely hides the quarter from view. Before the lesson, after the children are seated, walk around the circle and tell the children to look in the box and remember everything that it contains. After returning to your position, ask the students what they saw in the box. Ask them if there was anything else in the box. If they are absolutely certain, continue with the beginning of the story.)

Boys and girls, today's Bible story will teach us a lesson that is very important for us to learn.

Have you ever made a mistake? Now, I am not talking about putting on two different colors of socks in the morning when you are sleepy. I'm talking about a mistake—a big mistake—the kind of mistake you don't know how to fix.

Well, today you have all made a mistake. Hand the box to the first child in the circle. Remove the lid and allow the child to take the box this time. Let him or her examine it more closely. (Shake it and pick up the picture.) Allow all the children to come and see what this student has found.

Now, that wasn't such a big mistake, and I did trick you into thinking that was all there was in the box. But, what I need you to remember is how sure you were that you were right. Today's lesson is about a man who was sure he was right, while, all the time, he was making a very big mistake.

Saul Is Forgiven

Acts 9:1-22; 22:1-21; 26:9-29

(Show a picture of Saul. Place a flash light, blindfold, and picture of Jesus in the Wonders-of-God's-World box.)

Saul was a man who believed in finishing what he started. He was an angry man who was tired of hearing about the Jewish Christians who were going everywhere preaching about Jesus. Saul believed these people were wrong, and he didn't like them stirring up the people with their tales of Jesus coming back to life after dying on a cross. He believed so strongly that these Christians were wrong, that he went to the High Priest and asked for special letters giving him permission to put men AND women in prison if they continued to teach about Jesus. Saul did not believe Jesus was the Son of God.

He received special permission to go to a city called Damascus. There he would look for Christians and make them prisoners. Later he would take these prisoners to Jerusalem. Remember, Saul believed it was right to do this. He didn't know he was making such a BIG mistake.

The Bible tells us he was traveling with some other men who would help him. (Remove the flashlight from the box.) As they came near Damascus, (Turn the light on your own face and squint from the light.) a bright light, a VERY bright light shown down from heaven. Saul fell to the ground. He heard a voice calling to him saying, "Saul, Saul, why do you persecute me?" Saul answered the voice asking who was speaking to him. (Remember, he did not think it could be Jesus because Saul didn't believe in Jesus.)

The voice answered, "I am Jesus whom you are persecuting." Then, Jesus told Saul to get up and go into the city and wait to be told what he should do.

When Saul stood up again, he could see nothing. He was blind. The men had to lead Saul into the city.

I believe hearing from Jesus helped Saul realize he was making a mistake about gathering Christians and putting them in prison. How do you think Saul felt after being blinded by this light and hearing Jesus' voice? (Allow time for discussion.) Who looked up the word *forgiveness?"* (Allow the child to read what he found in the dictionary about forgiveness.) Repeat the definition and be sure the class understands.

The Bible tells us Saul was in Damascus for three days and would not eat or drink anything. He must have felt very sorry for what he had done to the people who loved Jesus.

Jesus asked a man named Ananias to go to Damascus and talk to Saul. Ananias was afraid, at first, but he knew when Jesus asked him to do something, Jesus would help him and keep him safe.

The Bible says Ananias went to see Saul. He placed his hands on Saul, and when Saul opened his eyes, he could see again.

Ananias told Saul that Jesus had a special job for him to do. Ananias told him he would travel to many cities preaching to people about Jesus. By now, Saul believed in Jesus. He had been thinking about all that had happened for three whole days. He remembered all he had done to hurt so many people, and he needed to have his sins forgiven. He was so sorry for the mistakes he had made. Ananias told Saul, "What are you waiting for? Get up and be baptized and wash your sins away, calling on Jesus name".

The Bible tells us Saul was baptized and after his baptism, he ate some food and gained some of his strength back. Then, Saul because a great preacher who spent the rest of his life traveling to many cities and teaching people about Jesus.

It is interesting that Saul's name changed. Who looked up Saul's new name ? Allow this child to answer—Paul.)

Teacher's note: Saul was both a Jew and a gentile. He was born of Jewish parents (Acts 23:6). However, he was born in Tarsus, a city of Rome (Acts 22:3; 25-29). It is believed that Saul was his Jewish name and when he became a teacher to the gentiles, he began using the gentile name Paul.

Application: Saul had made some pretty bad mistakes. He had put people in prison and even watched people die because he did not believe all that they were saying about Jesus.

Isn't it wonderful to know that God planned for Saul to be forgiven? Jesus had died for this man who was killing people who said they loved Jesus. When Saul accepted Jesus, he was baptized and the sins he had committed, all the mistakes he had ever made, were "washed away" to be remembered no more.

Listen to this verse of Scripture from the Psalms. (Have a child to read Psalm 103:12, 13.)

As far as the east is from the west, that's how far our sins have been taken away. We should praise our, holy, gracious God for forgiving our mistakes when we accept Jesus and live for Him. Clap your hands and say, "We praise You, God, for forgiving our sin. We praise Your holy name."

Have the children go to the tables and give them page 28 of the activity book.

5-8. *Choices:* Look carefully at the pictures. Then put an **X** on the picture that shows a child making the wrong choice.

8-10. *Saul:* Unscramble the letters to discover words from today's Buble lesson. Use the word list if you need it. Then look up the Bible verses listed under the heading, "Bible Verses to Know." What do these verses say about forgiveness?

When all have finished with the activity papers, have the children go to the Light Post on Memory Lane.

From cardboard and a paper fastener, make a spinner game like the one pictured. Let the students take turns spinning and performing the job indicated. Team up in pairs and have one pair challenge another pair before spinning. If the pair that is challenged cannot say what is indicated by the spinner and the challenging pair can, the challengers are given five points. The pair with the most points at the end of the game are declared the winners.

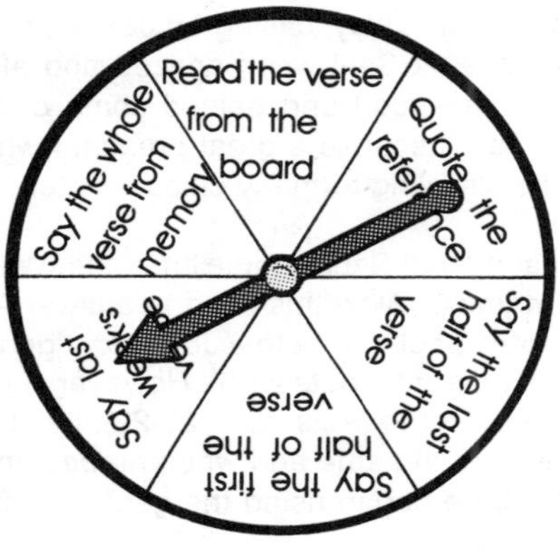

5-8. Cross Picture: Give each student a styrofoam meat tray (obtainable at meat markets or the grocery.) Place dots in the areas indicated by the illustration. Allow the children to punch holes with a pencil or pen by placing the point on the dot and being careful not to crack the tray. Wrap a piece of cellophane tape around the end of any color yarn chosen by the student to make a point like a needle. Weave the yarn in and out around the cross. (Just like you would connect the dots with a pencil.) Push the final tail of yarn down through the beginning hole and pull it to the back of the picture so you cannot tell where the picture weaving starts or ends. Glue rick rack or ribbon around the outer edge of the picture. Attach a loop of yarn and the picture is ready to hang. Type the memory verse on paper and glue beneath the cross.

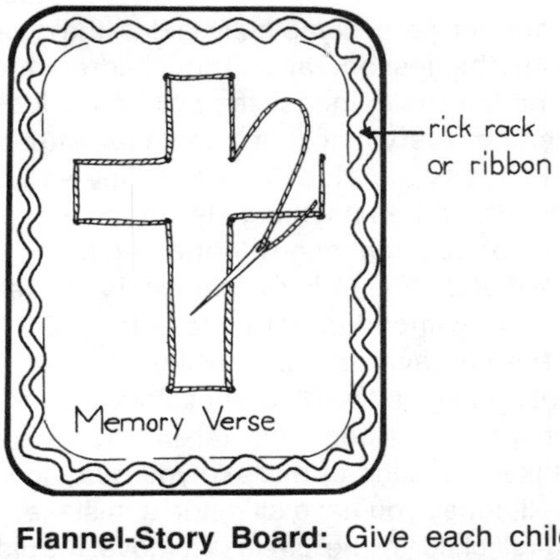

8-10. Portable Flannel-Story Board: Give each child a small size dress or shirt box with lid. On the inside of the bottom, glue a piece of construction paper across the width of the box and 4" to 5" tall to make a pocket for the flannel figures.

Cut a piece of blue flannel to cover the inside lid of the box. Glue this piece to the lid. It is not removable. (Be sure to place glue around the outer edges of the piece and none in the middle. The glued area may show through.)

Allow the students to cut pieces of flannel or felt appropriate for the colors of grass, clouds,, rocks, road, hillside. Use the patterns on pages 103-106 to cut out figures of Saul, two friends, the bright light, the city of Damascus, Ananias and a pool of water.

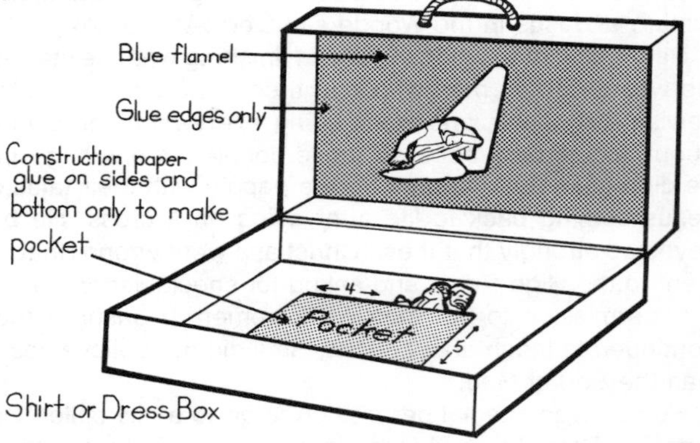

Use these figures to tell the story in your own words. Add as many felt pieces as time and creativity will allow. Decorate the outside of the box with any materials you choose. (Self-sticking shelf paper covers a large area easily.)

Add a handle by punching two holes five inches apart on the outside closing edge of the box. Push a 12" piece of yarn through both holes and tie a knot after measuring the handle to fit comfortably in your hand.

The felt pieces are stored in the inside pocket when the board is not in use. Enjoy telling this and other Bible stories to younger children and your friends. Write a play and present it on the board during family devotions. Keep the board and add to your felt pieces some rainy day when you need a good craft idea.

This has been the best day in Critter County! You could say we've made this trip one of the best of all because we've learned new things and shared old memories too! It's time to get in the Shuttlebug and head for home. (Discuss some of the children's favorite lessons, games, songs, memory verses and crafts from all their visits to Critter County.) It has been fun remembering.

Let's especially remember today's lesson because it is important for us to know God has promised to forgive our sins.

Here we are at home. This is where we'll practice what we have learned. Maybe we'll all have the chance to visit Critter County again soon.

Closing Prayer

God, we thank You and praise You for giving us life and for loving us so much that you sent Jesus to take away our sins. We praise You for providing for our forgiveness. Help us to grow in our understanding of Your Word. We love You and praise You for the knowledge we have gained and the fun we have shared together. Bless our teachers for the work they have done for You. Help us to always follow the example of our Master Teacher, Jesus. In His name we pray, amen.

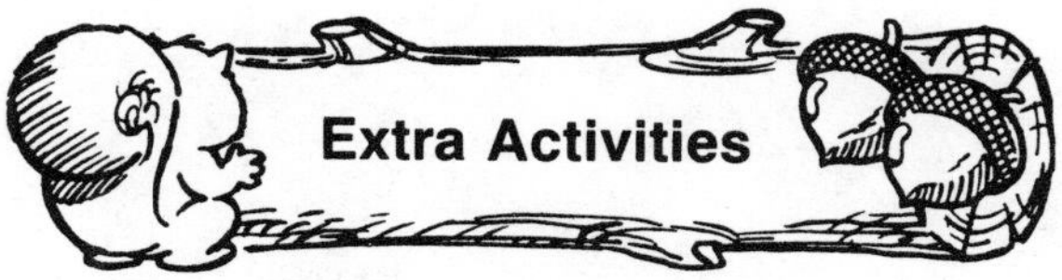

Extra Activities

Great Game Exchange: Gather some of the favorite games the children have enjoyed during this series of lessons. Divide the class into groups of three or four children. Allow ten minutes for the different groups to play the various games simultaneously. After ten minutes, ring a bell, play music or give some kind of signal for all the game players to rotate. Change players or have one entire group exchange games with another group, and the games begin again. Every ten minutes, rotate. The class will have fun recalling stories.

Forgive Me: Give every student a sock, some beans and a piece of yarn to tie around the sock. Allow everyone to make the beanbag before play begins. Divide the class into two teams. Each team sits in a circle on the floor. The first player will begin to pass the beanbags by saying, "Forgive me, I have them all,"He will pass each beanbag individually to the player on his right. The bags will travel around the circle until they all end up in the possession of the player sitting at the starter's left. That player says, "Forgive me, I have them all, and begins the routine again. This continues until every player on the team has obtained and passed all the socks. The team to complete the entire cycle, stands up and is declared the winner. Mix up the teams and play again.

Lesson 12

Praise God by Serving Him

Scriptures: John 13:1-17

Psalm References: Psalm 119:9-17; 86:11, 12; Psalm 150:5 (Pause-to-Praise verse)

Memory Verse: Serve the Lord with gladness; come before him with joyful songs.—Psalm 100:2 (NIV)

Lesson Aim: As a result of studying this lesson, the children should be able to

1) Know that Jesus became a servant.
2) Know that a servant willingly seeks the good of others disregarding himself.
3) Feel honored to serve God.
4) Thank God for Jesus' example.
5) Tell one thing he or she will do for someone else.
6) Sing or say the memory verse, Psalm 100:2

Materials Needed:
Pre-session. *Activi-Tree:* Write the following directions on slips of paper to fasten to the Activi-Tree before class. Materials suggested include window cleaner, rags, brooms, flowers

- Serve your teacher today's snack at snack time.
- Pick up paper outside during **Pre-session.**
- Wash two of the tables in our room. (2)
- Place the chairs against the wall after class so the church custodian can sweep.
- Get a drink of water for the teacher before the Bible story.
- Sweep the sidewalk in front of the building.
- Make a bouquet of flowers for the secretary's office.
- (Add suggestions of service that fit your church or class needs.)
- Look up Philippians 2:5-7 and be ready to read it later.
- Drive the Shuttlebug to Critter County today.
- Look up Psalm 150:5 and be ready to read it during **Pause to Praise.**
- Pretend to fix the Shuttlebug when it breaks down.
- Look up the word *resounding* in the dictionary. What does it mean?
- Look up Passover Feast; in the Bible directory. Tell us what it means for Bible Story Time.

Seeking to Serve: Construction paper, file folders, markers, stickers, clear self-sticking shelfpaper.

Preparation for Pause to Praise: Old pan lids, real cymbals from drum set, drum sticks, and drum brushes, pie tins, drawer knobs with screws, construction paper, glue, and markers.

Together Time. Posterboard with list of service projects that were on Activi-Tree, marker.

Snack Time. Ice-cream cups and fruit juice. Various toppings (optional)

Bible Story Time. Bible, Wonders-of-God's-World box containing wash cloth, soap, picture of Heaven, picture of Jesus washing disciple's feet.

Light Post on Memory Lane. Alphabet letters, posterboard for every two students, glue.

Crafts.
5-8. *Homemade Sachet:* Wallpaper, cottonballs, glue, spray perfume, ribbon or rick rack trim, pinking shears or scissors.

8-10. *A Basket Full of Love:* Pint size plastic fruit or vegetable baskets, ribbon, paper, markers.

Extra Activities. *Excessive Servanthood:* broom, waste basket, five pieces of paper, dust cloth, scarf, apron, and spray bottle of water.
Who is the Servant?: Chair for every player.

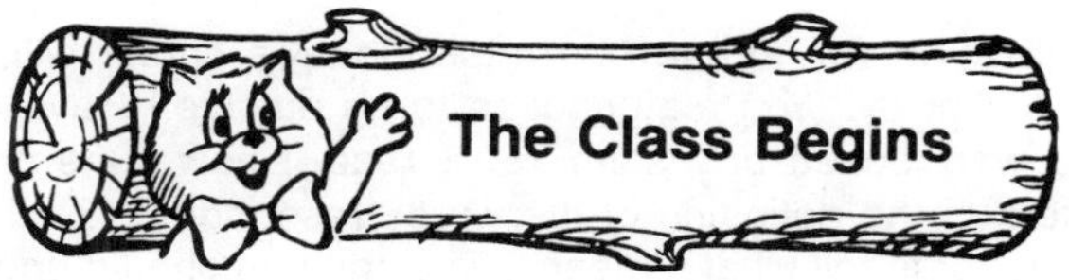

Welcome the Children
Greet each child by name and give each a slip of paper. Explain that you and the other teachers are here to serve them today. Tell them they may write a request at any time, on the slip of paper and give it to a teacher. That teacher will do all that she can to serve. Guide each child toward the Activi-Tree and be ready to give assistance as today's service projects are begun. (You may need to shorten the time spent at the Activity Centers today because the Activi-Tree projects will take more time than usual.)

Pre-session Activities
Activi-Tree. Today's tree will contain slips giving instructions for service projects. See the list at the beginning of this lesson. Be sure to think of the children's abilities as well as their safety as you add slips to the tree. You may also choose to invite other adults or responsible teens to assist the students if you feel they need help. For instance, the children picking up paper outside should not be sent outside alone. If anyone needs to stand on a ladder, be sure that an older teen or adult is available to assist.

A Servant I will Be. Prepare cards from manilla paper. The cards should be 2″ x 4″. Have the children print, "A Servant I Will Be" somewhere on one side of the card. Decorate around these words with the markers, stickers, or materials that the children suggest. The back of the card should have a line for the child to sign his or her name, and it should contain today's memory verse. Cover the front and back of the card with the clear adhesive shelf paper and trim the edges.

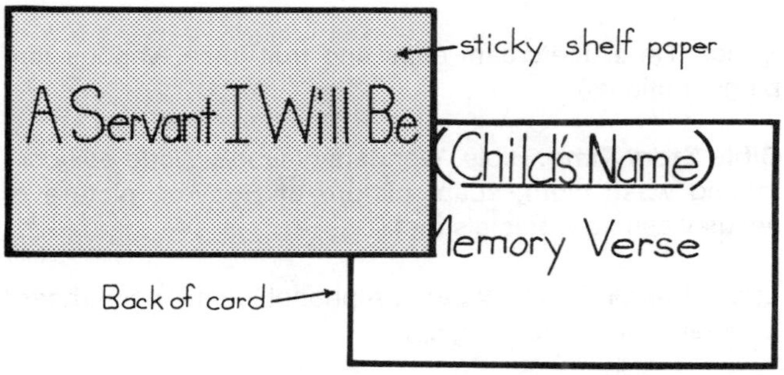

The card is to be used by the owner to give special service to others. Surprise a neighbor by giving them the card, and telling them that they are to keep the card until you complete your act of loving service. (Examples would include pulling weeds, sweeping sidewalk, walking their dog.) When the job is complete, the neighbor returns the card, and the child thanks the neighbor for allowing him or her to work as a servant. **Never accept money for the service you give.** Remember, this time you are willing to give of yourself to someone just because you love them, and you love Jesus.

Preparation for Pause to Praise. Today's center will be fun, but noisy. (You may choose to go outside.) Have the child who looked up Psalm 150:5 read it now. One child looked up the definition of the word "resounding." Call on him or her to tell what it means. The children should understand this is like an echo. One cymbal sounds, and the other cymbal answers it or repeats the first cymbal's sound.

Allow the children to tap the drum cymbal with the drumsticks, and then with the brushes. If you have real cymbals, allow the children to take turns clapping them together.

Explain to the children that cymbals do not give a pleasant sound when they are played alone. But, when added to an orchestra or band, it is the cymbal that brings the music to attention. People sit up and listen when the cymbals clash.

This Psalm has talked about many instruments. We are sure the cymbals are added because they will bring attention and emphasis to the power and greatness of our God.

If time permits, make a small hole in the center of each pie tin. Place the drawer knob on the outside and twist the screw into the knob from the inside. make several sets of these cymbals for the class.

Remember to have one child draw a picture of cymbals on a sheet of construction paper and add the words, "Praise Him with the clash of cymbals, praise Him with resounding cymbals." (This is the twelfth page of the scrapbook.)

Pause to Praise: Have the same child read Psalm 150:5. Then, have one child explain what we have learned about cymbals, and re-sounding cymbals.

Tell the class that we will be praising God that we can serve Him.

Divide the class in two groups and let them stand several feet apart in separate lines. Give half of the cymbals to one side, and the remaining cymbals to the other side. Say the following praise clapping the cymbals on the words in bold print.

Side One: We **PRAISE** you God.
Side Two: We PRAISE you God,
Side One: That **WE** can serve,
Side Two: That **WE** can serve.
Side One: We **PRAISE** you God.
Side Two: We **PRAISE** you God.
Side One and Two Together: We **PRAISE** your holy **NAME.**

All cymbals sounding together four times, last time vibrating. Close this session by reading the entire scrapbook as one child turns the pages.

Together Time: Have the posterboard prepared with the list of activities from the Activi-Tree. The board should be titled, "A Servant I Will Be." Talk with the children about serving and tell them they have all acted as servants as they have completed their assignments. Go around the class and allow each child to explain what his particular job of service involved. Let each write his or her name beside the activity he or she completed.

Allow the students who attended the A Servant-I-Will-Be center, share the cards they have made and explain their use. Encourage them to tell what special job they have in mind for the use of their card, and who they intend to serve first.

We just began our class time and already we are tired from all of the work! But, when you think about it, boys and girls, being a servant isn't like work because you feel as good inside when you are doing something for someone else. Who would like to do something for all of us now? (Allow the volunteer you choose to drive the Shuttlebug to Critter County.)

Let's all buckle up. We'll rest as we drive to Critter County. We're going to visit the Critter County Elementary School today. Cream Puff has a problem. A new critter at school is being unkind to her. We will see how Cream Puff learns to serve this new critter. There's the school up ahead. Everyone out of the shuttlebug to listen to the story.

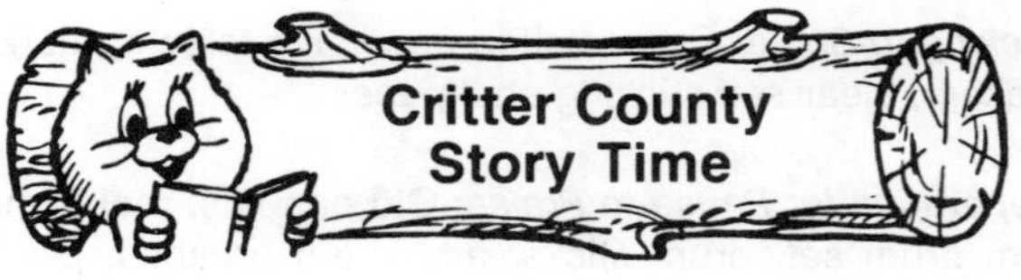

The first day of school is always exciting. Cream Puff loved school and was eager to go. However, this year she met someone who was very hard to like. She tried to be nice.

I'm sure that each of you know how Cream Puff felt. You have known people like that. What did you do? (Allow several children to answer.)

Cream Puff did not know what to do. Listen carefully to find out who helped Cream Puff solve her problem.

Cream Puff Learns to Love

Cream Puff, the kitten, woke up very early the first day of September. She jumped out of bed, ran over to where she had laid out her clothes the night before, and held up her new dress in front of her. She looked at herself in the mirror and twirled around. She was so excited!

Today was the first day of school. She looked out the window. The sun was already beginning to melt the dew which had formed overnight on the lawn and trees. Yes, it was going to be a beautiful day. She was glad since she had to walk several blocks to and from the Critter County Elementary School.

Cream Puff was one of the first critters to arrive at school. She skipped down the hall, looking for the sign above the door which read "Grade 2." She stopped and went inside.

"Good morning, Cream Puff," said Mrs. Turtle, the second grade teacher. "You're here bright and early. that must mean you like school."

"Oh, I do," said the little kitten. "I've hardly been able to sleep for days."

Soon the door flung open and in walked a new critter that Cream Puff had not seen before. He marched up and down the aisles looking for the desk which had his name on it. Finally, he stopped at the desk right behind Cream Puff's.

"Here's my place," he exclaimed.

"Oh," said Cream Puff, "You sit right behind me. What is your name? I've never seen you before."

"My name is Stinker," said the little skunk, pointing to his name tag on the desk.

"Welcome to our school," said Cream puff, trying to make him feel welcome.

Stinker looked at Cream Puff and said, "I don't know who you are, but I don't plan on being friends with any kitten who has short little ears, and a long skinny tail. You are ugly."

Then Stinker turned around and sat down at his desk. He didn't seem to care that Cream Puff stood there with tears in her eyes. Never before had she met a critter who was so cruel to her.

The next morning, Cream Puff was at school a little bit early again. She hoped that the hurtful things that Stinker had said were only because he was scared of going to a new school.

Maybe today he will be nicer to me, she thought as the bell rang. It was time for everyone to take their seats. But, Cream Puff was wrong.

At lunch time, Stinker called her names in the cafeteria in front of all the other critters. He even threatened to step on her tail. Cream Puff went home in tears.

That evening before bedtime, Cream Puff's daddy read a story from the Bible which told how she should, love her enemies.

"Daddy, why would Jesus tell us to love our enemies?" asked Cream Puff. "Does that mean I should try and love Stinker? How can I love him when he doesn't want to be my friend? It's so hard not to be mean back to him when he says such nasty things to me," sobbed Cream Puff, as she thought about what had happened in the cafeteria that day. "Oh, daddy, I'm starting to hate school. What am I going to do?"

"Now, now, Cream Puff," said the big, daddy cat. "Come here and sit on my lap. Let's talk about this. Sometimes Jesus asks us to do things that are very hard. It seems like His Word doesn't make much sense. But you know what Cream Puff? I'll tell you a secret."

Cream Puff straightened up a bit. She tried to stop crying so she could hear her daddy.

"What's the secret, daddy?" she asked in a small voice.

"The secret is that Jesus knows what is best for us because He made all of us. He really loves us. He would only tell us to do things that would be good for us, not bad. Let's try an experiment," said the wise daddy. Think of something really "special" you can do for Stinker. We'll figure out a way you can do what Jesus said when he says , "Love our enemies." Then we'll wait and see what happens."

Cream Puff's daddy suggested that maybe Cream Puff could plan a party just for Stinker for the following Saturday. She could invite lots of critters from her class. They would play games and have a big cake that said, "We love Stinker. Welcome to Critter County."

The rest of that week Cream puff was busy getting ready for the party. She sent out the invitations, made party decorations, and Friday after school, her mommy helped her make the cake.

The next morning all the critters arrived a little early. They all waited anxiously for Stinker to arrive. Just then there was a knock at the door. Tommy the turtle ran to open it. Stinker walked in, looked around, and said, "Wow, who's the party for?"

"It's for you," said Tommy. "This was Cream Puff's idea. She planned the whole thing and even made you the cake. Come and see it."

Stinker went with the others. He looked around at all the decorations. Finally he arrived at the table where the cake sat. Cream Puff had worked very hard to make it look pretty.

"Boy, what a great party! Thanks, Cream Puff," said Stinker.

The party was lots of fun. The critter who seemed to enjoy it the most was Cream Puff.

"May I ask you something, Cream puff?" said Stinker.

Cream Puff turned around to face him.

"Why would you want to give me a party when I was so mean to you? I mean, that doesn't make any sense," he said.

"Well," said Cream Puff, "Jesus said that I should try and love others even when they're mean. I can see my daddy was right. Jesus does know what is best for us. He only tells us to do things that will make us happy. And today, I am happy."

Have the children go to the tables and give them page 29 from the activity book.

5-8. *Hidden Pictures:* See if you can find the eight objects that Cream Puff will need for the party. Color the picture.

(The eight items are a balloon, a party cake, a party horn, a party hat, napkins, plate, cup, and party invitation.)

8-10. *Cream Puff Learns to Serve:* Start at the arrow and write every other letter on the lines. What is the message? (Thank you for planning such a nice party for me. I am sorry I was so unkind to you. Forgive me, please.)

When all have finished with the activity papers, have the children go to the Critter County Radio Station and sit in front of it. You will need someone to be Sydney and someone to be Rascal in the Critter County Radio Station.

Critter County Radio Station

Sydney: You're tuned into **WWCC**—the Wonderful World of Critter County. We'd like to express our joy in serving you, our listeners. Serving? We're hearing quite a bit about service today, aren't we?
Rascal: Hut, two, three, four, hut, two, three, four.
Sydney: Rascal, hello, won't you join us on **WWCC** for a few minutes?
Rascal: Why, Sydney, I'd love to! I was just pretending that I was in the Army.
Sydney: Oh, I see, and you were marching.
Rascal: Serving my county, Sydney. That's me.
Sydney: You know, Rascal, there are many types of service.
Rascal: Yes. Mother serves me my dinner every night, and my evening snack and my bedtime munchies, and then . . .
Sydney: And Poncho the pig serves us by putting gas in our cars at the gas station.
Rascal: And a critter can serve for many kinds of reasons.
Sydney: That's right! A critter sometimes serves because that's their job!
Rascal: Like my paper route!
Sydney: Or sometimes it's just because you feel like you should. But the best kind of service is when it's out of love.
Rascal: Like when all of Mrs. Bunny's friends helped her out when her baby fell! And when Cream Puff planned the special party for Stinker.
Sydney: Exactly! And that's how we want to serve you here at **WWCC**—out of love!
Rascal: Hut, two, three, four, Don't turn your dial, 'Cause we've got more,
Sydney: More of what you're looking for! Here on **WWCC!**

Snack Time

The suggestion for today's snack is ice cream. If you choose, purchase strawberry, chocolate and or butterscotch topping to have on hand. Write the names of all the students and teachers in the class on small slips of paper. (Exclude the teacher's name which was included on the Activi-Tree.) Allow the students to choose one name. They must take the spoon and cup of ice cream to the student or teacher whose name they have chosen. If the person being served would like one of the toppings, the server is to take the cup of ice cream to the topping area and prepare the ice cream for the one he is serving. Everyone in the class should be a servant as well as being one who is served. Talk about the feelings you have as a servant or as the one who is being served as you eat the delicious snack. The servants are to throw away the used cups of the ones that they served.

After clean up, have the children return to the story area.

Songs of Praise

Play the song "Sing Praise to Him," page 140, as the children assemble in the story area. When all have gathered, sing the song together.

Sing familiar songs as well as new ones: "Forever Will I Praise Your Name," page 138; "Be Kind and Compassionate," page 126; "O Give Thanks," page 128; and "I Can Do Everything," page 123; and "Serve the Lord," page 124.

Prayer Song: "Hear Us as We Pray," page 143.

Prayer. Ask God to help the children listen as we learn about being servants. Ask Him to help them desire to be like Jesus.

Bible Story Time

Today we all found out what it is like to be servants. We have been so busy doing things for each other and helping with special jobs around our class. I want you to put on your thinking caps for a minute and really think about your answer to my next question. Ready? Who do you think is the greatest servant who has ever lived? (Allow for time to think. If anyone quickly answers, "Jesus," immediately ask, "Why?" Encourage the children to think about how Jesus should be considered as a servant.) Show the picture of Heaven. Do you know where Jesus was before the earth was made? (Allow time for an answer.) The Bible says He was with God. Listen to this verse in Philippians. (Have child to read Philippians 2:5-7.) Jesus was with God, but when God needed Him to come to earth and live as a man, Jesus gave up his place with God in Heaven and came to earth. He left everything behind Him in Heaven and came to earth. Think about it! Nothing ever hurts you in Heaven. You never have to feel pain or be sad. Nothing bad ever happens because in Heaven, there is no sin. No one can hurt your feelings or steal what is yours. There is no sickness or suffering. Heaven is a wonderful place. Because God is there,

Heaven is the very best place anyone can live. Jesus left Heaven to come to earth, and live as a man. He did that, not because He had to, but because He wanted to. That is why Jesus is the greatest servant who has ever lived. Let's listen while I tell you what kind of servant He was on earth.

Jesus Washes the Disciple's Feet
John 13:1-17

The Bible tells us that this lesson from Jesus occurred when it was almost time for the Passover. (Ask the child who looked this word up to explain what he knows about the Passover.)

Jesus and His disciples had come together to eat. Jesus knew it was almost time for Him to die. He knew that He would be crucified during the days of the Passover celebration. The Bible tells us He had loved His disciples very much as He spent time with them on earth, and He decided to do something very special that would show them just how very much He loved them.

As the meal was being served, (Take the towel and soap from the **Wonders-of-God's-World** box.) Jesus got up from the table, took off the cloak that he was wearing, and wrapped a towel around his waist. After doing this, he poured water into a bowl and began to wash the disciple's feet.

You see, it was a custom in Jesus' day, to wash people's feet. People walked everywhere they went. They were always walking along dusty roads and traveling every day through the towns and countrysides. Most of the people wore sandals, and their feet would be very dirty most of the time. It was common to have a towel and basin close to the entrance of the house. People would wash their feet before they entered. A servant would wash the visitor's feet if the house was owned by someone wealthy enough to have servants to do the washing. Jesus moved from disciple to disciple, washing their feet.

When He came to Peter, Peter would not let Him wash his feet. Peter knew that Jesus was God's Son. He felt this was a task that Jesus was too special to do. Peter said, "You shall never wash my feet." But, Jesus made Peter understand that this was something He wanted each disciple to allow Him to do. Peter finally agreed, and Jesus washed Peter's feet while the other disciples waited. When Jesus finished washing each of them (even Judas who was about to turn Jesus over to the rulers to be killed), He explained why He had chosen to wash them. He reminded them that He was their Lord and teacher. He knew they would never expect Him to wash their feet. But because He was willing to do this humble task, He taught them how to behave as servants.

Jesus knew these men would be teachers and leaders in the church after He went back to Heaven. He wanted them to remember this lesson. He wanted each disciple to act as a servant to others. He knew if He showed them by His example, they would do what He had done.

Application: This is a wonderful lesson to learn, boys and girls. Remember how you felt today as you were serving others? Remember how it felt to be served?

Never forget that Jesus was the greatest servant of all. He was not too special to wash the feet of His disciples. He wanted them to be like Him, and he has asked us to follow His example, too. He showed us we should always be willing to be a servant.

Let's praise God that we can serve Him. Clap your hands together and say, "We praise You, God. Our service we give. We praise Your holy name!"

Have the children return to the tables and give them page 30 of the Critter County Activity Book.

5-8. *Things I Can Use to Serve Others:* Draw a line from the picture on the left to the tool you would use to serve others.

8-10. *Jesus' Tools:* Follow the dots to find out what tools Jesus used to serve His disciples. Color the picture.

Upon completion of their activity papers, have the children gather at the Light Post on Memory Lane.

Begin today's visit by singing "Serve the Lord," on page 124.

Divide the group by asking them to choose a friend because they will work together and serve each other with the project.

Give each set of friends one sheet of paper, and some glue. Write the verse on the board where everyone can see it. Pour the alphabet letters in the center of each group's work area. Encourage them to work together to construct the verse and glue it to the paper. (For beginning readers, pre-sort the letters into divided trays such as egg cartons.) After completing the verse, help each other memorize by taking turns saying the verse to one another.

5-8. Home-made Sachet: Cut various pieces of wallpaper samples with pinking shears. The finished pieces should be $4^{1/2}"$ x 8". Cut two per student. Have the children fold the sheets in half. Place a line of glue around the inside top, side and bottom of folded square. Spray 3 cottonballs heavily with cologne. Place these cottonballs inside the center of the folded square. Press the edges together allowing the glue to seal the edges completely. Decorated to outside edges with rick rack or ribbon.

Explain to the children that the sachet is used to bring a fresh scent to clothes in dresser drawers or in closets. Ladies, especially enjoy sachet. Listen to the children as they discuss who will receive the special gift.

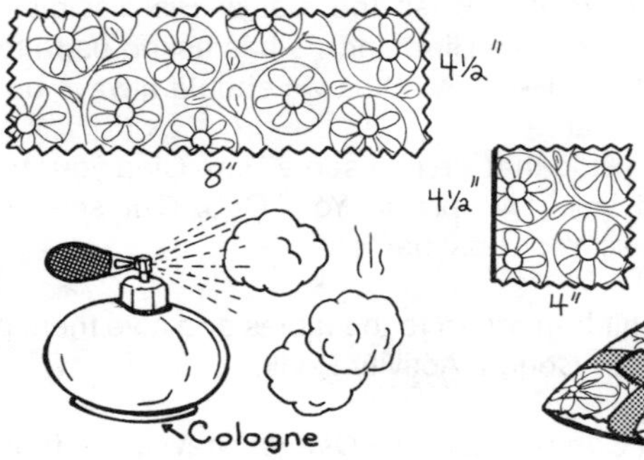

8-10. *A Basket Full of Love:* Ask your grocer if you might purchase large pint-size plastic vegetable or fruit containers for your class. Be sure the containers have a basket weave construction. Choose several colors of ribbon; ¼" ribbon should fit inside the lattice work of the basket. Encourage the children to weave their favorite colors of ribbon in and out around the basket. Weave ribbon around the top row, and bottom, and also center, if you choose. The more ribbon, the prettier the basket will be. After the basket is woven, cut squares of paper to fit each basket. Have the children to write notes of praise to God across the bottom of each paper or use the verse in Psalm 86:12.

Tell the children to think of someone special to give the notes to. Before giving the basket full of love, write one special job of service they intend to do for this person. Encourage them to tell the receiver they have been learning to be a servant.

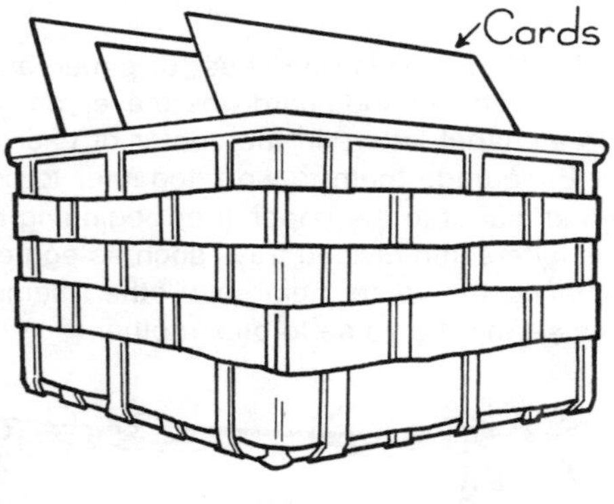

Shuttlebug Ride Home

Oh, I'm tired after this special day of learning to serve others. Let's get in the Shuttlebug and head for home.

On the journey home, review the events of the day, and lead the discussion toward servanthood. Ask the children what special ideas they will put into practice as servants at home. When you arrive at your destination, clap Your hands and praise God once more by saying, "We praise You, God, that we can serve. We praise Your holy name."

Closing Prayer

We praise You, God, for Jesus, Who was willing to come to earth and live among men. He taught us so many things as He lived on the earth. We especially praise You for His lesson about serving. Help us to remember His example and try to live like He did. Help us to take opportunities to serve others. In Jesus' name, amen.

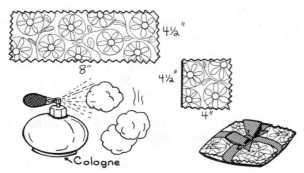

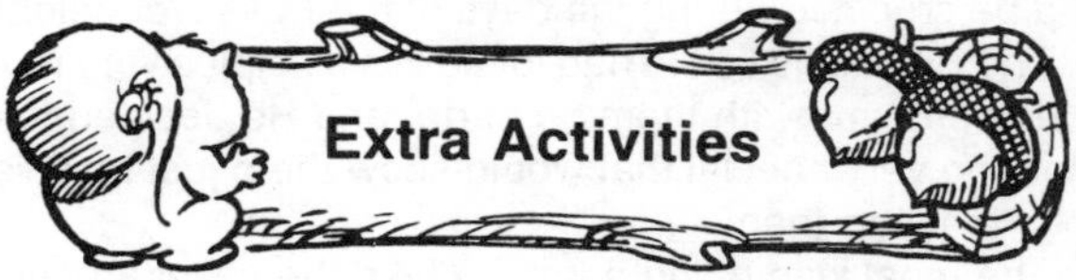

Extra Activities

Excessive Servanthood: Divide the class into two teams for this relay. At one end of the room, place two sets of the following: Broom, wastebasket, a scarf, a dust cloth, and spray bottle of water.

The teams will line up fifteen feet away from their set of objects. The game is played when the signal is given to start. The first person in each team must run to the objects. Put on the apron and scarf, dust the table, sweep the floor, put the paper in the waste basket, and spray the air pretending to clean a window. After going through all the motions, take off the apron and scarf, remove the paper from the trash can, and return to the end of the line. The first team to have every member complete the relay sits down and is declared the winner.

Who Is the Servant?: Line the chairs up in a straight line. Have the students sit down and number the students beginning with number one and continuing through the number of students present. (Place the numbers on the chairs.) Tell the class that each student must remember his or her number. The leader calls a number. (We will use number three as an example.) The person with that number stands and says, "Who, Sir? Me, Sir?" before the leader can say, "Number Three to the foot." (This is in reference to the end of the line of chairs.) If number three was successful at speaking first, the leader says, "Yes, sir, you, sir." Number three then says, "No, Sir, not me, sir," and the leader replies "Who then, Sir?" Number three calls another number, and the game begins again. If number three was not able to say, "Who sir? Me, sir?" before the leader said, "Number three to the foot," number three must go to the end of the line and everyone moves up and changes numbers. The chairs always remain the same number. So everyone who has to move, must remember a *new* number.

Note: This game works best with older children, and with a class of at least 10 students.

Lesson 13

Praise God for His Plan

Scripture: John 14:1-3

Psalm References: Psalm 111:9, 10; 101:1, 2; 103:13-22; Psalm 150:6 (Pause-to-Praise verse)

Memory Verse: We give thanks to you, Lord God Almighty, who is and who was, because you have taken your great power and have begun to reign.—Revelation 11:17 (NIV)

Lesson Aim: As a result of studying this lesson, the children should be able to
1) Know that God has planned for them to live someday with Him.
2) Know that Jesus will return.
3) Feel anticipation instead of fear of Christ's return.
4) Tell how he or she feels about Jesus' return.
5) Praise God for providing a plan for man.
6) Sing or say the memory verse, Revelation 11:17.

Materials Needed:
Pre-session. *Activi-Tree:* Slips of paper with the following suggestions attached to the tree before class. Be sure there is one paper for each child in the class.

- Help prepare the snack during snack time.
- Drive the Shuttlebug to Critter County.
- Be Sydney, the announcer, during Critter County on Radio.
- Hold the Wonders-of-God's-World box during Bible story time.
- Read John 14;1-3 during Bible story time.
- Choose one song to sing during Songs of Praise.

Heaven to Me: Magazine pictures, paper, glue, scissors, and crayons.

Preparation for Pause To Praise: Bible, magazine pictures, construction paper, and glue.

Together Time. The Heaven-to-Me scroll made during Pre-session.

Snack Time. Krispie Rice treats and fruit juice

Bible Story Time. Picture of family eating, picture of Last Supper; Wonders-of-God's-World box containing a sandal, money bag, plastic rooster, plastic dove, praying hands, and handkerchief.

Light Post on Memory Lane. Paper and pencils or markers.

Crafts.
5-8. *"Jesus Is Coming" Bumper Stickers:* Self-sticking shelf paper (any design), self-sticking shelf paper (clear), white butcher paper, markers, and cellophane tape.

8-10. *Wallet Witness:* Manila paper, credit card, pencils, newspaper, marker, small picture or sticker of face of Jesus, self-sticking clear shelf paper.

Extra Activities. *Glory-Hallelujah Band:* Rhythm instruments made during the past weeks of class, music, choruses.
To Go or Stay: Table, masking tape, ping-pong ball.

Welcome the Children
Greet each child by name as you welcome them to our last visit in Critter County. Tell them we will be talking about the most exciting event ever. Encourage them to choose a slip from the Activi-Tree and follow the instructions. Introduce any new student to one other child and the teacher in the activity center he/she chooses. Encourage each student to do their best and to ask for help if they need special assistance completing their assignment from the Activi-Tree.

Pre-session Activities
Activi-Tree. See the beginning of this lesson for suggestion of activities to place on the tree. Add special activities unique to your class situation. Be sure each student has a responsibility before choosing an activity center. Let the child know you are confident he or she can complete their responsibility with success.

Heaven to Me. Have a piece of butcher paper large enough to fit the length of one of the tables in your room. (Or choose a large work area in the hall.) Divide the paper by drawing lines to give each child in the class his own section. Write the words "Heaven to Me" across the top of the paper. Give the children magazines, markers and/or crayons. Have each child draw pictures or glue pictures from the magazines that show what things he hopes will be in Heaven or what he expects Heaven to be like.

Talk with the children about their thoughts concerning Heaven. Listen carefully to their conversation. You may hear something you will need to address during Together Time or Bible Story Time later. Save the paper to share with the class during Together Time. Roll it together to resemble a scroll.

Preparation for Pause to Praise. Have one child read Psalm 150:6. Quiz the children by asking,"How many things you can remember praising God for since we began studying in Critter County? How many instruments of praise do you remember?"

Let them work as a group to make one more collage for the scrapbook or give them individual papers for each to make his own. Use the magazines to cut pictures of breathing creatures mentioned in the verse. (If it breathes, cut it out!) Try to use many pictures of different people from various lands. Cover the entire page leaving room only to write, "Let everything that has breath, praise the Lord". Add one of these collages to the scrapbook and then add one more page that has large letters spelling out, "Praise The Lord!" The scrapbook should now contain the complete Psalm. Allow the group to read the book from beginning to end. Be sure to follow closely the words from a New International Version of the Bible to be sure you have correctly copied each phrase.

Pause to Praise: Have one child read Psalm 150:6. Have one child explain the collages made during the activity center. Talk about all the reasons to praise God we have discussed since our first class in Critter County.

If you have saved one instrument made each class period, hand out the instruments to each of the students. Assign each student a phrase from Psalm 150. As each child says the part of the chapter he is assigned, have one student turn the pages of the scrapbook. All the instruments are played together following the first two verses. When the instruments are mentioned, the child with that phrase will hold up and shake, strum, or blow into the instrument. All instruments are played together again after the closing verse, "Praise the Lord".

Allow every student to sign the last page. Display the book if you have a special parent night or closing program. Close this session by clapping your hands and saying, "We praise you, God, our Creator and Lord. We praise Your holy name!"

Together Time: Bring the Heaven to Me scroll made during Pre-session. Talk about Heaven as you ask the children what they know about it and where they believe it is located. Have each child explain his thoughts about Heaven as he expressed them on the paper.

Tell the children we will be talking more about Heaven as the class continues. Tell them to continue thinking about Heaven and remember any questions they will want to ask later.

Read Psalm 103:13-22 and close this session by saying that we may not know when Jesus is coming to take us to Heaven, but we can keep praising Him until we see Him. Praise God by clapping your hands and saying, "We praise You, God, Our Creator and Lord, We praise Your holy name!"

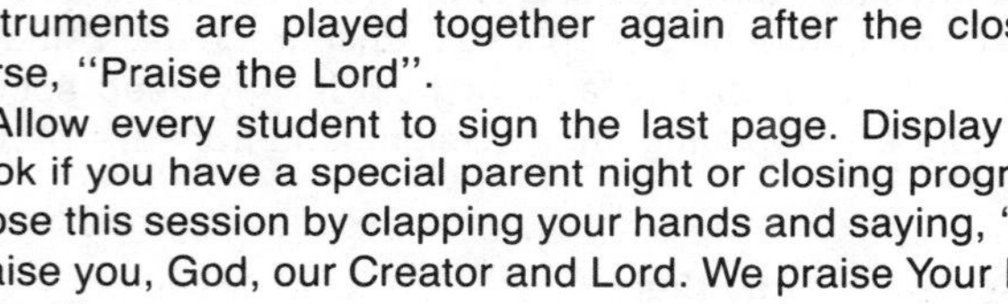

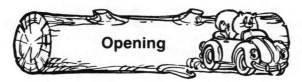

Well, we may not know when we'll take that trip to Heaven, but we do know we have a journey to take to Critter County today. Everybody into the Shuttlebug! We'll take our last ride to visit Sydney and his friends. Let's see how many stories we remember hearing during our visits as our driver drives for us today. (Call on the children by name as you ride and see if each will share his or her favorite story.)

Oh! There is Critter County up ahead. So much sharing has made this trip a very fast one. We're stopping at Lester and Liona Lou's house today. I wonder what Lunchbox can tell us about what is happening now. Let's go find out.

Sometimes life in this world gets so mixed up. We might wonder what it would be like to be alive when Jesus comes back to take us to live with Him. Lunchbox can understand that feeling a little bit. He has some very anxious moments just before his daddy comes to save him from trouble. Let's listen.

Please Hurry Back

"Good night, Lunchbox," said Liona Lou as she tucked her young son in bed. "Sleep tight and remember, Daddy will be back from his trip when you wake up in the morning."

Little Lunchbox reached up and turned out his night light. "Good night, Mother. I can't wait to see what Daddy's surprise is. I just hope he remembers to bring me something."

Liona Lou smiled because she knew that Lester had gotten Lunchbox a new soccer ball.

'Oh, I'm quite sure that your Daddy won't forget to bring his boy something special. Now you go to sleep, and we'll all have a good breakfast together," she said.

After a few minutes, Lunchbox was able to go to sleep. His mother read the latest issue of her favorite magazine, "Better Dens and Gardens." Then, she fixed herself a bowl of warm milk, lapped it right up, and decided to go to bed.

I'll leave the light on above the sink so Lester will know I was thinking of him when he pulls the car into the driveway, she thought.

She went upstairs and thought to herself, *It's so late and I'm too tired to take a shower. I think I'll just take a cat bath and go to sleep. Oh, I wish I could stay awake until Lester gets home, but I'm just so sleepy."*

Only minutes later, she was all curled up and quickly fell sound asleep. About an hour later, something strange began to happen in the kitchen. When Liona Lou had left the light on, she didn't know there was something wrong with one of the wires inside the light. The outside of the wire that protects it had worn away. On this night, because it had been left on for so long, it began to get very, very hot. Soon, a small amount of smoke began to curl and rise from the wire. A couple of minutes passed. Then more smoke began to rise up from behind the light, and it began to fill the kitchen. If someone had been downstairs, they would have seen it. They could have called the Critter County Fire Department. But both Liona Lou and Lunchbox were sleeping upstairs. No one knew that serious trouble was cooking in the kitchen.

Quickly the smoke filled the kitchen and then poured into the living room. It was so thick that if anyone had been in the room, they wouldn't have been able to breathe. Then, the smoke began to wind and curl up the steps. Fortunately, Lunchbox and Liona Lou each had their doors closed so it was harder for the smoke to get inside their rooms. Soon the entire hall and even the bathrooms were filled with the black smoke.

What would happen? If the lions didn't wake up, the smoke would surely go into their rooms, and they wouldn't be able to breathe. It would only take a few moments and dear Liona Lou and little Lunchbox would be dead.

Then it happened. The smoke found the crack under Lunchbox's door. It began to creep into the lion's room. It swept across the floor and then up the sides of his bed. The lion cub slept on.

Outside and just down the road came Lester's car chugging along. Of course, Lester didn't know his family was in so much trouble or he would have hurried. Instead, he was singing and whistling and taking his merry time.

By this time, the smoke was nearly filling Lunchbox's room. The little lion began to cough and choke. Still, he did not wake up. In only a few more minutes, he would not be able to breathe.

Lester's car rounded the bend in the road. He thought, *Oh, how sweet of Liona Lou to leave the light on for me. Hey, that light in the kitchen looks really strange.*

He had so sooner thought these words and he said out loud, "Oh no, our house is on fire!"

Quick as a wink, he turned off the car's engine and tried to open the kitchen door. But the thick smoke made him close the door again.

"Oh, no, I can't get in. What am I going to do?" he shouted.

Inside, Liona Lou heard her husband's screams and looked outside.

"Hurry and climb out onto the tree limb. The house is filled with smoke," instructed Lester.

As Liona Lou did just that, Lester went over and yelled, "Lunchbox, wake up. Hurry, son, wake up and come to the window."

The smoke was so thick that Lunchbox couldn't open his eyes. So he got down on all four paws an crawled over to the window. "Help, Daddy, I can't see!"

Lester yelled back, "It's OK. Just jump! You can trust me. I'll catch you.

So Lunchbox stood on his windowsill with his eyes closed tight. He counted to three and jumped. He landed safely in his daddy's arms. His daddy had returned home just in time to save his life.

Have all the children go to the tables and give them page 31 from the Critter County activity book.

5-8. *Lester Saves Lunchbox:* Look carefully at the picture. Outline with a crayon all the triangles you see in this picture of Lester saving Lunchbox from the terrible fire.

8-10. *Safe:* Look carefully at the code and sample puzzle. Now use the code to discover the message in the puzzle. Write the letters on the lines provided. (Answer: Lunchbox was saved from the fire by his daddy.)

When all have finished the activity sheets, have the children go to the Critter County Radio Station and sit on the floor in front of it. Remember to have the child who chose the responsibility from the Activi-Tree to be the announcer. You will need only Sydney to be the announcer today.

Sydney: WCC listeners, I want you today to think just a moment about the word, "return." When I finish the news or the weather, I usually let you know that we are returning you to our regular program. I'm simply letting you know that I have finished what I needed to do, and I am returning, or taking you back, to what you were doing before. Boys and girls, have your Mother or Dad ever gone on a trip? They hated to leave you, but they had to. And as soon as they had finished what they were doing, they returned to you! I rarely like good-byes, but I sure like returns! We at **WWCC** would like to thank you for returning to join us each week here on our station. We've done our best to make it an enjoyable time for you, and it's something that we've come to look forward to!

Children like crispy rice treats made form cereal and marshmallow topping. Make these before class and serve them with fruit juice as you talk with the children about their favorite snacks. Will there be snacks in Heaven? Will there be any food at all? Ask questions just to see what the children are thinking. Tell them you are glad God didn't tell us everything about Heaven because it will make things even more special when we can enjoy the surprises He will share. After clean up, have the children return to the Story area.

Play the song "Sing Praise to Him," page 140, as the children assemble in the story area. when all have gathered, sing the song together.

Sing: Allow the children to choose their favorite songs from this series of lessons. "How Much Do You Love," page 134; "O Give Thanks," page 128; "We Give Thanks," page 121; "My God Will Meet All Your Needs," page 123; and

"Seek First His Kingdom," page 127.

Prayer Song: "Hear Us as We Pray," page 143.

Prayer: Ask God to help the children understand that today's lesson is about the best promise of all. Help them to listen as we talk about how Jesus will come back to take us to be with Him.

One of my favorite times in the day to be with my family is meal time. (Show the picture of the family eating.) It seems like everyone is anxious to enjoy the supper and talk about all the events that have happened in the day.

During our last class time together, we talked about how Jesus washed the disciples feet when they met together for supper.

Today's lesson was given during that same meal. It is often called the "Last Supper". (Show picture.) Jesus had so many things to tell his disciples. They met together in a room at the top of a building, and they listened to Jesus all evening.

(Have the Wonders-of-God's-World box prepared with the items mentioned at the beginning of this lesson.) During the time they spent together, (Take sandal from box.) Jesus washed the disciples feet. (Remove money bag.) He sent Judas away to turn Jesus over to the rulers for the money they had promised him. (Remove rooster.) He told Peter he would say he did not know Jesus. (Remove dove.) He promised the Holy Spirit would come to be with the disciples when Jesus was gone. (Remove handkerchief.) He promised them they would only be sad for a little while and then they would be happy again. (Remove praying hands.) And He prayed for the disciples.

We're going to pretend that we are the disciples and we are having this meal with Jesus. (Give each one of the children one of the disciples names, if you choose.) We have seen Him wash our feet. He has eaten with us. He has sent Judas away, and now, He is talking about going away himself.

Jesus Will Return
John 14:1-3

Peter becomes upset because Jesus says He will only be with us a little while longer. He hears Jesus tell us that we are to love one another so that all men will know we are His disciples. Peter finally asks Jesus where He is going. Jesus doesn't tell him. He says only, "Peter, where I am going, you cannot follow now, but you will follow later".

Peter is so disappointed. He asks why he will not be allowed to follow ,and he tells Jesus he is willing to die for Him.

Peter is saying what all of us feel. None of us want Jesus to leave us. We want Him to stay and be our teacher. We do not understand why He has to go away.

Jesus tells Peter that before the rooster crows tonight, Peter will say three times that he does not even know who Jesus is. This causes Peter to be very sad. But, then Jesus shares the most wonderful news.

Let's pretend that (child who looked up Scripture) is Jesus. Listen to the words Jesus spoke to His disciples. (Allow child to read John 14:1-3.)

Jesus said two important things in those verses. Did you listen carefully? What did you hear Him say. (Allow children to explain: 1. He is going away to prepare a place for us, and 2. He is coming back again.)

Jesus knew what the disciples were thinking and feeling about His leaving them. They did not understand that He was going to die. They just knew they did not want Him to go away.

And so, He tried to help them feel better. He told them He was going to prepare a place for them so they could be with Him again.

Now, how do you suppose the disciples felt after hearing this? (Allow time for discussion.)

I know it makes me feel wonderful inside to know Jesus is making a place for me to live with Him. But . . . we need to remember that that is not all He said. Jesus went on to say, I will come back and take you to be with me that you also may be where I am.

Application: Boys and girls, what have we learned about the promises Jesus makes? (Allow time for them to explain Jesus keeps His promises.) When Jesus said this, was He just wanting the disciples to feel better? Or, does He intend to keep this promise? (Allow time for discussion.)

Help the children to know Jesus meant every word. He has been away preparing a home for all who will follow Him. Clap your hands and praise Him by saying, "We praise You, God, our Creator and Lord. We praise Your holy name!"

I want you to think back with me to our very first lesson and try to remember as many lessons as you can. (Place pictures of praise or craft objects around the room. They will serve as reminders.) Give the children time to recall as many lessons as they can.

Tell the children that every lesson was important because each event was part of God's plan. We needed to learn about each before we could understand the lesson for today.

God made the world. He created man to live in His world. Man disobeyed God and had to be taught how to live lives that would please Him. People needed to trust God's wisdom to provide for their needs, to take care of them as they lived, to help them make the right choices and to help them lead others to Him. Jesus came to be an example to man. He healed the sick; He raised the dead. He provided for forgiveness. He taught us how to be servants to one another. He showed us how very much God loves us.

All these lessons were part of God's plan. He has allowed the world to exist for man. He is preparing another place for man to live with Him forever.

I praise God for all He has done for us and all He has taught us in His Word. It will be the most wonderful day when Jesus comes to take us to our new home. Let's praise Him together, one more time. Clap your hands and say, "We praise You, God, our Creator and Lord. We praise Your holy name!"

Have the children go to the tables and give them page 32 from the Critter County activity book.

5-8. *A Special Message:* Begin with the letter **J** in the box in the center. Follow the arrows and write down each letter on the lines provided. (The message: Jesus is coming back again!)

8-10: *Word Search:* Find each of the words printed below in the word search puzzle. Look upl, down, backwards, across, and diagonally. *Special Messages:* Begin with the letter **J** in the center. Follow the arrows to discover two important messages. Write the letters on the lines provided. (Messages: 1. Jesus is coming back again! 2. He is preparing a place for me!)

When all have finished the activity papers, have them go to the Light Post on Memory Lane.

Explain that there are many ways to travel. We can go by car, boat, bus, taxi or plane. There is only one way we'll get to Heaven and that is by accepting Jesus and living for Him. He will come back to take us the way He plans for us to go. However, today, we are going to send His words by plane.

Give every student an 8½" x 11" sheet of paper. In five minutes, everyone must try to create a paper airplane and write the words to the memory verse somewhere on the plane.

Line the students up at one end of the room. Launch the planes and watch where they land. The owner of the plane that went the farthest is called upon to recite the memory verse. If he cannot, he removes his plane and waits for the second launch. The next student in line who's airplane is now the farthest takes a turn at saying the memory verse. Continue until all have said the verse. Begin a new launch after eliminating all those who cannot say the verse.

Sing, "My God Will Meet All Your Needs," on page 123.

5-8. Bumper Sticker: Give each child a piece of designed self-sticking shelf paper cut 3' x 15", one piece of white butcher paper cut 2½" x 14", and one piece of clear self sticking shelf paper cut 3" x 15". DO NOT PEEL THE BACK FROM THE DESIGNED SHELF PAPER.

Let the children write the words, (or teachers may help younger students) "Jesus Is Coming Again" and the Scripture reference John 14:1-3 under these words in the center of the butcher paper. Decorate around the lettering using markers and/or stickers. When a child is happy with his design, place this white sheet in the center of the designed shelf paper forming a border around the white sheet. Secure this with cellophane tape on each edge so it will not move when placing the clear shelf paper on top.

Peel the backing from the clear shelf paper and press this piece over the entire bumper sticker.(A teacher should assist.) Smooth out all the air bubbles to read clearly, "Jesus Is Coming Again". Encourage the children to take their stickers home and let their parents peel the backing that remains before putting the sticker in place.

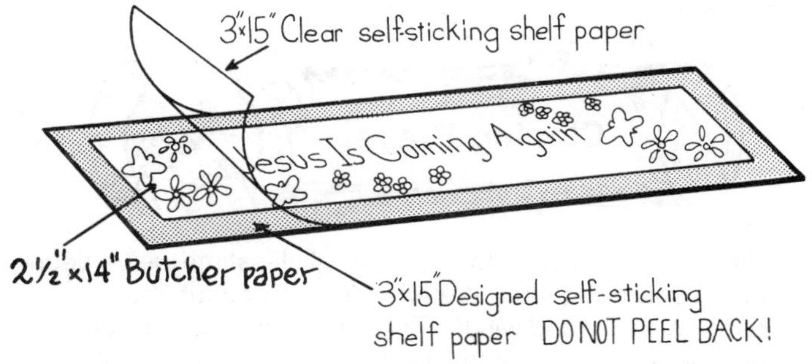

8-10. Wallet Witness: Give each child a card cut from old file folders. Use any credit card or driver's license as a pattern. Draw around the card and cut out the piece of file folder. Have the children draw around the file folder card on a piece of newspaper. Cut the newspaper and glue it to one side of the card. Write across the newspaper with red or any bold-color marker the words, "Great News". Turn the card over and place a picture of Jesus in the center and write the words, "Jesus Is Coming Again" somewhere above or below the picture. Peel the backing from the clear self-sticking shelf paper and cover the card entirely. Cut the excess shelf paper from the edges following the rim of the card.

Encourage the children to place this card in their billfold or give it to one of their parents to carry with other cards. Whenever searching for the proper credit card or looking through pictures, the "Wallet Witness" may provide an opportunity to talk to a new friend about Jesus. The great news is He *IS* coming again.!

Everyone to the Shuttlebug. It's time for our last ride home. This should be a sad ride knowing it is our last visit to

Critter County for awhile. But, you know what? After today's lesson, I know we really don't have anything to be sad about. We can all be happy as we think about Jesus coming again. I love to think about what Heaven will be like and how much time we will have to talk to all the people we've studied about. Aren't you anxious to meet Moses, David, the disciples, and Paul? Oh, we'll have so much to share. (Have the children take turns sharing who they will want to talk to first.)

Sing today's memory verse as you near the end of your journey.

We thank You, God, for this special classtime we've been able to share together. We have learned about Your greatness and power and wisdom. We have seen the lives of men and women who chose to follow You. God, we praise You for the plan You have shown us in Your Word. We praise You for sending Jesus to die for us so that we might come to live with You in Heaven. Thank You, God for loving us. Help us to remember the lessons we have learned. We praise You, God, our Creator and Lord. We praise Your holy name. In Jesus' name, amen.

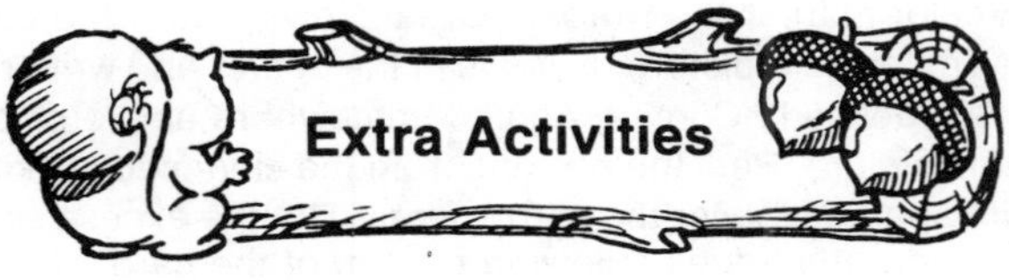

Glory-Hallelujah Band: Use the instruments you have made during the last few weeks of class and collect any rhythm instruments you can find. Play music on a tape recorder and try to keep the rhythm with all the instruments playing along.

Take turns choosing your favorite songs and memory verse choruses and allow the children to play as everyone sings. Emphasize that this special time of praise is to be a celebration of Jesus' return.

To Go or Stay: Have the children seated around a table. Divide the table in half with a masking-tape line. The children on one half become the angels of Heaven. The children on the other side represent followers remaining on earth.

Explain to the children that we live wanting to go to Heaven, But we stay here on earth to serve God for as long as He allows us to live.

Place the ping-pong ball on the earth side of the table. The children on this side blow the ping-pong ball toward Heaven as the children on the other side blow the ping-pong ball toward earth.

Each time you play, give the ping pong ball the name of one member of the class. See how long that member serves on earth by how long it takes to blow the ball off the Heaven side of the the table. (The teacher might want to keep time with a stop watch.)

If the ball falls off the earth side, it is replaced on the earth side of the table, and the race continues. The ball must be blown off the Heaven side of the table while, at the same time, the angles of Heaven are trying to keep the ball (person serving on earth). Allow the children to rest between plays. The blowing will use more air and energy than they realize.

Critter County Program

A Time of Praise

This program has been written to provide flexibility as it brings an understanding of worship and praise to both the audience and participants.

It will be important for the program director to choose children who are good readers to fill the position of Narrators One and Two. Parts that require memorization should be given to the children early. The children who accept the monologue pieces should be encouraged to pretend they are the actual characters and try to convey, through expression and tone of voice, how they believe the character would feel about what is being said. The program will flow smoothly if everyone is committed to doing their best work.

The program has been designed to allow audience participation. You might find it helpful to provide a printed program that will instruct the audience. Or, the program director might choose to have a few words of explanation before the program begins.

We suggest using posterboard cut outs of creation to decorate the auditorium. Have the audience stand when they are singing or participating in the "litany". Allow trio groups or quartet groups to sing some of the songs suggested. Add favorite songs your children particularly enjoyed as they studied the lessons.

This program suggestion is a guideline. Add other Bible dramas or puppet sections. Remove monologues we have prepared and encourage some of the children to write their own.

Above all . . . enjoy the time you spend praising God with the children. Lift His name, read His Word and re-commit your life to His service. May His Name Be Praised!

Characters Needed:

Narrator One	Child Two
Narrator Two	Bible Child
Boy or Girl to present the world	Children to act out the Prodigal:
Noah	Father
Moses	Two Sons
Child One	Servants
Children of Praise—5 children	Friends
Scrapbook—2 children	Saul

A Time of Praise

All of the children file into the auditorium singing (or stand and sing) "Praise Ye the Lord" (page 116).

Narrator One: Read Psalm 117.
Praise the Lord, all you nations; extol him, all you peoples. For great is his love toward us, and the faithfulness of the Lord endures forever. Praise the Lord.

Narrator Two: Read Psalm 113:1-3.
Praise the Lord. Praise, O servants of the Lord, praise the name of the Lord. Let the name of the Lord be praised, both now and forevermore. From the rising of the sun to the place where it sets, the name of the Lord is to be praised.

Sing: "Clap Your Hands" (page 119)

Narrator One: During the class sessions we have studied thirteen lessons of Praise from the Scriptures. We invite you to join us as we share the memories, lessons and Scriptures we have discovered. Let's worship and praise God together.

Narrator Two: Please join us as we sing. (Choose a well-known hymn and sing as many verses as you feel is fitting. Be sure to give the page number in your hymnal.)

Narrator One: Read Psalm 105:1-4.
Give thanks to the Lord, call on his name; make known among the nations what he has done. Sing to him, sing praise to him; tell of his wonderful acts. Glory in his holy name; let the hearts of those who seek the Lord rejoice.

Presentation of World—(Boy dressed in blue choir robe and holding a globe, or girl in white with stars pinned to the robe holding globe.)
In the beginning God created the heavens and the earth. The Bible tells us that God is the creator of all living things. "Through Him all things were made; without him nothing was made that has been made." (John 1:3)

Sing: "Give Glory to the Lord" (page 137) and "The Heavens Are Telling" (page 114)

Narrator Two: Read Psalm 105:5, 7.
Remember the wonders he has done, his miracles, and the judgments he pronounced . . . He is the Lord Our God; his judgments are in all the earth.

Monologue One: Noah. (This child should be dressed authentically and carry a walking stick. A smaller child could stand beside Noah and hold a posterboard model of the Ark.)

Years passed after God First created man. He saw how wicked and sinful man had become, and the Scriptures say He grieved that He had ever created man. It humbles me to know that I found "favor" in His eyes.

God talked with me. He told me of His plan to destroy

man and remove him from the earth. He gave me instructions telling me how to build a large boat.

My three sons worked with me for many years, and when we finished, the ark was large enough to hold two of every living creature. I called the animals to the ark two by two.

My sons and their wives entered with their mother and I, and God closed the door to keep us safe from the terrible flood. My name is Noah.

Sing: "We Give Thanks" (page 121)

Monologue Two: Moses. (This child should be dressed authentically and hold the ten commandments. Smaller children could stand beside Moses holding posterboard figures of manna and birds that represent raven.)

The people of God had much to learn as they began to multiply on the earth. Walking with God and trusting Him brought them peace and prosperity. When they turned away from Him they found themselves bound by slavery and ruled by harsh kings.

God gave me the task of leading His people through the wilderness. For forty years they depended on God daily for bread (point to manna) and meat (point to raven) provided by His hand. As we walked ... we learned. My name is Moses, and I praise God for His faithfulness.

Child One: (This child is to be dressed in the type of clothing worn in the day of Moses and will quote Psalm 105:4.) "Look to the Lord and his strength; seek his face always."

Narrator One: Turn to Psalm 136:1-16, 23-26 in your Bibles. I invite you, the audience, to respond after each statement with the words of the Scripture, "His love endures forever."

Give thanks to the Lord, for he is good.
His love endures forever.
Give thanks to the God of gods.
His love endures forever.
Give thanks to the Lord of lords:
His love endures forever.
to him who alone does great wonders,
His love endures forever.
who by his understanding made the heavens,
His love endures forever.
who spread out the earth upon the waters,
His love endures forever.
who made the great lights—
His love endures forever.
the sun to govern the day,
His love endures forever.
the moon and stars to govern the night;
His love endures forever.
to him who struck down the firstborn of Egypt
His love endures forever.
and brought Israel out from among them
His love endures forever.
with a mighty hand and outstretched arm;
His love endures forever.
to him who divided the Red Sea asunder
His love endures forever.
and brought Israel through the midst of it,
His love endures forever.
but swept Pharaoh and his army into the Red Sea;
His love endures forever.
to him who led his people through the desert,
His love endures forever.
to the One who remembered us in our low estate
His love endures forever.
and freed us from our enemies
His love endures forever.
and who gives food to every creature.
His love endures forever.
Give thanks to the God of heaven.
His love endures forever.

Child of Praise: Read Psalm 139:1-4.
O Lord, you have searched me and you know me. You know when I sit and when I rise; you perceive my thoughts from afar. You discern my going out and my lying down; you are familiar with all my ways. Before a word is on my tongue you know it completely, O Lord.

Child of Praise: Read Psalm 139:7-10.
Where can I go from your Spirit? Where can I flee from your presence? If I go up to the heavens, you are there;If I make my bed in the depth, you are there. If I rise on the wings of the dawn, if I settle on the far side of the sea, even there your hand will guide me, your right hand will hold me fast.

Child of Praise: Read Psalm 139:14-16.
I praise you because I am fearfully and wonderfully made; your works are wonderful, I know that full well. My frame was not hidden from you when I was made in the secret place. When I was woven together in the depths of the earth, your eyes saw my unformed body. All the days ordained for me were written in your book before one of them came to be.

Child of Praise: Read Psalm 139: 17, 18, 23, 24.
How precious to me are your thoughts, O God! How vast is the sum of them! Were I to count them, they would out number the grains of sand. When I awake, I am still with you.

Search me, O God, and know my heart; test me and know my anxious thoughts. See if there is any offensive way in me and lead me in the way everlasting.

Narrator Two: Each time we met for class we studied one verse of Scripture from Psalm 150. We compiled a scrapbook that illustrates the Scripture.

Presentation of Scrapbook: (Allow two children to share the scrapbook. One could turn the pages while the other child reads the verses.)

Sing: "Sing Praise to Him" (page 140).

Child Two: Says from memory John 3:16.

Monologue Three: (Child dressed as a child in Jesus' day)

I grew up in the area of Nazareth and Galilee where Jesus lived. I loved playing on the hillsides where He taught, and I loved to visit the city of Jerusalem. I remember one day when I was very small. I went with my parents to hear this teacher the people called the Messiah. He spoke of loving our neighbor and being kind instead of returning evil for evil. On this day when Jesus had stopped teaching, my mother took me close to meet Him. The men who worked with Jesus thought He was too busy to bother with children. But, I will never forget how He picked up a small child beside me. He placed His hand on my back and told the men, "Let the children come to me and do not hinder them, for the kingdom of heaven belongs to such as these".

I love Jesus. And . . . when I grow up . . . I shall teach my children to love Him and serve Him also.

Sing: "The Builders" (page 120)

Narrator One: Read Psalm 119:9-11

How can a young man keep his way pure? By living according to your word. I will seek you with all my heart; do not let me stray from your commands. I have hidden your word in my heart that I might not sin against you.

A Bible Story: (Music plays as children prepare to present the story of The Prodigal Son.) This can be done with puppets or with children "walking through" the character's parts as the narration is read from Luke 15:11-24.

Sing: "Praise the Lord for His Forgiveness" (page 125) and "My God Will Meet All Your Needs" (page 123)

Narrator Two: Read Psalm 18:1-3.

I love you, O Lord, my strength. The Lord is my rock, my fortress and my deliverer; my God is my rock, in whom I take refuge. He is my shield and the horn of my salvation, my stronghold. I call to the Lord who is worthy of praise.

Monologue Four: Saul (dressed authentically)

"The Lord is my rock." How true those words are today! I am sorry that I was not always able to hear those words and understand. I thought the Christians were so foolish. I believed they were enemies of Rome and should be completely destroyed before the word of this Jesus they spoke of spread too far. I stood by and held the coats of my fellow countrymen as they stoned one of the Christian leaders named Stephen.

It wasn't until I was traveling to Damascus to arrest Christians and deliver them to Jerusalem that I fell down before the same Lord these Christians worshiped.

Jesus talked to me from Heaven and helped me see how wrong I had been. I went into Damascus and repented for three days before a man named Ananias came. He taught me more about Jesus and led me to be baptized that my sins might be washed away.

I am Saul. I turned from punishing Christians to joining them in praise. Together we watch for the return of Jesus Christ our Lord!

Child of Praise: Says from memory, Psalm 118:46.

The Lord Lives! Praise be to my Rock! Exhalted by God my Savior!

Sing: (Include the musical instruments made during class if possible)
"He Is the King" (page 141) and "Sing and Shout It" (page 136)

Closing Comments: By teacher or minister.

Everyone Sing: Select a hymn of praise that your congregation knows well from your church's hymnal.

Patterns

WWCC

1 Block = 1 Foot

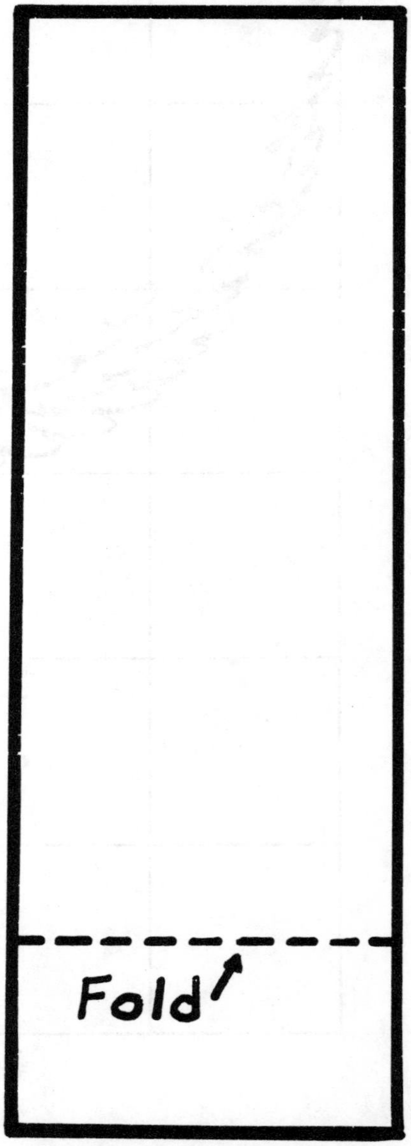
Fold

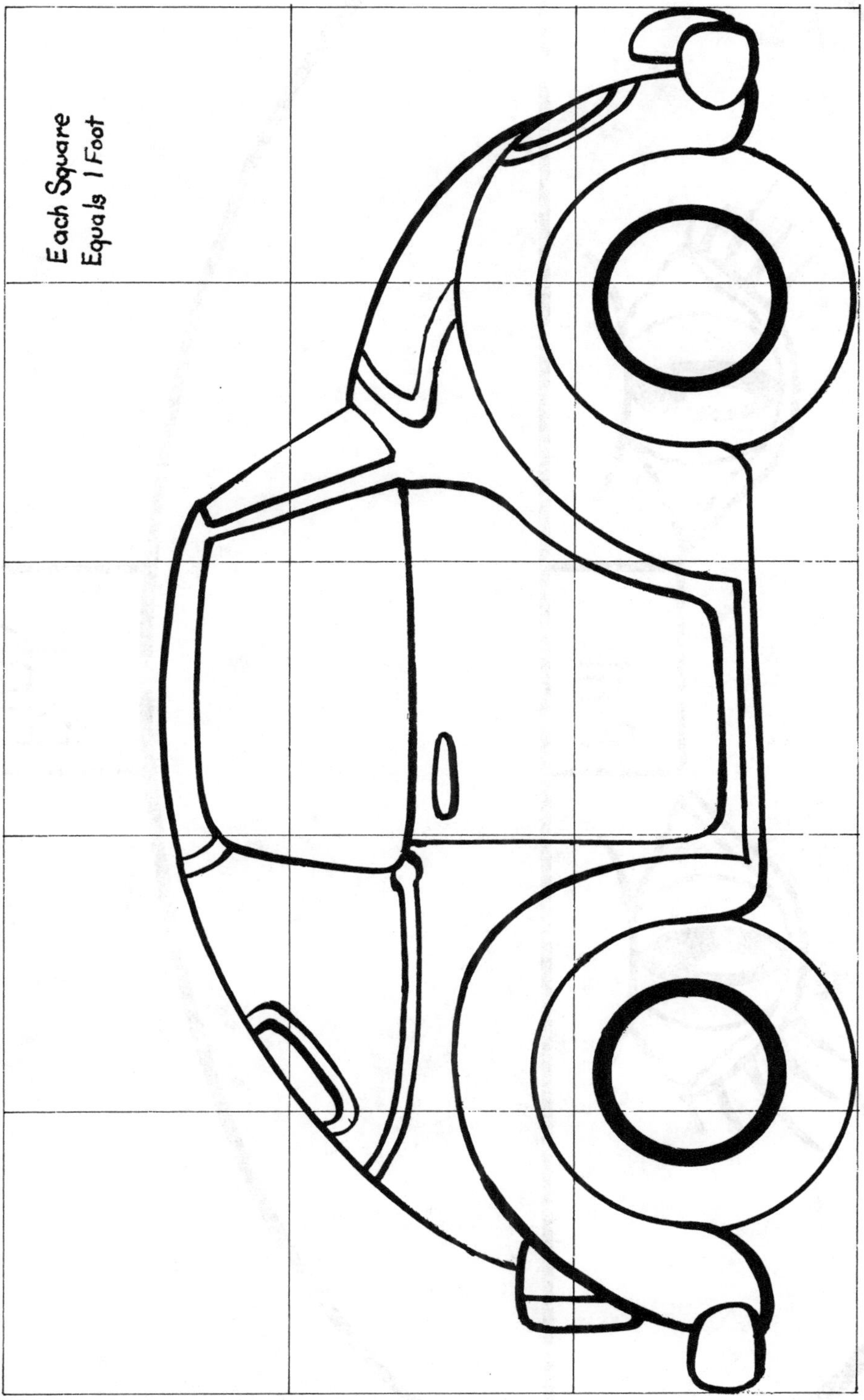
Each Square
Equals 1 Foot

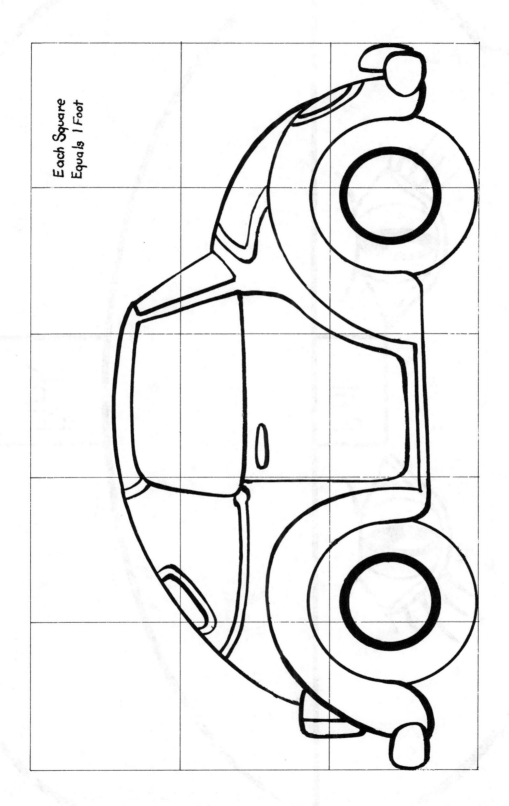

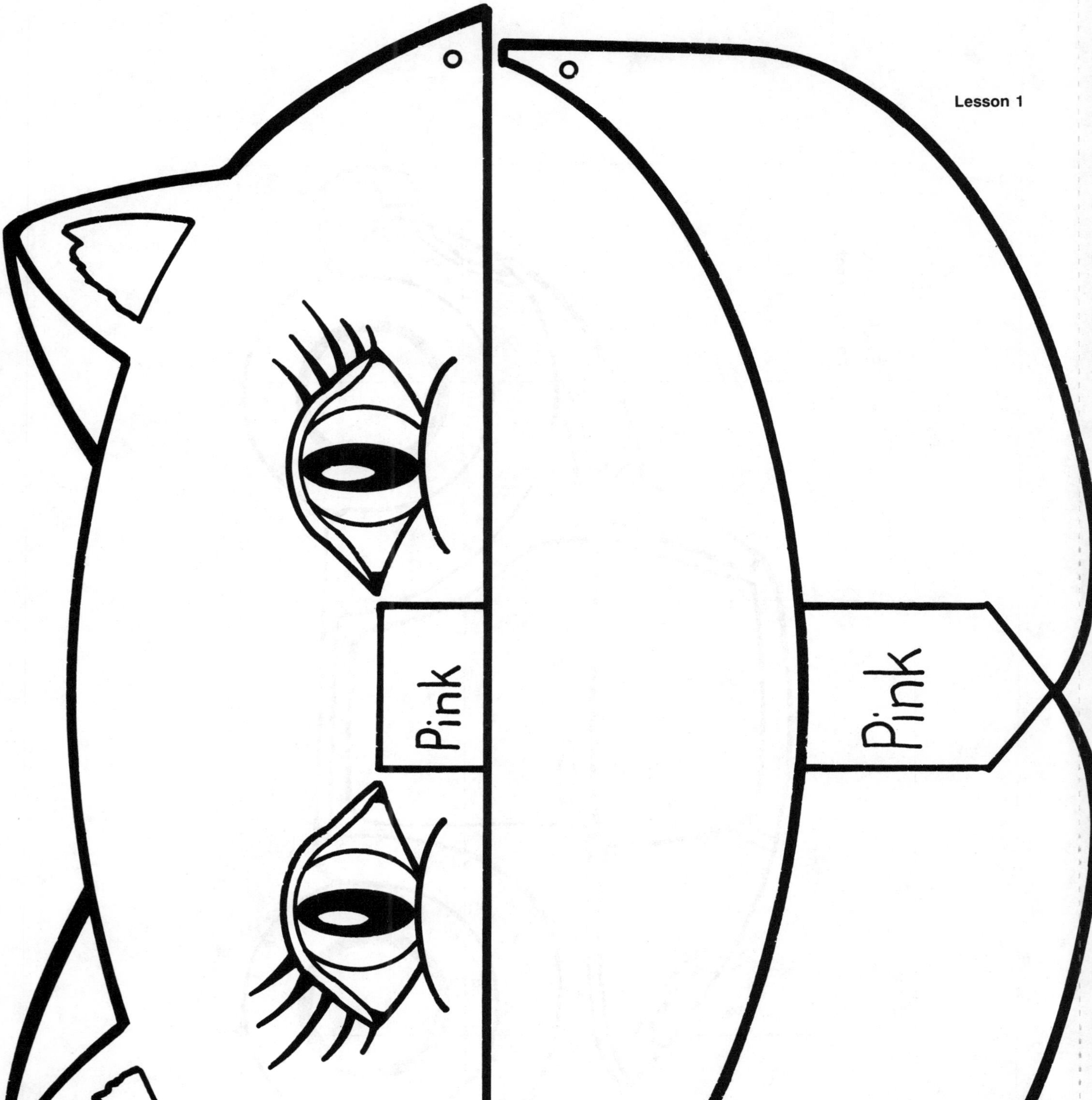
Pink
Pink

Lesson 3

Lesson 2

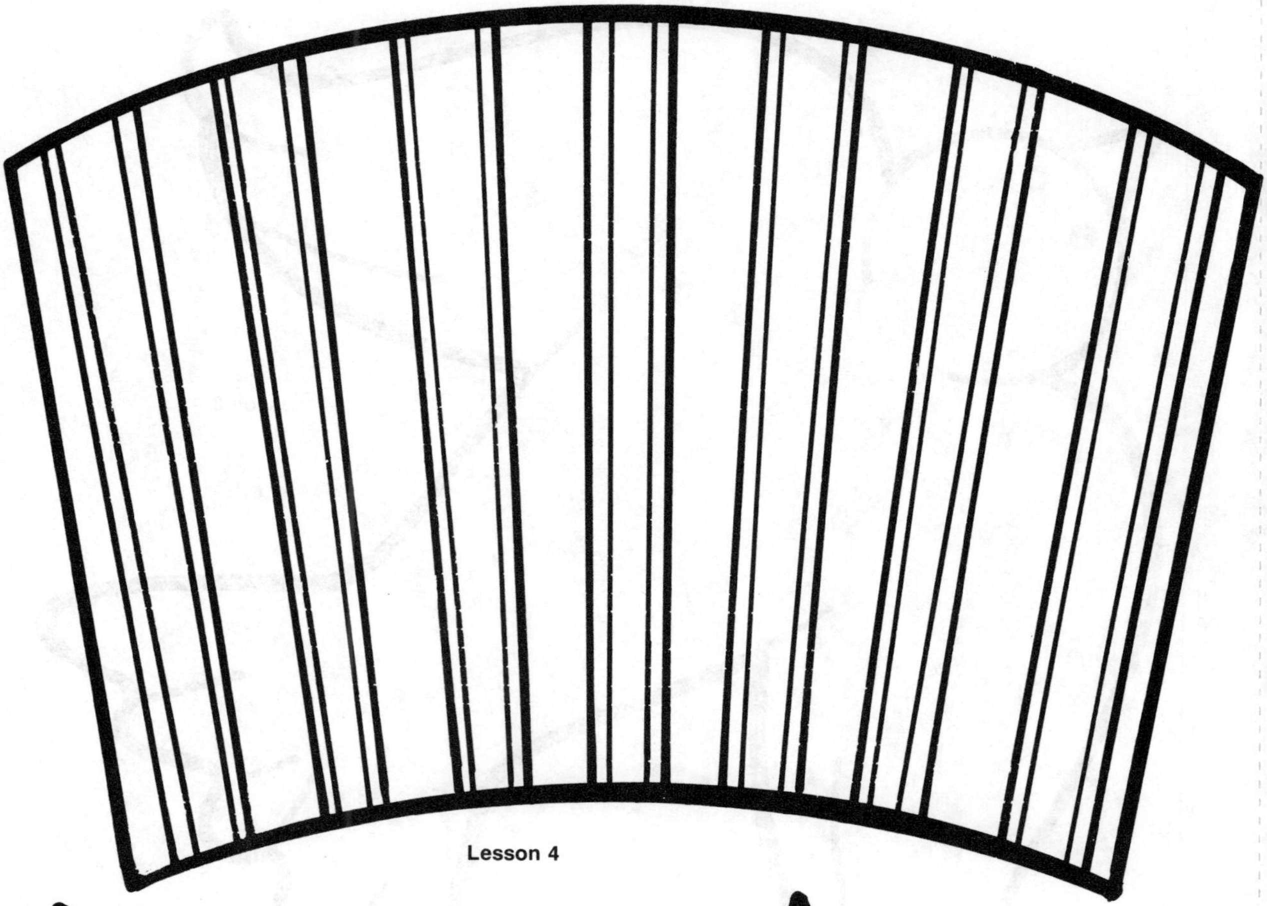

Lesson 4

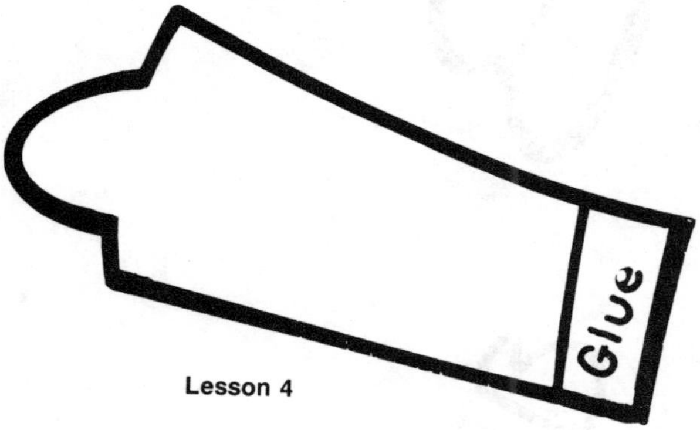

Lesson 4

Lesson 10

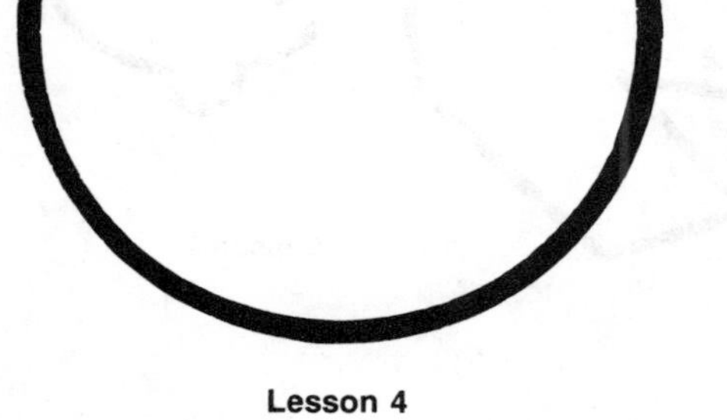

Lesson 4

Saul's friend

Lesson 11

Ananias

Lesson 11

Saul

Saul's friend

Lesson 11

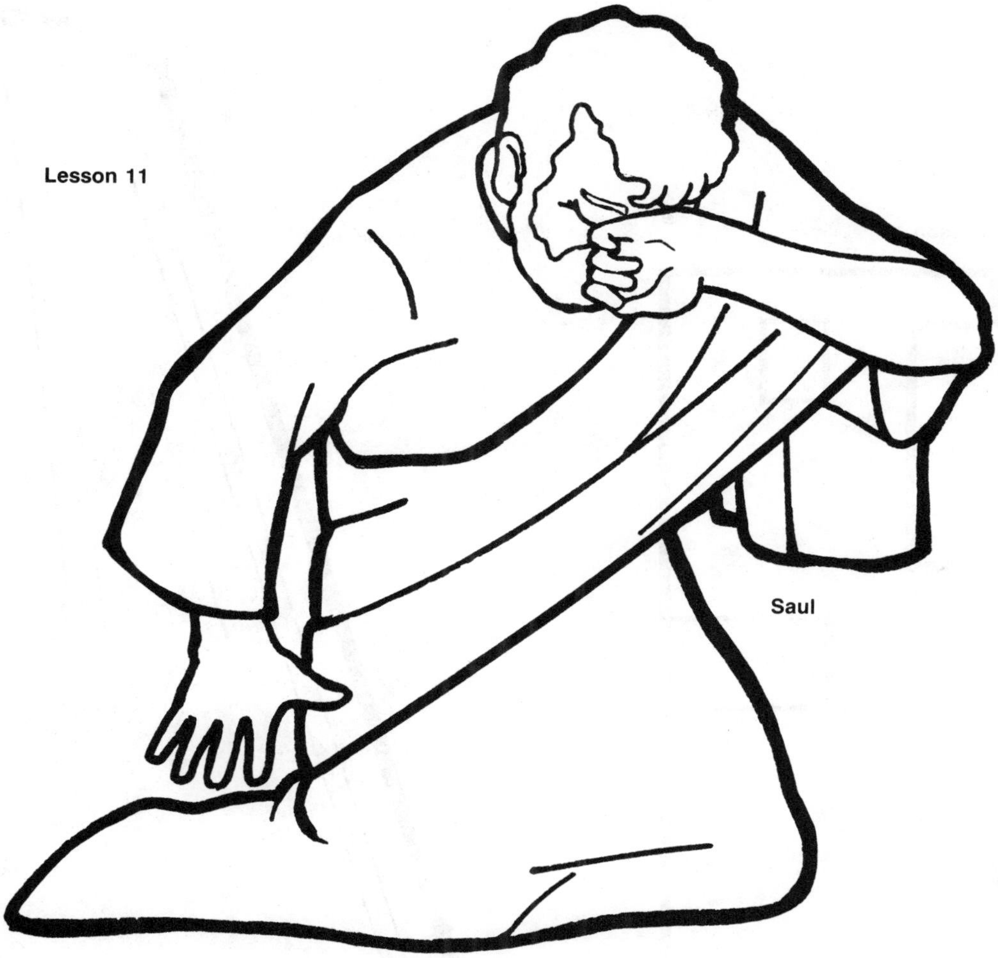

Saul

Lesson 11

pool

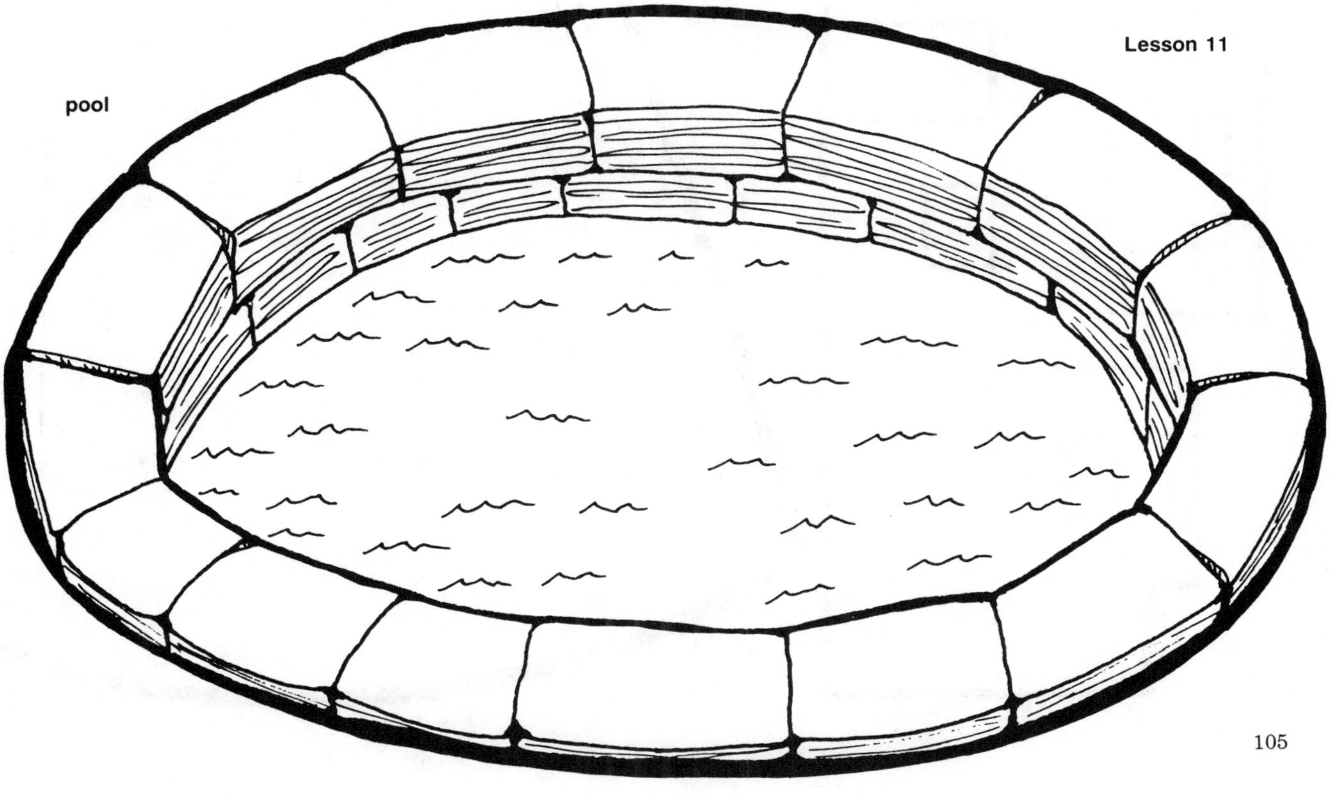

Lesson 11

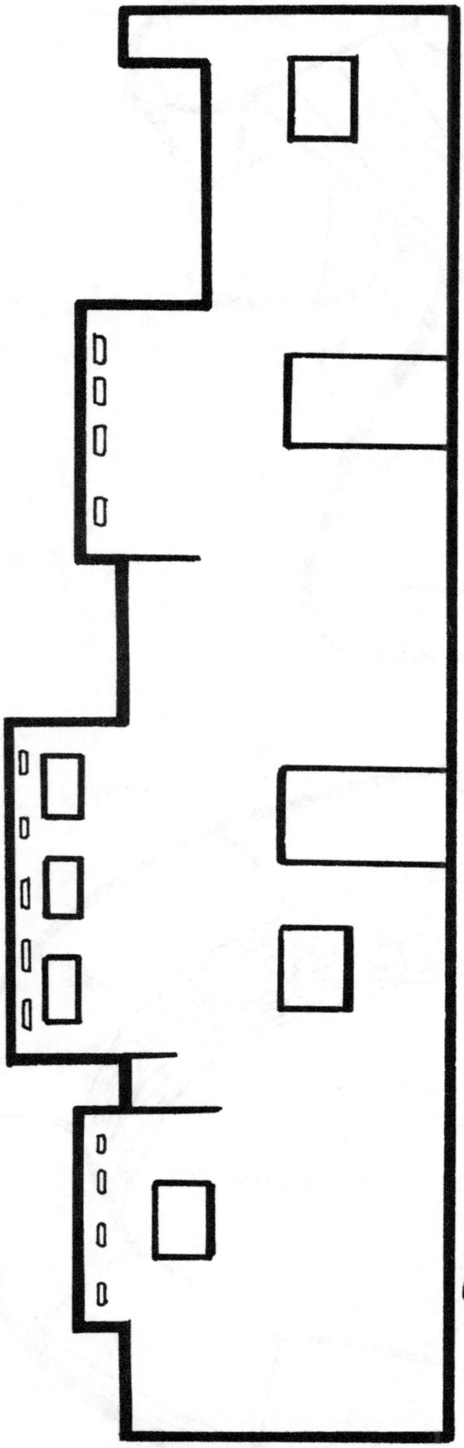

Lesson 11

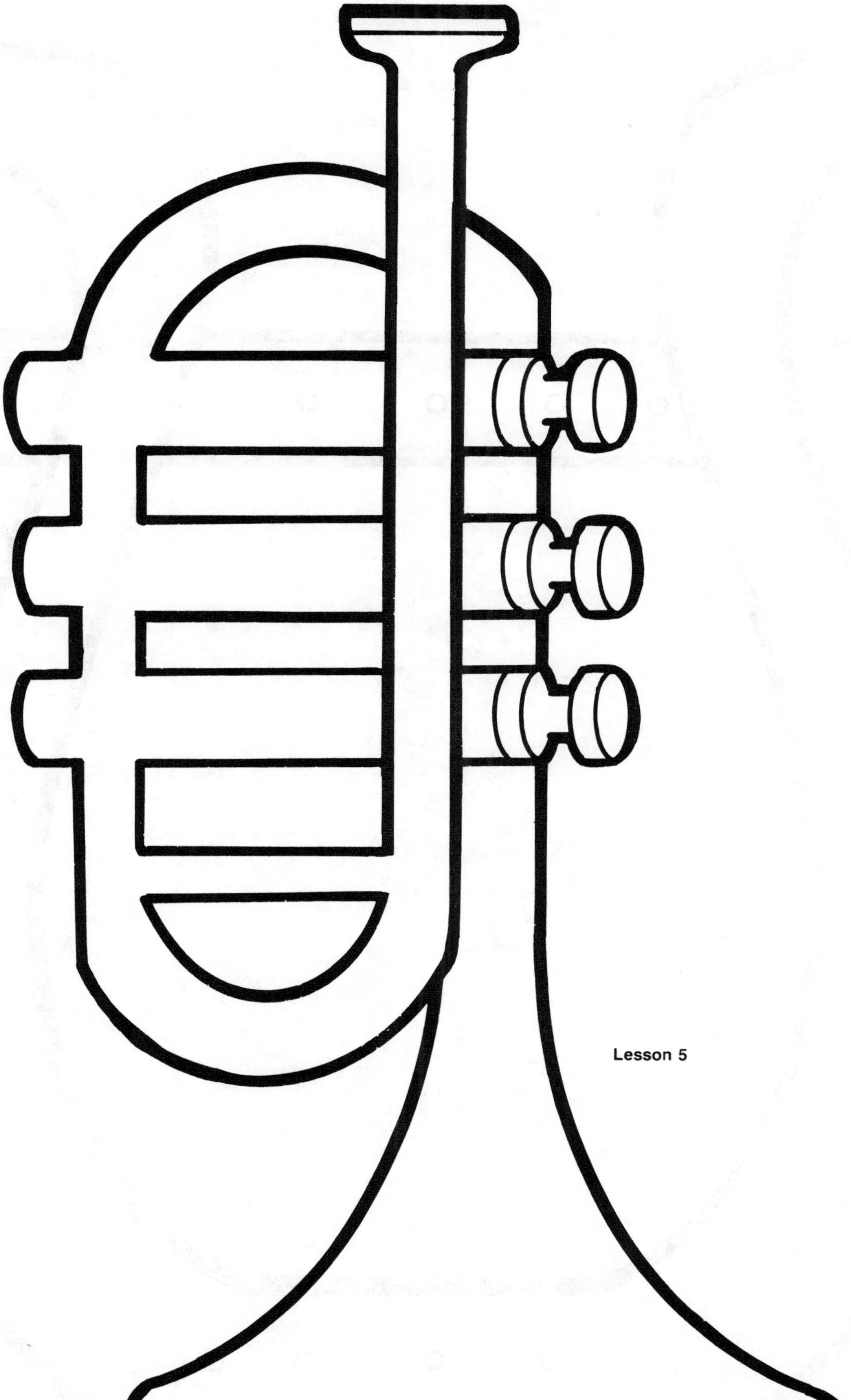

Lesson 5

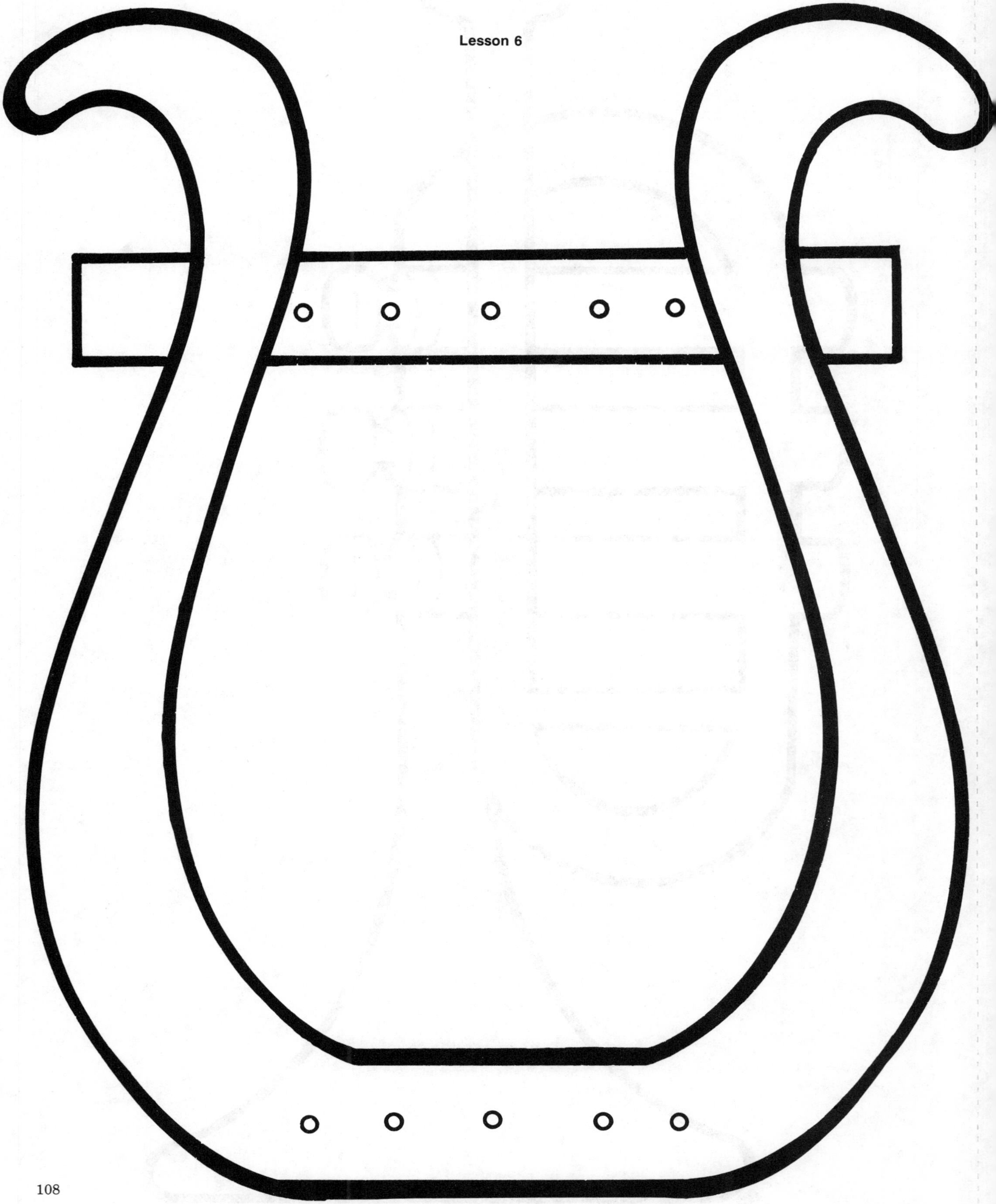

Jesus Brings Life

Lesson 10

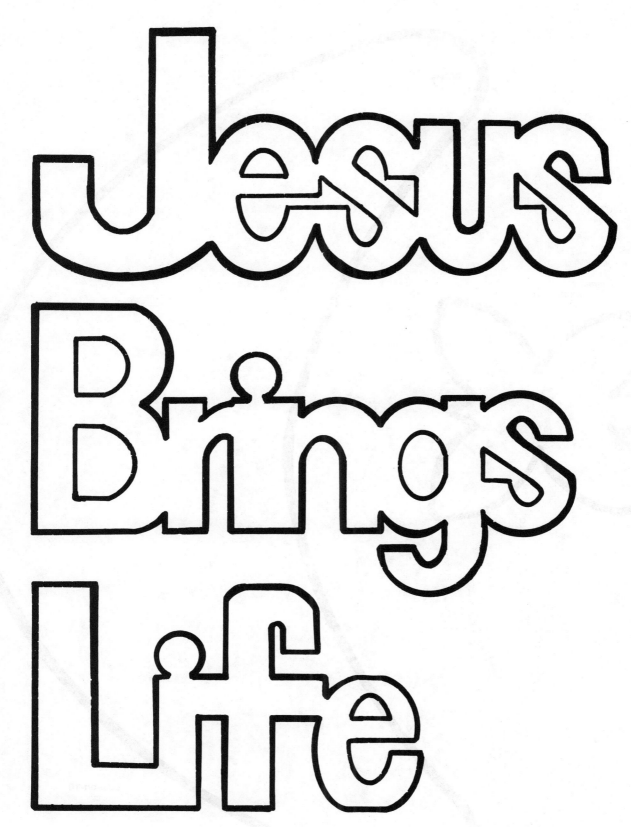

Lesson 10

Lesson 10

Lesson 7

Lesson 10

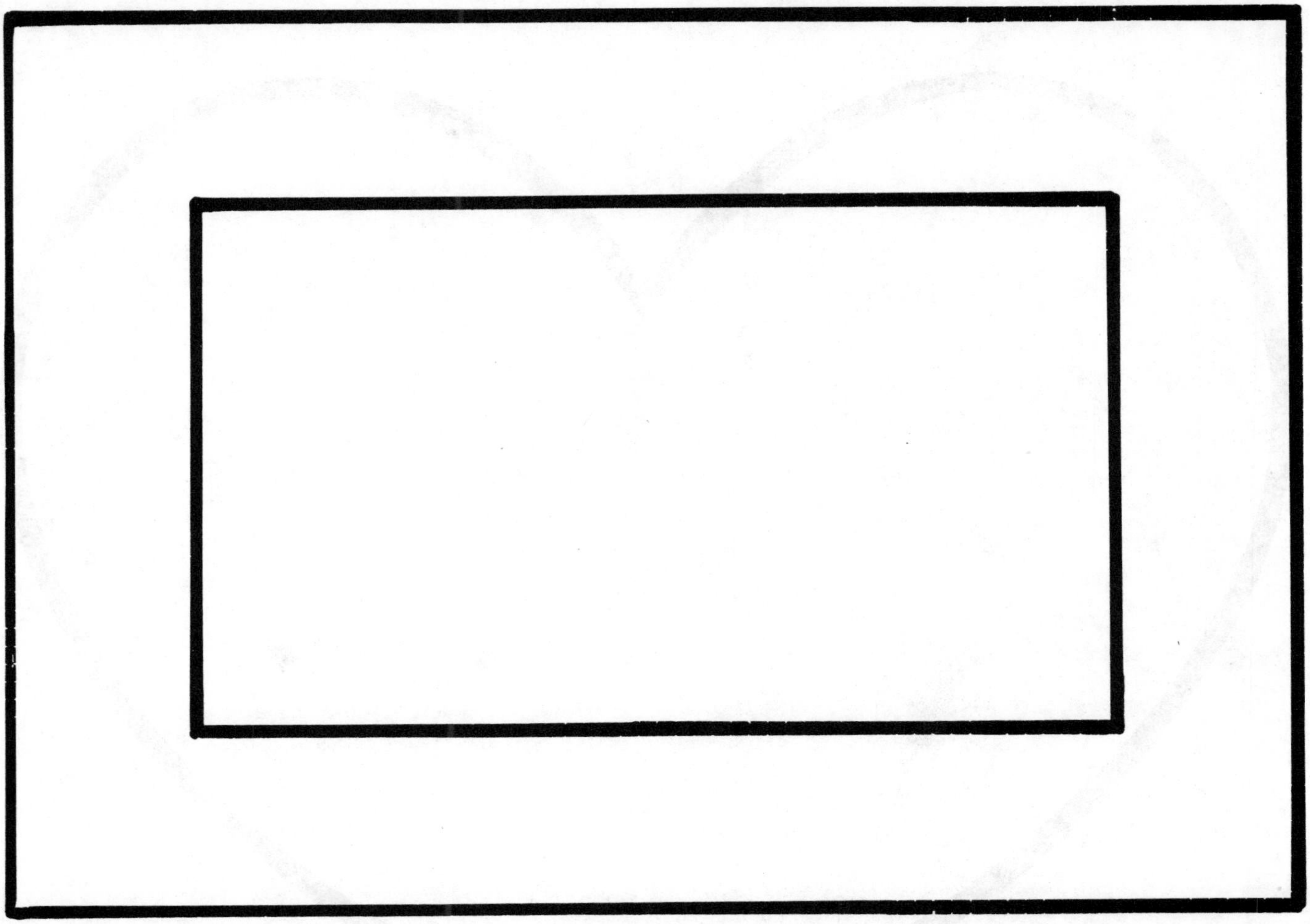

Lesson 9

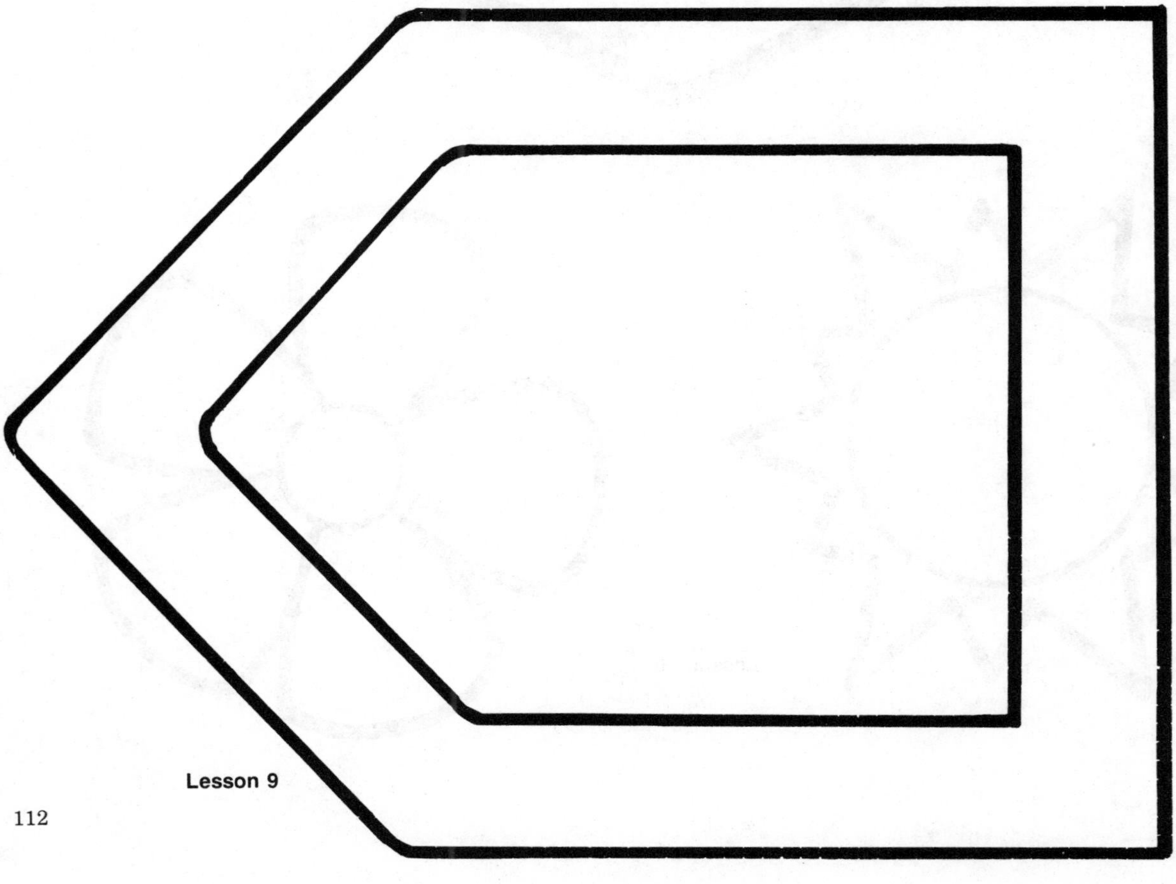

Lesson 9

Songs of Praise

The Heavens Are Telling

Psalm 19:1

Christine Wyrtzen

The heav-ens are tell-ing the glo-ry of God, the
glo-ry of God, the glo-ry of God, The
heav-ens are tell-ing the glo-ry of God. They're de-
clar-ing the works of His hands.
Fine

Great Is Our Lord

Psalm 147:5

Christine Wyrtzen

Great is our Lord and wor - thy of praise. His
un - der - stand - ing has no lim - it. Great ___ is the Lord!
Now to our God, Now to our Fa - ther, A - men.
Fine

Our God and Father

Philippians 4:20

Christine Wyrtzen

Promises

2 Peter 3:9 — Christine Wyrtzen

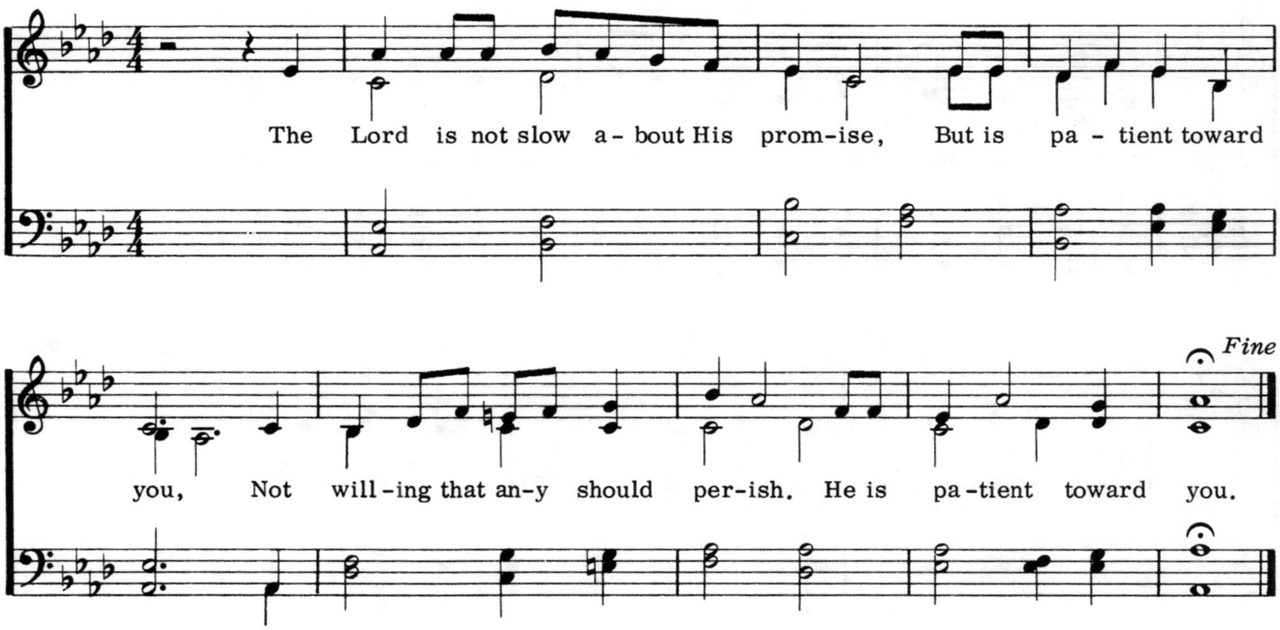

The Lord is not slow a- bout His prom-ise, But is pa - tient toward
you, Not will-ing that an-y should per-ish. He is pa-tient toward you.
Fine

Praise Ye the Lord
Praise ye the Lord, for it is good to sing prais - es un - to our God,
Repeat 3 times

Psalm 147:1 — Christine Wyrtzen

God's Wisdom

Colossians 2:3

Christine Wyrtzen

In Him are hid - den all the trea - sures
of wis - dom and know - ledge. In Him are hid - den
all the trea - sures. They are hid - den in
Him. They are hid - den in Him.
Fine

He Hath Done Great Things

Deuteronomy 10:21 | Christine Wyrtzen

He is your praise; (clap, clap) He is your God. (clap, clap)
He hath done great things for you. He is your
praise; (clap, clap) He is your God. (clap, clap) He
is (clap, clap, clap) your God.
Fine

Clap Your Hands

Psalm 47:1

Christine Wyrtzen

The Builder

Psalm 127:1

Christine Wyrtzen

Un - less the Lord builds our house, ___
___ our la - bors will all be in vain.
Un - less the Lord builds the house, ___
___ our la - bors will all be in vain. ___
Fine

Victory

1 Corinthians 15:55, 57

Christine Wyrtzen

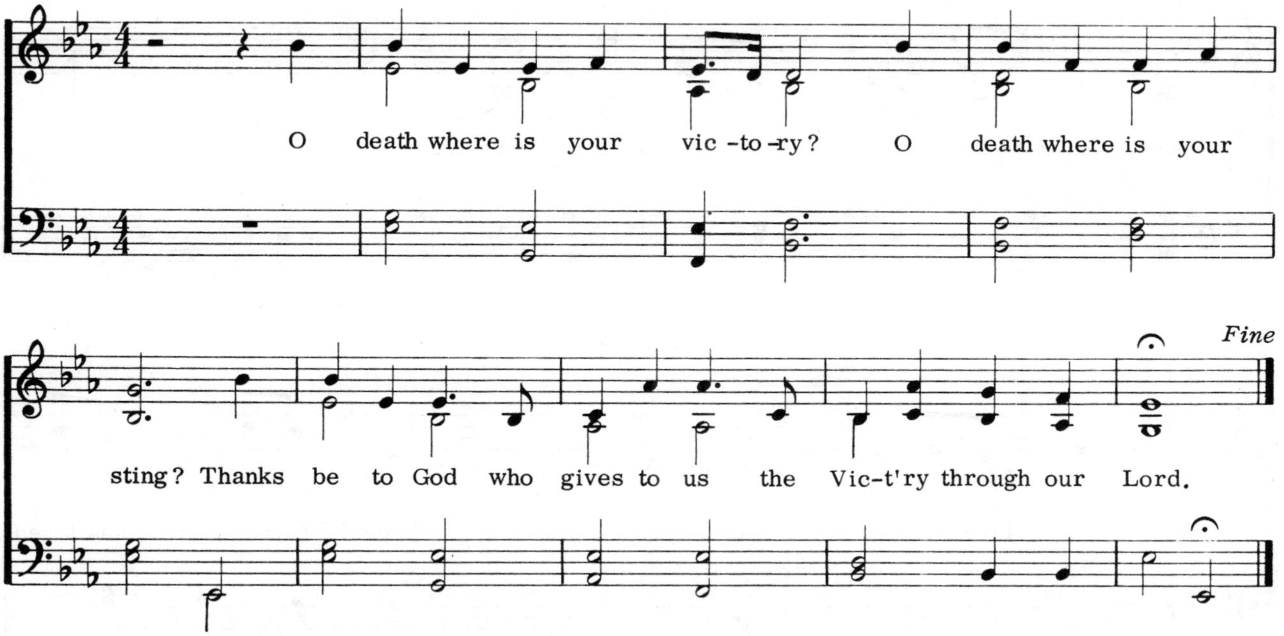
O death where is your vic-to-ry? O death where is your
Fine
sting? Thanks be to God who gives to us the Vic-t'ry through our Lord.

We Give Thee Thanks

Revelation 11:17

Christine Wyrtzen

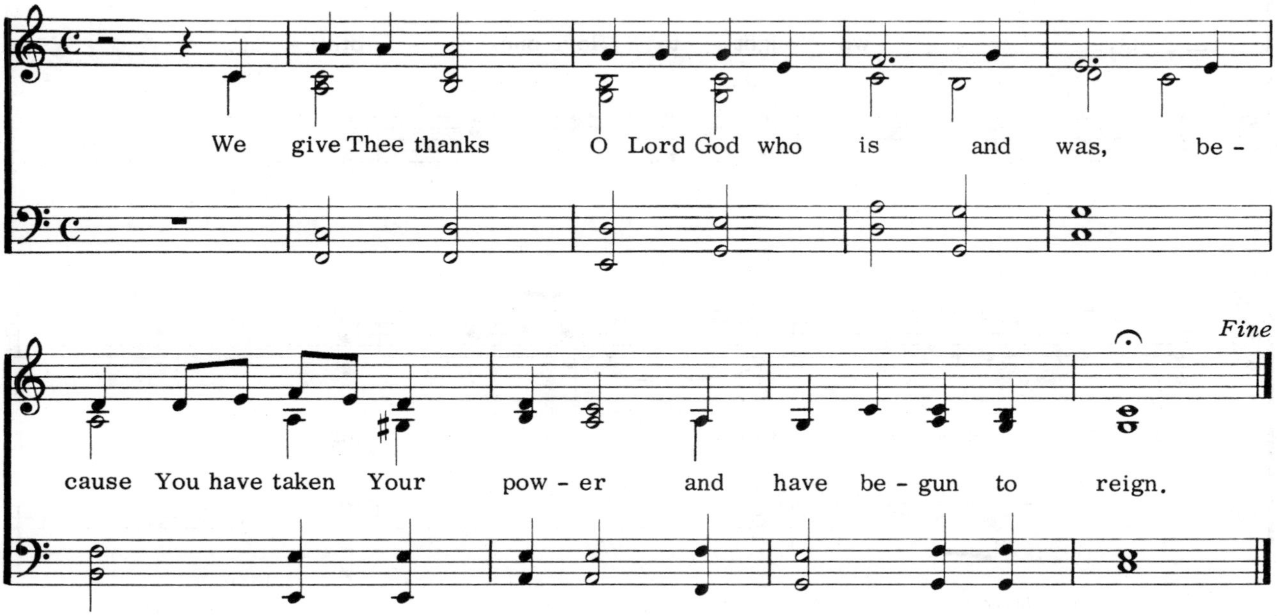
We give Thee thanks O Lord God who is and was, be-
Fine
cause You have taken Your pow-er and have be-gun to reign.

Since God Has Loved Us

1 John 4:11

Christine Wyrtzen

Since God has loved us, we
ought to love one an - oth - er. Since God has loved
us, we ought to love one an - oth - er. We
Fine
ought to love one an - oth - er.

I Can Do Everything

Philippians 4:13

Christine Wyrtzen

I can do ev-ery-thing, ev-ery-thing, ev-ery-thing! I can do ev-ery-thing thru Him.

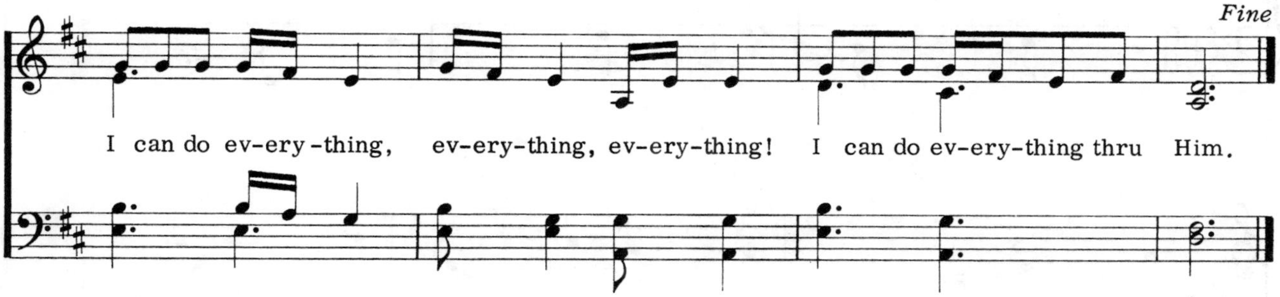

Fine
He will take care of you. My
He will take care of you.
I can do ev-ery-thing, ev-ery-thing, ev-ery-thing! I can do ev-ery-thing thru Him.

My God Will Meet All Your Needs

Philippians 4:19

Christine Wyrtzen

Serve the Lord

Psalm 100:2

Christine Wyrtzen

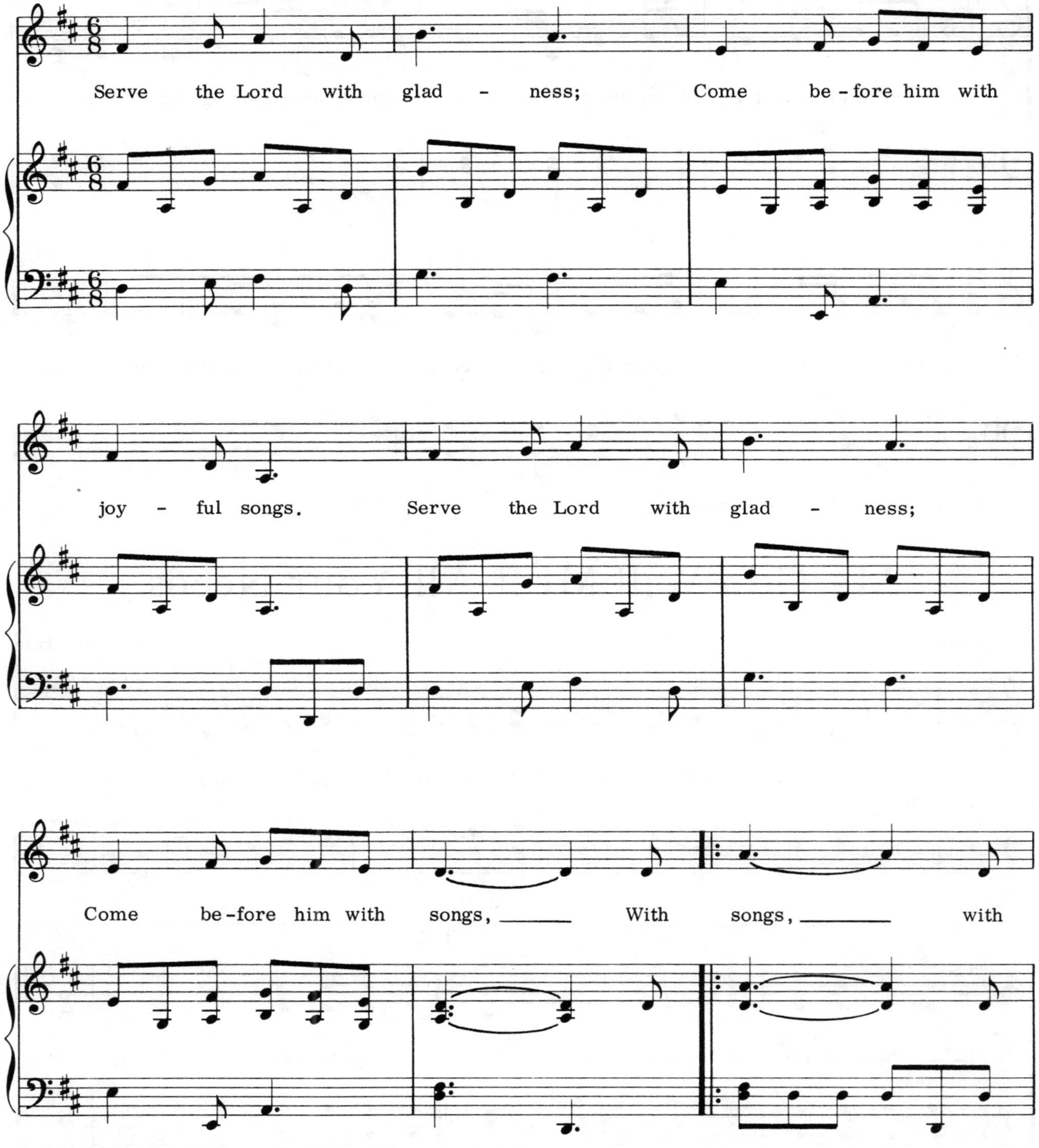

1.
2.
Fine
songs. Come be-fore him with songs, ___ with songs.

Praise the Lord for His Forgiveness

Psalm 103:1, 3

Christine Wyrtzen

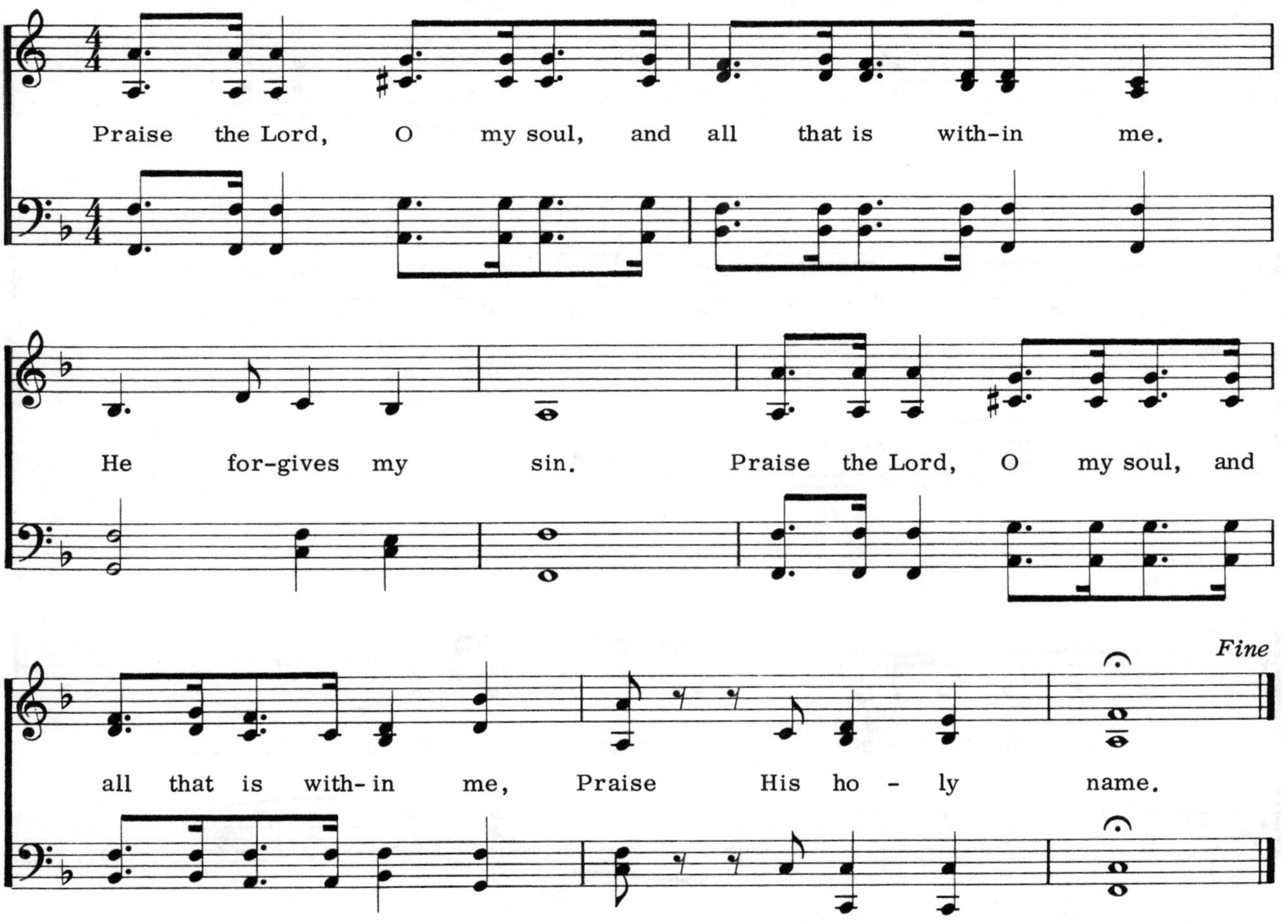

Praise the Lord, O my soul, and all that is with-in me.
He for-gives my sin. Praise the Lord, O my soul, and
all that is with-in me, Praise His ho - ly name.
Fine

Be Kind and Compassionate

Ephesians 4:32

Christine Wyrtzen

Seek First His Kingdom

Matthew 6:33

Christine Wyrtzen

Seek first His king - dom, Seek first His
right - eous - ness, And all of these
1.
things will be ad - ded un - to you,
2.
Fine
Be ad - ded un - to you.

O Give Thanks

Psalm 136:1

Christine Wyrtzen

Exceeding Great

2 Peter 1:4

Christine Wyrtzen

Memory Lane

Words and Music by Christine Wyrtzen

Shuffle

C C/E F
fun and the games?_ There's not a thing_ that
C/E Dm7 G C
Fine
I'd ra-ther do_ than to walk down Mem-o-ry Lane._

Speaking the Truth

Ephesians 4:14

Christine Wyrtzen

C F G4 3 F C
Speak-ing the truth in love, we will in all things grow up in-to Christ.
C F Dm G4 3 F C
rall.
Fine
Speak-ing the truth in love, we will grow up in - to Christ.

What Time I Am Afraid

Psalm 56:3

Christine Wyrtzen

Even a Child

Proverbs 20:11

Christine Wyrtzen

G G B7 C C
E - ven a child is known by his do -
G C G
- ings. You can tell if he loves the Lord, and Is
A D G G
walk - ing on the nar - row way. E - ven a child
B7 C G C
is known by his do - ings. He will be sen-si-tive to
G Am7 D G
the truth in the things You hear him do and say.

How Much Do You Love?

M. K. B. | Mary Kay Bottens

Quickly
F
How much do you love? How much do you love? How much do you love my
C7
Je - sus? How much do you love? How much do you love? How
F
F
much do you love my Lord? How much do you love? How
A
Dm
Bbm/Db
much do you love? How much do you love my Je - sus? How
F
Dm
G9
C7
F
Fine
much do you love? How much do you love? How much do you love my Lord?

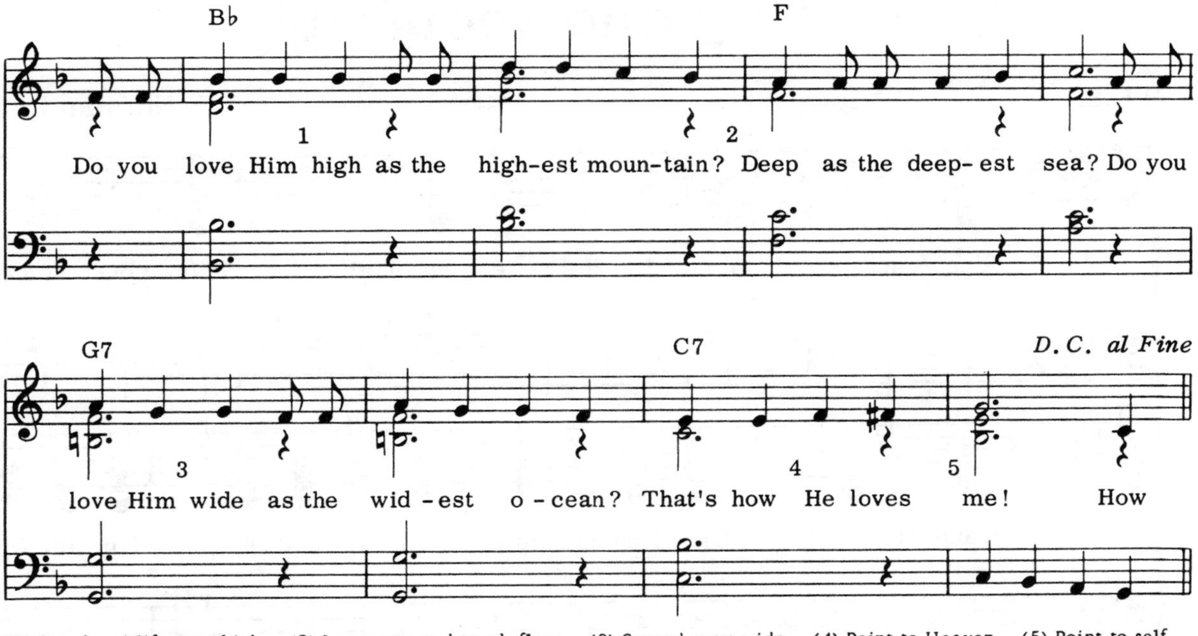

Bb
F
Do you love Him high as the high-est moun-tain? Deep as the deep- est sea? Do you
G7
C7
D. C. al Fine
love Him wide as the wid - est o - cean? That's how He loves me! How
1
2
3
4
5

(1) Stand and lift arms high (2) Lean over and touch floor (3) Spread arms wide (4) Point to Heaven (5) Point to self

Never Will I Leave You

Hebrews 13:5

Christine Wyrtzen

D
G
Em
A
G
D
Nev - er will I leave ___ you; nev - er will I for - sake you.
D
G
Em
A
A7
D
Nev - er will I leave ___ you; nev - er will I for - sake you.

Sing and Shout Out

N.L.S.

Norman L. Starks

Sing and shout out, * Hal - le - lu - jah! Lift your voice and
* praise the Lord! Give Him ear now, * all ye peo - ple; Lis - ten to His
* Ho - ly Word! God's sal - va - tion, free from trib - u - la - tion, Un-to
ev' - ry na - tion be His love pro - claimed! We are broth - ers, let us
tell to oth - ers Of the won - der - ful power of Je - sus' name!

All Lessons

Give Glory to the Lord

P.J.W. **Phyllis J. Warfel**

F F/C F/A F/G F F/C
1. Let us shout from the top of the moun - tain. Let us
2. Let us sing hal - le - lu - jah in wor - ship. Let us
3. Oh, re - joice, for the Lord, He is our God. Oh, re -
F F/C F/A Gm/F Gm C7
shout from the top of the hills Let us
sing hal - le - lu - jah in praise. Let us
joice, for the Lord, He is King. Oh, re -
F D♭6
shout from the riv-ers and val - leys. Let us
sing hal - le - lu - jah for- ev - er. Let us
joice, for the Lord, He is Sav - ior. Let us
F/C C7 C7sus6 F
give glo - ry to the Lord.
give glo - ry to the Lord.
give glo - ry to the Lord.

Forever Will I Praise Your Name

M.K.B. | Mary Kay Bottens

F
1. It was a hap - py time in - deed When one
2. So now a hap - py song I raise, As I
Bb Bb/G C7
day I stopped to read All the sto - ries that my Bi - ble had to
lift my voice in praise To my Lord and Sav-ior, Je - sus, King of
F
tell! For I learned that Je - sus came, Lived and
kings! For He healed the blind and deaf, Won the
Bb Bb/G C7
died, and rose a - gain. And be - cause He lives I'll nev - er be the
vict'- ry o - ver death, And He lives to - day. That's why I glad - ly
F CHORUS Bb/G C7
same.
sing.
Je - sus, I just praise Your name!

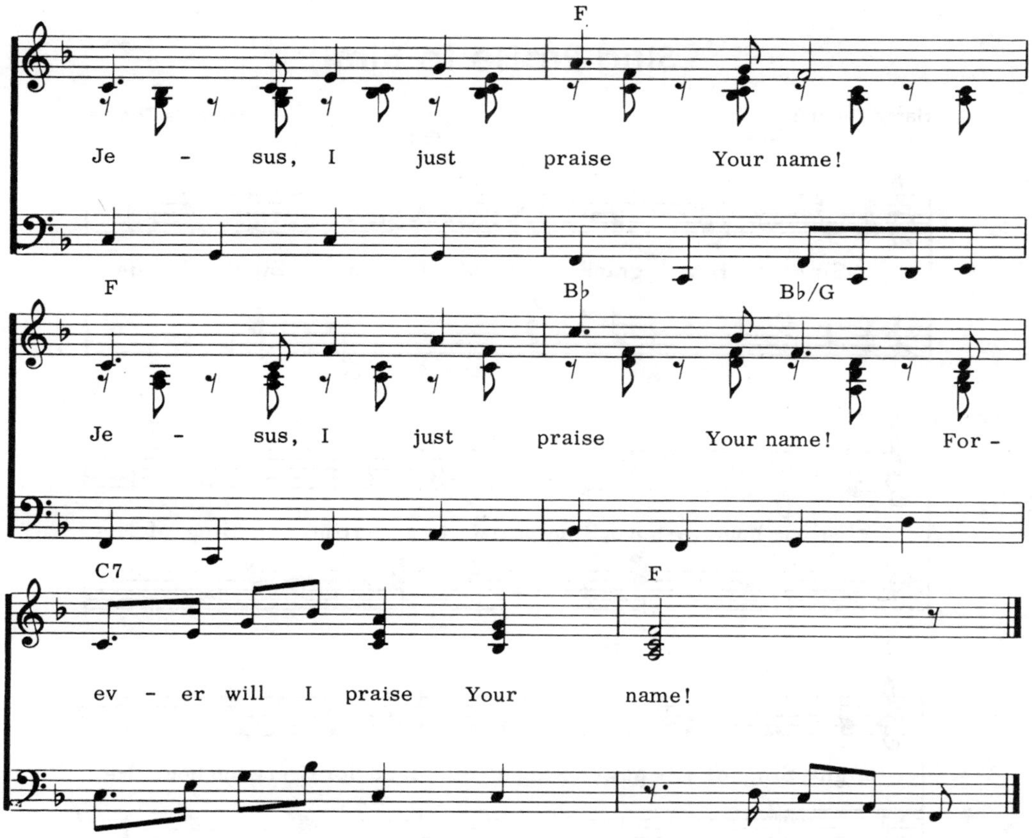
F
Je - sus, I just praise Your name!
F
Bb
Bb/G
Je - sus, I just praise Your name! For -
C7
F
ev - er will I praise Your name!

Sing Praise to Him

Harry Thomas | Minerva Thomas

3
Sing of His grace, Sing of His love, Sing of His
glo-rious home a-bove, Sing praise to Him. Sing of His
might, Sing of His power, Sing of our need for Him each hour, He
saves from sin. He gives me peace and joy to - day, And
life that nev-er fades a - way.—Sing of His grace, Sing of His love,
Sing of His glo-rious home a-bove, Sing praise to Him.

He Is the King

P.J.W.

Phyllis J. Warfel

When Group 1 reaches B, Group 2 will begin at A.

Praise Ye the Lord Forever

M.K.B. **Mary Kay Bottens**

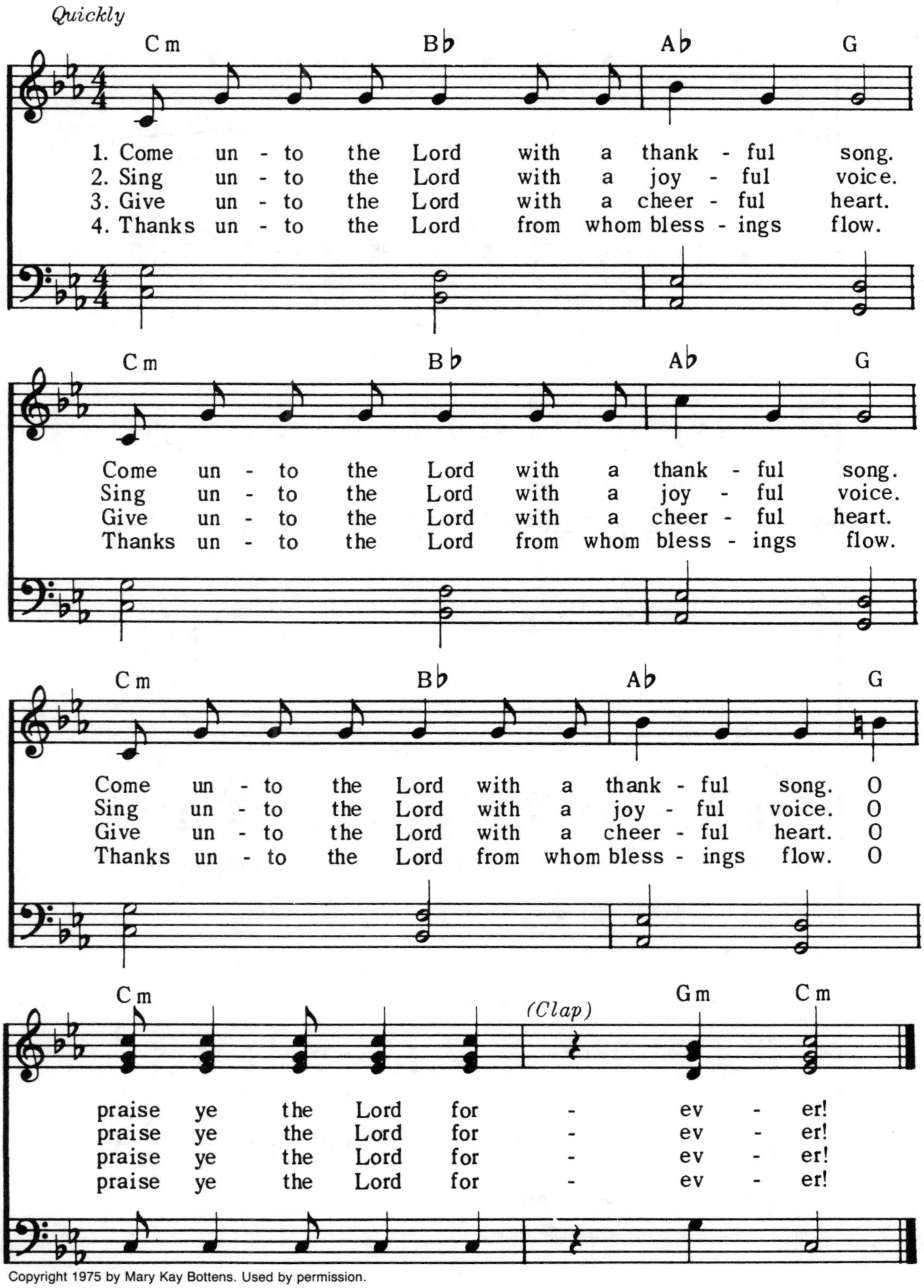

Hear Us as We Pray

M.K.B. | Mary Kay Bottens

Song Index